The Making of the Past

Biblical Lands

by P. R. S. Moorey

ELSEVIER·PHAIDON

Advisory Board for
The Making of the Past

p.2: Church of the Nativity, Bethlehem.

Planned and produced by Elsevier International Projects Ltd, Oxford, © 1975 Elsevier Publishing
Projects SA, Lausanne. All rights reserved. No part of this publication may be reproduced, stored in a
retrieval system, or transmitted, in any form or by any means, electronic, mechanical, photocopying,
recording or otherwise, without the prior permission of the Publishers.

Printed and bound by Brepols - Turnhout - Belgium

Biblical Lands

Preface to the series

This book is a volume in The Making of the Past, a series describing in comprehensive detail the early history of the world as revealed by archaeology and related disciplines. Written by experts under the guidance of a distinguished panel of advisers, it is designed for the layman, young people, the student, the armchair traveler and the tourist. Its subject is a *new* history – the making of a *new* past, freshly uncovered and reconstructed by skilled specialists like the authors of these volumes. Since these writers are themselves leaders in a rapidly changing field, the series is completely authoritative and up-to-date; but it loses nothing of the excitement of earlier discoveries. Each volume covers a specific period and region of the world and combines a detailed survey of the modern archaeology and sites of the area with dramatic stories of the pioneer explorers, travelers and archaeologists who first penetrated it. Part of each book is devoted to a reconstruction in pictures of the newly revealed cultures and civilizations that make up the history of the area. As a whole, the series not only presents a fresh look at the most familiar of archaeological regions such as Egypt and Classical Greece, but also provides up-to-date information and photographs of such archaeologically little-known areas as the Islamic world, the Far East and Africa.

Contents

Introduction

The Lands of the Bible were rarely rich in material things, and seldom politically or economically powerful. Therefore the following pages are not concerned with buried treasures. You will not find here gold and silverwork from princely graves nor even great architectural monuments as in ancient Egypt or India, Greece or Rome, Mexico or Peru – not at least until, towards the end, the narrative reaches the Persian palaces of Persepolis. The excitement here is provided by the legacy of men's minds more than by the creations of their hands, though these are by no means absent. This legacy may be less obvious, less tangible, but is all the more influential and vital to the gradual development of the world in which we live today. These men created in turn the creeds of Judaism, of Christianity and of Islam, and with them a literary legacy of supreme sensitivity and universal relevance. Above all, a millennium before Homer, they devised the idea of an alphabet. And without the alphabet much of their intellectual and religious achievement would have remained crippled for want of a simple means of record and transmission – a means that in time all men might use to write whatever language they spoke.

Numerous statements in the historical chapters of this book rest upon, or are illuminated by one of the many archaeological discoveries of the last 150 years, even when there is also some mention of it in the Old Testament or other ancient literary source. The earliest excavations in this region, when not undertaken to find beautiful objects for museums, were intended to shed new light upon the Bible. The work was often unmethodical and ill-conceived. But with time and growing experience, a new emphasis on systematic investigation, and meticulous attention to detail, has shifted the focus of interest to more general problems: to a broad-based investigation of the mosaic of ancient societies in the area. The Old Testament, still a unique source for much of the period, has now been supplemented by archives of baked clay tablets from the second millennium BC, inscribed in various languages and found at cities like Ugarit, Alalakh and Mari in Syria, and Nuzi in Iraq, and also a wealth of inarticulate objects that, properly studied, constantly yield new information.

It is all too easy to overlook how remarkable was the conviction which first led men to excavate and interpret the ancient mounds of Palestine and Syria. To the untutored eye these mounds suggest nothing more than unusually regular natural hillocks. Indeed many of the most significant of them now lie in areas long lost to human settlement: "Her towns have been turned into desert, parched land, a wilderness: no one lives in them, no man goes that way" (Jer. 51:43). No less formidable was the intellectual climate against which such early archaeologists had to struggle, an opposition clearly expressed by the great French writer Chateaubriand in 1812 in his description of a journey to the Holy Land:

"The first travellers were indeed happy; they were not obliged to enter into these difficult problems: firstly, because they found in their reading the religion that never disputes with the truth; secondly, because everyone was persuaded that the only way of seeing the country as it is was to see it with its traditions and memories, and it is in fact with the Bible and the Gospel in hand that the Holy Land should be visited. If you wish to bring there a contentious and intriguing frame of mind, there is no need to seek so far afield. What would you say of a man who, travelling through Greece or Italy, occupied himself only with contradicting Homer and Vergil? Yet this is how we travel today: our self-conceit makes us wish to appear clever and only renders us arrogant."

Some of the earliest discoveries, fortunately, were the most fatal to this complacent and formidable skepticism: Layard's discovery of the "Black Obelisk" naming Jehu, King of Israel; the library of King Ashurbanipal written on clay tablets that spoke of a flood so like the Biblical one; the Moabite Stone which recorded campaigns obliquely mentioned in the Old Testament; the inscription in Hezekiah's tunnel in Jerusalem; and the letters from Tell el-Amarna in Egypt. All of these have a vital place in the following account.

The archaeology and history of no other region have been, and sadly all too often remain, so much the victim of religious or political sectarian interests, or mythmakers and magicians seeking eternal truths, or buried treasure in mystical measurements or Biblical ciphers. Methods have been deplorable; indeed Sir Mortimer Wheeler has gone so far as to describe Palestine as the place "where more sins have probably been committed in the name of archaeology than on any commensurate portion of the earth's surface." It would be unfortunate – as it would be untrue of most contemporary excavations – if such activities were to overshadow the very diverse and fresh information appearing year by year from work of great integrity and an increasingly sophisticated methodology. Man's perennial fascination with the past has always been so compulsive that legends have often been created when facts could not be known; when facts can be known it behoves us to seek every way of establishing them.

Chronological Table

Readers used to modern history with such pivotal absolute dates as 1453, 1789 or 1939 AD may well be bewildered to find that in ancient history dates in years BC vary, often markedly, from one book to another. Although margins of error grow narrower and narrower as modern research proceeds, absolute certainty before about 500 BC is rarely possible, and even after that only for outstanding events. Dates for Palestine and Syria are dependent on Egyptian chronology which, very broadly speaking, is based upon astronomical observations that can be correlated with our modern calendar. From about 1550 BC the recorded regnal years of Egyptian kings may be fitted into an absolute chronology, though a margin of error varying between a few years and a decade or two has still to be allowed for. Even after the establishment of the monarchy in Palestine, when the sequence of regnal years may be given absolute dates BC, slight variations are still possible with the available evidence.

No less curious may seem an endless inconsistency in the spelling of many personal and place names. The languages involved here, both ancient and modern, often differ so markedly from English in their use of consonants and vowels that no universally accepted "scientific system" of transliteration has yet been devised. Here the simplest or most familiar forms have been adopted.

(The absolute chronology used here is that adopted by BRIGHT, J., *A History of Israel* 2nd Edn, London, 1972.)

EGYPT

XIIth Dynasty

Middle Kingdom	BC
Amenemmes I	c. 1991–1962
Sesostris I	c. 1971–1928
Amenemmes II	c. 1929–1895
Sesostris II	c. 1897–1878
Sesostris III	c. 1878–1843
Amenemmes III	c. 1842–1797
Amenemmes IV	c. 1798–1790
Sobkneferu	c. 1789–1786

XIIIth to XVIIth Dynasty
IInd Intermediate Period (*Hyksos*)
XVIIIth Dynasty

New Kingdom	BC
Amosis	c. 1552–1527
Amenophis I	c. 1527–1507
Thutmosis I	c. 1507–1494
Thutmosis II	c. 1494–1490
Thutmosis III	c. 1490–1436
Amenophis II	c. 1438–1412
Thutmosis IV	c. 1412–1403
Amenophis III	c. 1403–1364
Amenophis IV (Akhenaten)	c. 1364–1347
Smenkhare	c. 1349–1347
Tutankhamun	c. 1347–1338
Ay	c. 1337–1333
Horemheb	c. 1333–1306

XIXth Dynasty

Ramses I	c. 1306–1305
Seti I	c. 1305–1290
Ramses II	c. 1290–1224
Merneptah	c. 1224–1211
4 rulers	c. 1211–1185

XXth Dynasty

Sethnacht	c. 1185–1184
Ramses III	c. 1184–1153
Ramses IV	c. 1153–1146
Ramses V	c. 1146–1142
Ramses VI	c. 1142–1135

ASSYRIA

Tiglath-Pileser I	c. 1116–1078
Adad-Nirari II	c. 912–892
Assurnasirpal II	c. 884–860
Shalmaneser III	c. 859–825
Tiglath-Pileser III	c. 745–727
Shalmaneser V	c. 726–722
Sargon II	c. 721–705
Sennacherib	c. 704–681
Esarhaddon	c. 680–669
Ashurbanipal	c. 668–627

BABYLON

Nebuchadnezzar II	c. 605/4–562
Nabonidus	c. 556–539

THE ACHAEMENIAN PERSIAN DYNASTY

Cyrus	c. 550–530
Cambyses	c. 530–522
Darius I	c. 522–486
Xerxes	c. 486–465
Artaxerxes I	c. 465–424
Xerxes II	c. 423
Darius II	c. 423–404
Artaxerxes II	c. 404–358
Artaxerxes III	c. 358–338
Arses	c. 338–336
Darius III	c. 336–331

PALESTINE

	BC
Saul	c. 1020–1000 ?
David	c. 1000–961
Solomon	c. 961–922

Kingdom of Judah

Rehoboam	c. 922–915
Abijah	c. 915–913
Asa	c. 913–873
Jehoshaphat	c. 873–849
Jehoram	c. 849–842
Ahaziah	c. 842
Athaliah	c. 842–837
Joash	c. 837–800
Amaziah	c. 800–783
Uzziah	c. 783–742
Jotham	c. 742–735
Ahaz	c. 735–715
Hezekiah	c. 715–687/6
Manasseh	c. 687/6–642
Amon	c. 642–640
Josiah	c. 640–609
Jehoahaz	c. 609
Jehoiakim	c. 609–598
Jehoiachin	c. 598/7
Zedekiah	c. 587–586

Kingdom of Israel

Jeroboam I	c. 922–901
Nadab	c. 901–900
Baasha	c. 900–877
Elah	c. 877–876
Zimri	c. 876
Omri	c. 876–869
Ahab	c. 869–850
Ahaziah	c. 850–849
Jehoram	c. 849–842
Jehu	c. 842–815
Jehoahaz	c. 815–801
Jehoash	c. 801–786
Jeroboam II	c. 786–746
Zechariah	c. 746–745
Shallum	c. 745
Menahem	c. 745–738
Pekahiah	c. 738–737
Pekah	c. 737–732
Hoshea	c. 732–724

1. Landscape, Archaeology and History

One single question underlies the perpetual fascination of Palestine's history – how did a country so small and ill-blessed by nature come to have so profound an effect on the history of western civilization, producing both Judaism and Christianity, and playing no small part in the early history of Islam? There is, of course, no single, simple answer. But from the subtle interplay of stimuli which served at one time or another to create conditions favorable for such developments, a few may be singled out.

Palestine, if small, was significantly placed as a land-bridge between Africa and Asia, and was intimately involved from earliest times with the political, commercial and cultural life of a region very much greater in size and physical resources than it was. To the southwest, across Sinai, lay Egypt; to the east and northeast, across the great Syrian desert, lay Mesopotamia. Both were lands with large rivers where good communications and irrigation agriculture had supported flourishing urban civilizations since the 4th millennium BC. These were the poles between which the history of ancient Palestine and Syria oscillated. Egyptian and Mesopotamian armies and imperial aspirations molded the political experience of both. No less were the religion, literature and learning of Palestine and Syria profoundly influenced by both regions. Even the most superficial study of the documentary legacy of Egypt and Mesopotamia reveals constant parallels, either with the style or the content of the Old Testament, while Canaanite and Phoenician art owed much to Egypt.

If geographical factors facilitated, they also muted foreign influences, especially in Palestine. The great caravan routes which brought luxury goods westwards from the distant shores of India, Arabia and the Persian Gulf largely bypassed Palestine, converging on the major cities of Syria; and only under unusual political circumstances, as under David and Solomon, was she involved with them. The one highway she had – the *Via Maris* – ran from Egypt up through the coastal plain, then eastwards through the plain of Esdraelon to the Syrian heartland, and it was used as much by invading armies as by traders. Peoples penetrating eastwards from this route, or westwards from the Arabian desert, reached a land naturally divided into many self-contained plains and valleys, their differences intensified by variations of soil and climate. Though always open to infiltration, there flourished here a sturdy independence and a variety of race and culture rarely met with in so small an area of land. Foreign ideas were sifted and tried in the area, before they were assimilated into the existing body of beliefs and practices. Never for long subjected to one single central authority, even less often achieving great material prosperity, its people, once settled and variously integrated, were often to excel their richer and more powerful neighbors in religious and literary sensibility.

The land in which they met and mingled did not yield its fruits easily or predictably. There was no great river here with a regular regime. Fertility depended upon a rainfall that, if generally regular and adequate, was often enough irregular and inadequate. Disastrous famines, pestilence and locust invasions were by no means infrequent. The religion of Canaan reveals a profound preoccupation with gods of storm and fertility; Israel's doctrine of moral Providence is, in its own way, equally explicit on the matter:

"For the land which you are to enter and make your own is not like the land of Egypt from which you came, where you sowed your seed and watered it by waterwheel like a vegetable garden. No, the land into which you are to cross to make it your own is a land of hills and valleys watered by the rain from heaven. . . . I will give your land rain in season, autumn rain and spring, so that you may harvest your corn, your wine, your oil; I shall provide grass in the fields for your cattle, and you will eat and have all you want. Take care your heart is not seduced . . . or the anger of Yahweh will blaze out against you, he will shut up the heavens and there will be no rain. . . ." (Deut. 11:10–17).

If this were all, it might then be easy to explain Palestine's unique historical role: but geographical situation and circumstance are not everything. A country is profoundly affected also by its historical experience, by a long succession of men and events. The following historical chapters do not directly seek an answer to the question with which

we started. But they guide the reader towards his, or her own answer by providing the primary archaeological and historical information now available for understanding the role of Palestine and the adjacent lands from about 2000 to 330 BC. This is approached gradually through an exploration of the landscape and its resources, through a brief examination of archaeological methods in the region, and finally through an account of the gradual rediscovery of ancient Palestine in the last 400 years. Although this quest is fascinating enough in itself, familiarity with the changing aims and achievements of earlier scholars will also serve to set the present state of knowledge in true perspective.

Above: the modern hill town of el-Jib (ancient Gibeon). Seen from a distance the ancient town would have looked very much the same.

Left: a typical stretch of Galilean landscape near the Sea of Galilee.

Title page: city gate at Megiddo designed and built by Solomon's masons, who used exactly the same layout at Hazor and Gezer (see I Kings 9:15–16).

Below: view across the Dead Sea towards the mountains of Moab, from a cave in cliffs overlooking its western shores.

The landscape. Syria, Palestine's large northern neighbor, is not a natural unit. To the west it consists of massive mountain ranges, the Ansariyeh in the north, the double range of Lebanon and Anti-Lebanon in the south. A deep valley runs down the eastern side of the Ansariyeh range and on between the two Lebanon ridges, known as the Ghab in the north, the Bekaa in the south. It is drained by the rivers Orontes and Litani. Here the climate is typically Mediterranean with warm, moist winters and hot, dry summers. Eastern Syria, taken as part of Mesopotamia in this book, offers a marked contrast. It is continental in character with great ranges of temperature and absolute aridity for six months annually. Diagonally through the midst of it runs the Euphrates. To the north the foothills of the Taurus mountains flank the river, then southwards a tableland with low detached mountains merges into a great expanse of steppe and desert. In the far south the distinctive volcanic area of Hauran and Jebel Druse runs on into Jordan.

In Syria, as over much of Palestine, vegetation has been radically modified by the activities of men and animals. Deforestation, and prevention of forest renewal by intensive grazing, not only reduces woodland plants but leads first to the spread of those plants capable of withstanding dry, exposed habitats, and then to a disastrous erosion of soil cover. In antiquity, as ancient records and modern studies of plant remains from excavations clearly show, a far greater area was cultivated than today and the country's considerable prosperity then depended on its agricultural

The desert landscape of southern Jordan, renowned in antiquity for its copper mines. The overland spice trade from Arabia passed through this region.

The rolling landscape of northern Palestine, once more forested than it is today, with sufficient water for fairly intensive cultivation in the valleys and foothills.

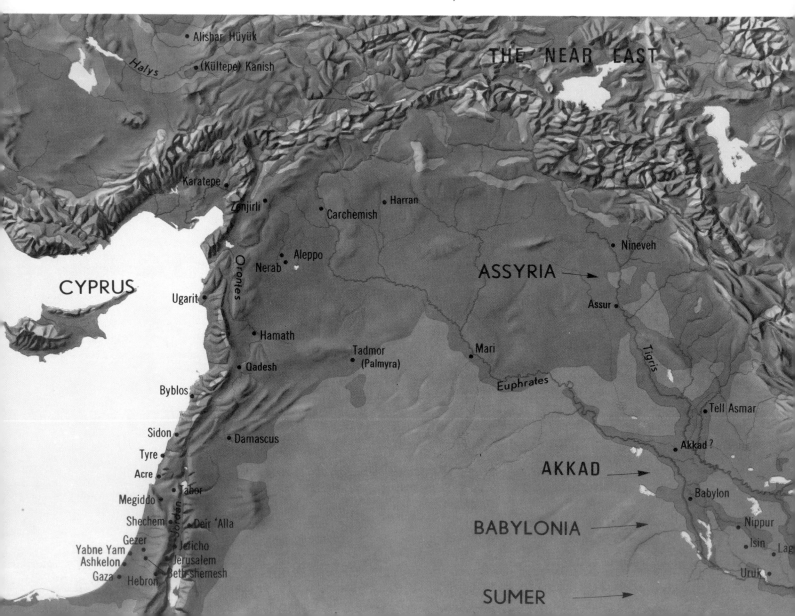

produce. Although water supply is abundant from rivers, springs, wells and rain, it is sporadic, and well-controlled irrigation is vital in a number of regions. At Palmyra, the greatest of the caravan cities in the middle of the desert, a slightly sulfurous spring created an oasis. A great dam or barrage, in existence by at least the later 2nd millennium BC, regulated the upper course of the river Orontes and created a reservoir for the surplus waters of springtime, which could then be used for irrigation in the dry summer months. Two rivers with an elaborate network of irrigation canals supported the large and rich oasis of Damascus.

The Phoenician coastal region, modern Lebanon, is very narrow: the mountains rise abruptly only a short distance from the sea and the hinterland forms an almost impassable barrier. This strip varies from 60 to a few miles wide and is mostly contained below the 20-meter contour. But water for irrigation is ample and simple canal systems, with well-terraced mountain fields, gave the land great fertility and a wide range of agricultural produce.

Different again is Palestine, a small land with richly contrasted landscapes. The coastal plain is a region of great fertility, save where in the south sand-dunes overlie the earth. Several wadis and watercourses, mostly dry except for a few days in the rainy season, and accessible ground water, provide sufficient water for irrigation to grow corn, vines and olives. To the southwest the Wadi Ghazzeh leads into Sinai and the region of semi-nomadic communities, where rainfall decreases and desert prevails. Southeastwards lies the Negev, a massive triangle of land with its apex at Aqaba and its base on a line from Gaza to the southern end of the Dead Sea. Level or slightly undulating in the west, it becomes a rough, deeply eroded wilderness in the east, where cultivation is only possible in years of ample rain, and even then only in wadis and depressions where sufficient soil has gathered. Cultivation without irrigation is only possible around Beersheba. Yet often in the past, through careful control and regulation of water supplies, the region has supported a sedentary population.

To the east the coastal plain is bordered by the low range of foothills running from north to south known as the Shephelah; behind them rises the limestone ridge of much higher hills, with intervening valleys, which extends northwards to form the geographical and historical backbone of the country, for here lay Judah, Samaria and Galilee. Limestone ravines reach up to Jerusalem at 2,500 feet; Bethel and Hebron lie 500 feet higher. The hills of Judah are relatively barren, but those of the Shephelah support vines, trees and fruit crops. A major break through the mountain ridge is provided by the fertile plains of Megiddo and Jezreel, providing a low and easy route through from the coastal plain to Transjordan. Galilee, the highest and most northern of the mountain terrain, is as fertile as the Lebanon. Although its southern limits are rugged, and were heavily forested in antiquity, the major northern part running up to the gorge of the Litani river is a spacious tableland with many springs and rich vegeta-

Shepherd with his donkey and flock of sheep grazing in the Judaean wilderness – a sight virtually unchanged since antiquity.
Unchecked grazing is one factor contributing to soil erosion.

tion. Olive, fig and other fruit trees, as well as wheat and vines, flourish here.

Passing down into the great rift valley running from north to south, where the river Jordan flows, involves descending 3,750 feet to the lowest point on the earth's surface at 1,246 feet below sea level near the Dead Sea. There is a marked contrast in landscape and vegetation. The subalpine of the high hills is replaced, where ground water is available (as at Jericho), by a rank subtropical oasis with plantations. The river Jordan rises gently in the Hermon foothills and unites with other streams to flow into Lake Huleh through swamps and reed beds. Then between the Sea of Galilee and the Dead Sea it has a strong, even current which has cut sinuous curves deep through the clay and marl subsoil. It is a river too deep for navigation, with high banks overgrown by willow and canebrakes. Normally the west bank of the Jordan is rather desolate, but the east is fertile, irrigated by a number of perennial streams. On the western shores of the Dead Sea, where there is now a small oasis in the wilderness known as En-Gedi, surveys of ruined terraces and aqueducts as well as excavations have given substance to ancient accounts of the area's great fertility, when palms and balsam plantations made it an important center for the production of unguents and perfumes.

East of the Jordan a steep escarpment rises to a plateau, with a mean height of 2,000 feet, that shades away eastwards into the great Arabian desert. On this to the south ancient Edom and Moab had considerable agricultural resources, valuable copper deposits, like those on the western side of the Arabah recently explored by Israeli archaeologists, and a vital position on the caravan routes from

Above: fragment of limestone inscribed in an early form of Hebrew by a schoolboy. His verse records the farmer's yearly routine, as in the adjacent translation.

Below: the mound of the Biblical city of Abel-beth-maacah near Dan in northern Israel.

Arabia. Northwards Gilead produced grain, vines, olive, oak and pine, with Bashan beyond it renowned for its cattle and grain.

Throughout the timespan of this book the whole region was sustained by agriculture and the population was predominantly rural. Even the towns, as in medieval Europe, were intimately linked to the countryside. On the western escarpments and plains of Palestine agriculture depended on the seasonal winter rains and the heavy spring dews; elsewhere on irrigation from perennial wadis and springs. In general heavy rains late in October and early November soften the earth for plowing and sowing in a single operation; harvesting takes place in April or May depending on the crop. About 925 BC a schoolboy at Gezer scratched on a fragment of soft limestone an exercise in Hebrew that reads like a verse-mnemonic reminding children of the farmer's year. In Albright's translation it reads:

"His two months are (olive) harvest
His two months are planting (grain)
His two months are late planting;
His month is hoeing up of flax (?)
His month is harvest of barley
His month is harvest and feasting
His two months are vine-tending,
His month is summer fruit."

This was only one side of the rural scene. As the conflict of Cain and Abel in Genesis graphically illustrates, the sedentary tillers of the soil were complemented by the keepers of sheep and goats, the pastoralists. Their year, like the farmers', was determined by the seasons. From winter until late spring the rains supported grazing in the steppe highlands, but in summer and autumn the sun withered them, driving herdsmen to seek forage in the river valleys and other likely spots. Here were the seeds of that age-old conflict between the desert and the sown. As settled farming communities expanded and political organization developed, the dwellers in the marginal areas and beyond found themselves deprived and gradually squeezed out. It was their reaction and the gradual absorption of the nomad and semi-nomad into Palestinian society that over the centuries provided it with a regular influx of fresh peoples with their own distinctive cultures and traditions.

Archaeology and history. Whereas the pioneer excavators of the 19th century were drawn to Egypt and Mesopotamia in the hope of recovering great works of art or by dreams of revealing legendary ancient civilizations, they came to Palestine for a very special and rather different reason. Indeed they were sent by bodies of subscribers, as one such American society put it, "for the illustration and defense of the Bible." Admirable as was this intent, and remarkable the discoveries made, such an approach could easily lead to special pleading. Modern archaeologists working in the area would happily accept the term "illustrate," but few would now care to use the

The harbor of Byblos through which the vital trade in timber between the Lebanon and Egypt passed for thousands of years.

word "defense." The Bible – and it is unique among the great religious books of the world in this – provides a very special religious interpretation of history. Archaeology can only establish more exactly our knowledge of the historical facts upon which these ancient authors, often long after the events in question, based their theological interpretation. An archaeologist today will not generally, as in an earlier time, excavate a site simply because it had a known role in the Old Testament, but will undertake it because it is likely to throw fresh light upon obscure aspects or periods in the life of those ancient societies for which the Bible happens to be a uniquely vivid and accurate witness – contemporary, or near contemporary..

The most striking feature of the Near Eastern archaeological landscape is the artificial mound (Arabic: *tell*) – so often all that remains of a once large and vigorous city. When houses of mud or mud-brick or stony rubble, with plastered walls and roofs, collapse they leave little or nothing to salvage and a newcomer will merely level off the ruins and build over them. In the course of time accumulating debris forms a mound in which the sequence of remains can be observed and recorded by cutting trenches into it. Stratigraphy – observing levels in the mound's growth – enables changes in architecture, in techniques (potting,

metallurgy, stone-working, etc) and domestic equipment to be placed in order of time and related to observed interruptions or alterations in settlement. In Palestine and Syria, during the periods described here, knowledge of ancient pottery styles has advanced to a point where, even without an associated historical inscription, it is possible to give approximate absolute dates, in years BC, to a relative sequence. It is also these distinctive pottery types which allow levels on one site to be correlated with levels on others, thus providing the basis for establishing the history of human settlement over wide areas.

Such tells are innumerable in the region, and even more so are those briefly occupied sites or cemeteries whose very presence may be hidden from all but the well-trained eye. How does an archaeologist decide where to dig? On not a few occasions, and some concerning the most famous and significant sites, chance takes a hand. In 1928 a Syrian peasant, plowing near the Mediterranean shore in Syria, turned up evidence of a tomb containing pottery which an experienced archaeologist recognized as Mycenaean Greek of the 13th century BC. The grave was seen to be part of a cemetery, and an adjacent mound, known locally as Ras Shamra, was recognized as a tell. In April 1929 a French expedition under Dr C. F. A. Shaeffer began to dig the

cemetery, at Minet el-Beida, but soon moved to the tell. Within five days of starting work there clay tablets were found, the first of thousands that were to give ancient Ugarit a very special importance in modern understanding of Canaanite religion and society.

Some years later a bedouin, digging for stones in the mound of Hariri by the Euphrates far away in eastern Syria near the Iraqi border, found a headless stone statue which he gave to the lieutenant responsible for the area under the French mandate. Within four months a full-scale archaeological expedition had been organized from France under André Parrot. On 23 January 1934 just over a month after work began, a statue was found inscribed "Lamgi-Mari, King of Mari, great governor, has dedicated this statue to the goddess Ishtar." Here was quite exceptional evidence for the site's ancient name, reflected, it may be noted, in its modern one. But this was only the beginning. Late in the same year came the first traces of a great mud-brick palace and in it the first batch of an enormous archive of clay tablets which was to reveal so much about the diplomatic, social and economic life of the area at a crucial time in the first half of the 2nd millennium BC. Excavations at both Ras Shamra and Hariri continue.

The eventual discovery of another important archive of the 2nd millennium BC was less a matter of chance, for the excavator chose his site with the care and intuition bred of a lifetime's involvement in Near Eastern archaeology. Sir Leonard Woolley wrote:

"After the conclusion of work at Ur, I was, in the spring of 1935, commissioned by the Trustees of the British Museum to look for a new site for excavation. The object that I had in view was, primarily, to trace early cultural relations between the Aegean and the Asiatic mainland, throwing light, if possible, upon the development of Cretan civilization and its connexions with the great civilizations of Nearer Asia; this meant that my search must be conditioned by political and economic history, by harbours and overland trade-routes. Geographical considerations led me to the Amq plain in north Syria, a plain dotted with something like two hundred ancient mounds, through which the river Orontes flows before breaking through the barrier of the Amanus mountains to reach the Mediterranean. Finally I selected one mound, Tell Atchana, which I believed to be the site of a royal city commanding the principal trade-routes, including the pass to the sea, and controlling too the timber-supplies of the northern mountains – the continuation of the Lebanon forests exploited by the Phoenician cities of the south coast; and also the insignificant little mound of Sheikh Yusuf at the mouth of the Orontes, which I believed to have been the port of the capital city." Thus was discovered the ancient city of Alalakh and the port of al Mina, though one had flourished in the 2nd millennium BC, the other four or five hundred years later.

Whereas in Syria the archaeologist has generally to work with sites whose ancient names are unknown until inscriptions found in excavations reveal them, in Palestine Biblical and Classical sources provide a wealth of information with which to locate ancient cities whose role in antiquity may often be relatively well known from the

Yet to other scholars the mound at Hesi remained Biblical Eglon, while a much more impressive mound, whose location better fitted the Biblical evidence, Tell ed-Duweir, was taken to be Lachish. In 1935 when a British Expedition found there a series of "letters" written on potsherds during Nebuchadnezzar's invasion, their geographical content indeed showed that Duweir, not Hesi, was Lachish. Matters are not always so complex. In his study Clermont-Ganneau identified Biblical Gezer with modern Tell Djezer; then in the field he discovered rockcut inscriptions close to the site, saying in Aramaic "boundary of Gezer".

New horizons. In the years since World War II excavators have returned to some of the outstanding Biblical sites for various reasons. Pritchard went to modern el-Jib hoping to prove whether or not it was indeed ancient Gibeon, where "the sun stood still, and the moon halted, till the people had vengeance on their enemies" (Jos. 10:12), and where "at the pool of Gibeon" the young men of Joab and Abner fought it out. He not only found the pool, but in its debris many baked-clay jar handles inscribed with the name "Gibeon" – very rare and absolute confirmation of the el-Jib/Gibeon equation. In 1956 Wright was attracted to Shechem as an ideal training ground for a fresh generation of American Biblical

p.16: the mound of Megiddo from the east showing the trench cut by the American excavators.

Above: aerial view of the great 18th century BC palace at Mari in Syria, source of an outstandingly important archive of inscribed tablets.

Below: rock-cut stairs descending into the great water-pool at Gibeon (el-Jib), excavated by Dr J. B. Pritchard.

Old Testament. Correlating ancient information and modern geography is not always as simple as it looks, save in the most obvious cases, and even then there are pitfalls, for a name may move with successive settlements. At Jericho, for instance, the tell marking the Old Testament city is some distance away from the New Testament town of the same name on the one hand, the modern town on the other. In locating Biblical sites account has to be taken of a variety of evidence. The ancient literary sources for its name and position must be carefully checked one against the other and, where there is a contradiction, established principles of textual criticism applied. The modern place-names in the required locality are then checked over to see if they help, and here a knowledge of changing sounds in language is essential. Local traditions or folklore may also be useful. When all this has been sifted, it remains to be seen whether the archaeological evidence fits in with the site's history as known from ancient documents.

In 1838, in quest of ancient Lachish, Robinson investigated whether the existence of a modern Umm Laqis three miles northwest of Tell el-Hesi indicated that Hesi was ancient Lachish; but its size and situation, he decided, were against the identification. As about two kilometers north of Hesi there was a ruin called Khirbet 'Ajlan, he thought identification with ancient Eglon more likely. But when in 1890 Petrie conducted excavations at Hesi he took it to be Lachish, an identification thought to be confirmed two years later when Bliss found at Hesi a tablet of the 14th century BC referring to ancient Lachish.

scholars, who would find there not only numerous archaeological problems but also a site rich in literary tradition. It was the Philistines who drew excavators to Tell Areini (thought to be Gath until digging suggested otherwise) and to Ashdod. Yadin took a major Israeli expedition to Tell-el-Qedah, whose very shape, size and situation command attention. Here is a site in northern Israel which, as ancient Hazor, is mentioned not only in the Old Testament but also in pre-Biblical literary texts from Egypt and Mesopotamia, as well as Palestine, way back to the 19th century BC. In the course of this work Yadin excavated about one four-hundredth of the site, estimating it would take 800 years at about four to five months a year to clear it all.

Dr Kenyon's intentions at Tell es-Sultan, ancient Jericho, were more varied than its name might immediately suggest. Certainly she went to obtain additional evidence, negative as it turned out, on the date of the fall of the latest Bronze Age city to Joshua. But she was also interested in obtaining a wide range of material from tombs and in clearing the important Neolithic remains discovered there earlier by Garstang. In the event these provided the highlights of her excavation. However careful the planning, archaeology is never predictable.

Yet still there is much in the ancient history of Palestine that must be studied without the aid of documentary clues, and here it is that the changing forms and decoration of pottery have so long held a crucial role. Fragments (sherds) of pottery are virtually indestructible. Concentrations of them on the ground will indicate an ancient settlement, their type the probable date of its occupation. By careful surveying of wide areas the trained archaeologist is able to identify in general the distribution of ancient settlements at various periods. By selective digging he can then add precision to this record, since sherds on the surface may only indicate the latest phase in a site's history. This method of survey, pioneered in Transjordan and the Negev by Nelson Glueck, led, among many other things, to the most probable dating for the early Patriarchal narratives in Genesis, associated particularly with Abraham. Recent extensions of such work have assisted understanding of Israelite penetration of Galilee during the Conquest and the course of human activity in Sinai from earliest times.

Scrupulous as may have been an excavator's approach to his site, every excavation raises quite as many questions as it solves, often more. At every step the archaeologist is challenged by his own work, as by that of his colleagues, to reconsider his current hypotheses in the light of fresh evidence. When, for instance, Glueck first surveyed the southern Arabah in the 1930s a distinctive type of pottery, regularly encountered, was dated to the 10th century BC or later. Subsequent excavations at Tell el-Kheleifeh were believed to have identified a copper refinery associated with King Solomon's exploitation of local mines and his trading activities in the Red Sea. Recent exploration,

mainly by Rothenberg, has shown that the pottery is earlier, of the late 13th and 12th centuries BC, and that the refinery was no such thing. Local mining went back to prehistoric times, but it had come to a temporary halt sometime before Solomon's reign. In its final stages it was associated with a small temple erected to their patron goddess, the Egyptian Hathor, by miners controlled from Egypt during the 19th and 20th dynasties. It was the occurrence of the distinctive pottery together with objects bearing Egyptian royal names of this period that provided the crucial new dating evidence, evidence not available through the earlier field surveys and restricted excavations. Similar radical reappraisal of previous archaeological conclusions about the Late Bronze Age city at Jericho followed Dr Kenyon's work there.

Archaeology, like any growing study, changes steadily in its emphasis. In the last decade or two the pace has quickened, with radical modifications of aims and methods. Until very recently all archaeology in Palestine and Syria was directed to unraveling the chronological development and spatial distribution of ancient societies, as defined by their material remains. The archaeologists have thus concentrated either on large-scale excavations on sites long and intensively occupied (tells) or on the surface sampling and test digging of numerous small sites. Methods of excavating, of sampling, recording and grouping the information recovered have steadily improved, most recently under the impact of statistical method and theory. At the same time the growing involvement of natural scientists of all kinds in archaeological fieldwork has seen a much greater focus of attention not only on the analysis of artifacts to reveal composition, methods of manufacture, sources of raw material etc, but also on the recovery and detailed study of material like bones, seeds and other organic matter previously ignored.

In broader terms the involvement of geographers, geologists, hydrologists and ecologists, to name but the most obvious, has transformed our knowledge and understanding of ancient settlement patterns and land use. For obvious reasons the impact of such work has so far been greatest in the study of the prehistoric periods; but its relevance to historic times is no less, particularly those so-called historic periods, like the time-span of this book, when written sources are still so meager. Even newer, and still matter for lively debate, is a move to push archaeological evidence to its potential limits by using methods borrowed from the social sciences, such as ethnology, community and environmental studies to explain archaeological phenomena which archaeologists of previous generations were just content to describe. What directions this will take in the area of concern under discussion here remain to be seen; but if the pace of theoretical innovation keeps up with the rate of discovery in the field, the next century of archaeological exploration in Palestine and Syria will be even more fascinating than the last. And this, as Chapter 2 will show, was fascinating enough.

2. The Progress of Archaeological Studies

Pilgrims and crusaders. St Paul, it will be remembered, saw no virtue in knowing Christ as a historical person, "after the flesh." (2 Cor. 5:16.) It was only after the Emperor Constantine, in the earlier 4th century AD, had initiated an extensive program of church building in Palestine that pilgrims first went there to venerate the places associated with the ministry of Christ. So it is that even the oldest traditions about the Holy Places are separated from the time of Christ by a long interval. To this initial period of interest belongs the famous *Onomasticon* compiled by Bishop Eusebius (c. 260 to 339 AD) as a record of all the geographical names in the Holy Land mentioned in the Bible and their identification at the time he was writing. Thereafter, for 1,500 years, men and women came to Palestine not to acquire knowledge of its antiquities, but to extend their own religious experience through contemplation and prayer at the sacred sites, whose authenticity was never challenged.

Typical of such pilgrims, a remarkable number of whom have left us accounts of their private adventures, was one of the earliest, a lady known as Egeria, who visited the East about 381–384 AD. An enormously energetic and enthusiastic traveler, as indeed most of them were, she was keenly observant of detail, but deeply credulous. After reading her account, it comes as no surprise to realize that sacred places and suitable legends multiplied over the centuries to meet the demand of Christian travelers. A brief extract from Egeria's account of her visit to Sinai catches the spirit of these pilgrim journeys. Wilkinson renders it:

"So this was our plan. When we had seen everything we wanted and came down from the Mount of God, we would come to the place of the Bush. Then from there we would return through the middle of the valley now ahead of us and so return to the road with the men of God, who would show us each one of the places mentioned in the Bible. And that is what we did."

Century after century pilgrims covered the same ground, passing from one Christian shrine to the next without much attention to anything else. Their accounts were written in an increasingly stereotyped form. When the crusaders occupied Palestine in 1099 AD and pilgrims gained new facilities and fresh obligations, the flow of detailed accounts increased. Valuable as these documents are for students of medieval travel and piety, they offer virtually no archaeological information. The most striking single impression for the modern reader is the formidable hazards of the journey – did not Chaucer, to give the full measure of that remarkable woman, record that the Wife of Bath had been three times to Jerusalem? In marked

Map of Palestine in mosaic laid in a church in Madaba in Jordan about 560 AD, at a time when the Christian Church was a pioneer in mapmaking. This map contains a wealth of information of great value to archaeologists and historians. Jerusalem, set at the center, has been exaggerated in size (to a scale of about 1/1,600) and offers a surprisingly accurate plan of the city in Byzantine times.

p.19: part of the excavations at Jericho photographed sometime after work had finished, when erosion was already beginning to destroy the sections cut through the mound to reveal the superimposed levels of ancient settlement. The steps are modern.

contrast the Arab geographers of the 10th to 12th centuries strove to write comprehensive surveys of the land and its resources, each incorporating the work of his predecessors, but adding personal observations and experiences as appropriate. This information is far fuller, better digested and arranged than anything to be found in pilgrim accounts until the very late Middle Ages. Even archaeological observations slip in, as in an Arab account written in 1047 AD:

"[I]n various parts of Syria there may be seen some five hundred thousand columns, or capitals and shafts of columns, of which no one knows either the maker or can say for what purpose they were hewn, or whence they were brought."

By the late 15th century the pilgrim records begin to show discrimination and a more critical spirit. Sea routes to Palestine were now open under Venetian control and the increasing flow of pilgrims eastwards is reflected in the use of the new invention of printing to multiply William Wey's *Informatyon for Pylgrymes* and to print, in Bernhard von Breydenbach's *Peregrinationes* the first accurate drawings of the Holy Land and its shrines by Erhard Reuwich of Utrecht. The transition to the more objective accounts of later travelers may best be seen in the travels of the Dominican Friar, Felix Fabri of Ulm, between 1481 and 1483, published in 1556. He was not much more of a geographer or archaeologist than his predecessors, but he presents his account carefully, attempts discussion and is very comprehensive, indeed formidably so. He seems to have consciously sought the evidence for doubtful and conflicting statements and traditions, testing them against his own experience of life in Palestine. For instance, in rejecting the tradition that Christ was crowned with "seathorns," he writes:

"[T]hey would have used thorns from the nearest bushes, or perhaps they found them in the kitchen of the house [of Pilate] among the faggots of wood for the fire for I have seen with my own eyes that even at the present day they have no firewood save thorns, and their kitchens are full of exceeding sharp thorns for burning in the fire."

This tradition of writing reached its summit in Francesco Quaresmio's massive *Historica theologica et moralis Terrae Sanctae Elucidatio*, published in 1639. This is a compendium of traditions about the Holy Places, largely false, that had accumulated over centuries. The author's learning was impressive, but neither critical nor selective. How sane Fabri's comment seems in the face of a whole chapter in this book devoted to the discovery of the crown of thorns and the nails used in the crucifixion, followed immediately by another on the crown's condition and the number of the nails. Happily by the time this book appeared the tide of scholarship was beginning to run strongly in quite another direction.

Merchants, travelers and gentlemen-scholars. By the 16th century merchants, envoys, scholars and travelers had begun to replace the earlier soldiers and wandering men and women of the church. In a book by the Fleming Johann Zuallart (1585), careful drawings of towns, landscapes and buildings were provided, which for the first time exhibited a genuine archaeological intent. So popular did they become that contemporaries used them freely to illustrate their own travels. What may fairly be described as the earliest archaeological report based on first-hand study was written by the French scholar de la Rocque after his visit to Baalbek in 1688. Yet still it was premature.

More in tune with the times was Henry Maundrell's *A Journey from Aleppo to Jerusalem at Easter A.D. 1697* which very rapidly became, and long remained, a standard guidebook. He was by no means wholly uncritical nor devoid of antiquarian interests, but, as one example will show, his work was not very profound:

"[W]e came to Jacob's well, famous not only on account of its author, but much more for that memorable conference which our blessed Saviour here had with the woman of Samaria. If it should be questioned whether this be the very well that it is pretended for, or no, seeing it may be suspected to stand too remote from Sychar for women to come so far to draw water, it is answered, that probably

A restored wall and gateway in the Crusader castle of Belvoir, northern end of the Jordan valley overlooking the Sea of Galilee.

Left: modern drawing of the design on the seal of Baldwin of Boulogne, first King of the Latin Kingdom of Jerusalem (100–118 AD), created by the Crusaders. It shows, from left to right, the Dome of the Holy Sepulchre, the Tower of David in the citadel, and the Dome of the Rock with a cross placed on it by the Crusaders.

p.23, below: one of Borra's engravings for Wood's epoch-making *Ruins of Baalbec* (1757), showing a small temple of the Roman period rather romanticized.

the city extended farther this way in former times than it does now, as may be conjectured from some pieces of a thick wall, still to be seen not far from hence."

Even when this book was published, in 1703, the architect Nicholas Hawksmore casually supplied illustrations, more dramatic than exact, of the temples at Baalbek, and these were borrowed direct from Jean Marot's *L'Architecture française* published some years earlier. Topographical accuracy in plates, and in text, remained to be achieved.

Throughout the 18th century the Near East became more accessible to Europeans, and consequently the traveling nobleman, extending his almost obligatory Grand Tour of Europe, slowly replaced the traveler. He was frequently accompanied by artists and architects. Travel books, compilations of miscellaneous information, with a growing emphasis on visible antiquities, proportionately increased. Of these, Richard Pococke's *A Description of the East* (1743 to 1745), recounting a journey through Egypt, Palestine, Syria and Cyprus, is preeminent, in Gibbon's words, for its "superior learning and dignity," and for its greater range of plans, drawings and copies of inscriptions than any previous traveler had offered. This brief extract captures its charm. Of Baalbek he writes:

"Sweetmeats and coffee were brought . . . in the afternoon I went to see the famous temple. In the evening I was elegantly entertained . . . in an open mocot in his court, a fountain of water playing into a basin in the middle of the court. We had for supper a roasted fowl stuffed, pilaw, stewed meat with the soup, a dulma of cucumbers stuffed with forcemeat, and a dessert of apricots, apples and mulberries both red and white. On the 16th I viewed the two other temples and went round part of the walls." This was the life of an 18th-century gentleman-scholar on his travels.

A sense of adventure and a desire to increase his knowledge of classical architecture inspired the journey of Robert Wood (1716–1771) to Syria in 1750. Wood, later to become an English Under-Secretary of State, was accompanied by his two friends, John Bouverie, who succumbed to the journey, and James Dawkins, son of a wealthy Jamaican merchant, who with Bouverie initiated the project and financed it. An Italian draughtsman, Borra, was enlisted at Rome to provide the beautiful and epoch-making drawings of Palmyra and Baalbek for two magnificent volumes, *Ruins of Palmyra* (1753) and *Ruins of Baalbec* (1757), published after hazardous and exciting visits to both sites. Wood's introduction to Palmyra reveals a new and very practical interest in the monuments of antiquity.

"Our account of Palmyra is confined merely to that state of decay in which we found those ruins in the year 1751. It is not probable that the reader's curiosity should stop there: the present remains of that city are certainly too interesting to admit of our indifference about what it has been: *when and by whom it was built, the singularity of its situation (separated from the rest of mankind by an uninhabitable desert), and the source of riches necessary to the support of such magnificence,* are subjects which very naturally engage our attention."

These are the first modern surveys of monuments in the Near East based on first hand inspection and accurate survey of the existing remains. No attempt was yet made to excavate the debris. These two books had an immediate impact on artists, architects and scholars, becoming the inspiration for many of the forms and details of Neo-Classical architecture and interior decoration.

Explorers and pioneer excavators. In the following 80 years it was still the travelers, intent on exploring beyond well-trodden paths, who unveiled more and more of the region's standing monuments of antiquity. The German Seetzen in 1805 to 1807 explored Transjordan, rediscovering Philadelphia (Amman) and Gerasa (Jerash) and describing Caesarea Philippi for the first time since the Crusades. The outstanding Swiss explorer and scholar Johann Ludwig Burckhardt, in 1810 to 1812, rediscovered Petra, explored the Greek cities of Apamea and Larissa in Syria, and systematically recorded Arabic place names correctly for the first time.

Less enthusiastic were their contemporaries, the Englishmen Captains Irby and Mangles who, writing of a visit to Palmyra, observed:

"[W]e judged Palmyra to be hardly worthy of the time, expense, anxiety and the fatiguing journey.... We suspect that it was the difficulty of getting to Tadmor [the Biblical name for Palmyra], and the fact that few travellers have been there, that has given rise to the great renown of the ruins." The strains and hardships of such journeys can hardly be overemphasized to a generation for whom travel in such regions has become a matter of routine, and religion no bar to it.

Among these pioneers was Lady Hester Stanhope (1776–1839). Her role among the earliest excavators is rarely remembered because it was her many other exploits that are emphasized in Kinglake's masterly account of her in *Eothen* (1844). She took to excavation for no ordinary reason. When a manuscript came into her possession concerning three million gold coins, reputedly buried at Ascalon, she not only secured the Sultan's permission to dig for them but at one point had a ship of the Royal Navy placed at her disposal to facilitate the operation. Her doctor's account of this escapade, for to Lady Hester it was little more, deserves to be quoted in full as it provides such

Above: a contemporary drawing of Lady Hester Stanhope (1776–1839) arriving at Palmyra (Biblical Tadmor), the great caravan city in the Syrian desert which superseded Petra when the latter was taken by Rome.

Above: the tower built by Crusaders over the present entrance to the Church of the Holy Sepulchre in Jerusalem.

Right: stepped street in the medieval city of Jerusalem, virtually unchanged since it was built.

a good illustration of a style of excavation that, sadly, was to persist far too long in the Near East.

His letter is dated at Jaffa, 26 April 1815, and runs in part:

"This mosque was the spot to which our attention was to be particularly directed, but like the rest it was in so ruinous a state that even the outline of the edifice could not be made out. The Southern Wall alone just peeped above the rubbish, and the Mahr-ab or niche in it, which Musselmans hold in view when they pray, assured us of a very essential point, that we had not been deceived by the peasantry so as to mistake a wrong place for the right one. The peasants worked in corps of two hundred or three, according to the business of the day, to the sound of pipes and tabors; and the knowledge of what they were digging for gave them a degree of spirit to their work impossible otherwise to have existed. Piles of entablatures, capitals, fragments of pottery and lapis specularis, one or two lamps, and foundations of masonry more recent than the original building were the things that were by turns thrown up. Still from the very dilapidated state of the whole, it was impossible for Lady Hester, until some days had elapsed, to bring the marks with which her old manuscript furnished her, to bear.

"I think it was on the seventh day, that in excavating to the depth of twelve feet near the South Wall, we discovered a marble statue without a head. It measured 6½ feet in its mutilated state and represented, as I conjecture, a deity or deified person. For near the spot, in searching for the head, we found the emblem of Serapis, that from its dimensions had evidently belonged to the Statue, and on the shoulders were sculptured the thunderbolt, as you see it in the Eagles' claws at Baelbeck, with a meduses head on the breast. The trunk otherwise was naked. . . . But you know what circumstances led to its destruction; and however much we may regret the loss the fine arts have sustained, we cannot but admire the bold stroke by which Lady Hester crushed all the surmises of doubting minds, and the malicious reports of evil-disposed ones. [Lady Hester had in fact had the statue broken up so that, in her own words, 'it might not be said by illnatured people I came to seek for statues not treasure for the Porte,' that is for the Sultan] . . . Succeeding days brought us down to the original pavement of the temple, which was of fine slabs of white marble. It was on the ninth that we cherished some hopes of having found what we were in search of. Towards the Western foundations the labourers discovered an extraordinary kind of trough; not like the sarcophaguses to be seen near Latakia, which are evidently from their size and place, intended to contain human corpses; but longer and narrower, in proportion, and fit for no purpose easily conceivable except that of hiding treasure. Besides over it appeared to have been some kind of covering that had cost great trouble in removing. This trough must have been rifled of its contents by some of the Pashas and governors who have rummaged the ruins, and ostensibly for stones, really perhaps, for something more precious. So that our labours having proved ineffectual, we returned to Jaffa seventeen days after leaving."

Lady Hester's treasure hunt, though a sign of things to

View of Bethlehem, still much as it would have appeared to such Victorian artists as Lear and Wilkie.

come, was at the time untypical. The moment had not yet come for exploration by excavation, and during the following decades attention was directed to historical topography, particularly to the true location of cities mentioned in the Bible. As long ago as 1714 a Dutchman, Adrian Reland, had compiled a monumental handbook, critically digesting all relevant information from sources ancient, medieval and modern with the descriptive title, *Palestine Illustrated by Ancient Monuments*. As he had written in Latin, then still the international language of scholarship, his work lacked the popular appeal of contemporary travelers' tales. But in the early 19th century religious revivalism accelerated the development of the scientific study of Palestine at a time when political conditions in the Turkish Empire permitted the entry of missionaries.

It was one of these, the American Edward Robinson, who with his traveling companion Eli Smith transformed understanding of the ancient geography of the Holy Land and prepared the way for systematic archaeological study of individual sites. Robinson, Professor of Biblical Literature in New York College, was long familiar with previous publications, his friend Smith with Arabic. They were an ideal team for recording and evaluating the many Arabic place names that preserved so much information about ancient topography. In the three months spent traveling over the country in 1838 Robinson had in mind some fundamental principles of research clearly stated in his renowned *Biblical Researches in Palestine, Mount Sinai and Arabia Petraea* (1843):

"*All ecclesiastical tradition respecting the ancient places in and around Jerusalem and throughout Palestine IS OF NO VALUE, except so far as it is supported by circumstances known to us from the scriptures or from other contemporary sources* . . . On the same general principle that important work the *Onomasticon* the production of the successive labours of Eusebius and Jerome, which gives the names and describes the situation of places in the Holy Land, can be regarded in a historical respect only as a record of the traditions current in their day . . .

In view of this state of things we early adopted two general principles, by which to govern ourselves in our examination of the Holy Land. The *first* was to avoid as far as possible all contact with the convents and the authority of monks; to examine everywhere for ourselves with the Scriptures in our hands; and to apply for information solely to the native Arab population. The *second* was to leave as much as possible the beaten track, and direct our journeys and researches to those portions of the country which had been least visited.*"

As with so many seminal books, the full impact of Robinson's approach was not felt for some time, though it was agreed that his work superseded all previous studies of Palestinian historical geography.

Meanwhile in England popular attention was also turning towards Palestine, stimulated by the sketches and engravings of men like Sir David Wilkie, David Roberts and Edward Lear, and by such books as Kinglake's *Eothen*, Warburton's *The Crescent and the Cross* (1845) and Curzon's *Visits to Monasteries in the Levant* (1849).

More popular and more significant for the future was

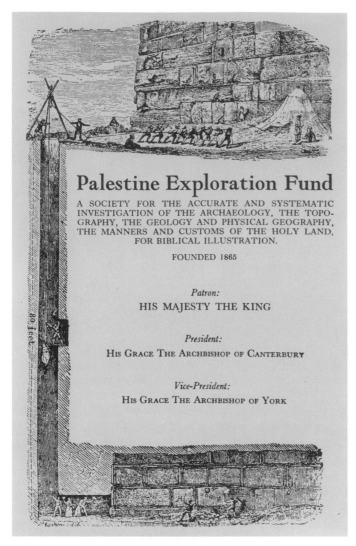

Above: a near contemporary drawing of visitors using the shaft and tunnel with which Warren explored the great Temple platform in Jerusalem.

Below: the Royal Engineers at rest during the great survey of Palestine about 1885 (Kitchener at lower right).

Nineveh and its Remains (1849), in which the young Austen Henry Layard so vividly described his pioneer excavations in the great Assyrian royal palaces at Nimrud in northern Iraq. One passage was to be of particular interest to those concerned with the Bible's accuracy for (although at the time Layard could not read the names on the "Black Obelisk," now in the British Museum) he had found the first ancient monument not only to mention but also to depict a king known from the Old Testament: Jehu of Israel paying tribute to Shalmaneser III, King of Assyria (c. 859 to 825 BC). Layard recounted the discovery thus:

"November, 1846. . . . I had business in Mosul, and was giving directions to the workmen to guide them during my absence. Standing on the edge of the hitherto unprofitable trench, I doubted whether I should carry it any further; but made up my mind at last not to abandon it until my return, which would be on the following day. I mounted my horse; but had scarcely left the mound when a corner of black marble was uncovered, lying on the very edge of the trench. This attracted the notice of the superintendent of the party digging, who ordered the place to be further examined. The corner was part of an obelisk, about six feet six inches in height, lying on its side, ten feet below the surface.

An Arab was sent after me without delay, to announce the discovery; and on my return I found the obelisk completely exposed to view. I descended eagerly into the trench, and was immediately struck by the singular appearance, and evident antiquity, of the remarkable monument before me. We raised it from its recumbent position, and, with the aid of ropes speedily dragged it out of the ruins."

An even more spectacular discovery was to follow in 1850 when, in excavating on the mound of Kuyunjik at Nineveh near Nimrud, sculptured reliefs were found showing, in Layard's own words:

"[T]he actual picture of the taking of Lachish, the city, as we know from the Bible, besieged by Sennacherib, when he sent his generals to demand tribute of Hezekiah, and which he had captured before their return (2 Kings 18:14; Isaiah 36:2); evidence of the most remarkable character to confirm the interpretation of the inscriptions, and to identify the king who caused them to be engraved with the Sennacherib of Scripture. This highly interesting series of bas-reliefs contained, moreover, an undoubted representation of a king, a city, and a people, with whose names we are acquainted, and of an event described in Holy Writ. They furnish us, therefore, with illustrations of the Bible of very great importance." These reliefs are now also in the British Museum.

Not only books but more forcefully the Crimean War (1853–1856), which in its beginning involved national rights in the Holy Places, called public attention to the often desperate state of these Holy Places. In the event it was a fusion of outraged piety and philanthropy that promoted action. The vigorous controversy arising from the publication of Darwin's *On The Origin of Species* in 1859 accelerated a demand for scientific reaffirmation of Biblical truth and close examination of the origins of the Christian faith. In 1864 the way was opened when Baroness Burdett Coutts, wishing to provide Jerusalem with a good water supply, arranged for Captain Wilson of the Royal Engineers to draw up an accurate survey of the city and its neighborhood.

Within a year the Palestine Exploration Fund had been set up to unite popular and academic interest in "investigating the archaeology, geography, geology and natural history of Palestine." Its initial program of research was twofold, to produce a modern map of the entire country and to begin the systematic investigation of Jerusalem through excavation. These plans were exceedingly ambitious. A preliminary survey by Wilson led eventually to the outstanding Survey of Western Palestine by Conder, Kitchener and others between 1872 and 1878. Perhaps no other single undertaking has contributed more to the right understanding of the archaeology and ancient history of Palestine than this magnificent map, scaled one inch to the mile, with its complementary *Memoirs*. Equally vital, though for political reasons less comprehensive, were the later surveys of eastern Palestine, Sinai and the Arabah.

The excavations in Jerusalem had a more equivocal legacy. In 1867 Captain Charles Warren, another Royal Engineer, was sent to investigate a whole set of problems associated with the ancient topography of the city. His task was far more formidable than his sponsors in England were in a position to realize, not only on account of the suspicions of local religious authorities, but also due to the accumulation of debris, in places 80 to 100 feet deep, which had to be plumbed. However good Warren's methods might have been, without any criteria for dating the

masonry or pottery his digging revealed he stood little chance of resolving the problems set him. He dug, in the only way his military training suggested, by sinking shafts and driving galleries through the debris adjacent to the ancient walls he wished to examine at their foundations. His vivid description of this operation, with its memorable opening paragraph, has since become a classic illustration, in textbooks on method, of how *not* to excavate. In acknowledging the truth of posterity's strictures it should be said in Warren's defense, as the following extracts show, that he executed his impossible task to the best of his ability with remarkable courage, resource and pertinacity. In *The Recovery of Jerusalem* (1871), edited by W. Morrison, Warren wrote:

"The system adopted in excavating at Jerusalem was that ordinarily used in military mining; therefore it is unnecessary to describe the details, as these can be obtained in any book of reference.

The work was one of considerable danger, for we were frequently subject to being blown up by the loose shingle which in an instant would destroy our galleries; to being smashed by the large pieces of masonry which lay huddled together above us, loosely lying one over the other, and ready to collapse at the slightest movement beneath them; or else to having our skulls stove in by the stones and iron bars which the fellahin, in their anxiety to be smart, occasionally allowed to fall back on us from the mouth of the shafts. . . . They were simply square pits sunk in the ground from 50 to 100 feet in depth, and sheeted round with wood, to keep the earth from falling in. . . .

One of the most ticklish pieces of work we had was in sinking a shaft down alongside the corner of an old wall; when, after passing its foundations, we sunk thirty feet, and, coming on rock, drove galleries in two directions.

The so-called "Alexander Sarcophagus," made of marble, found in Sidon. Probably made on one of the Greek islands for a Persian aristocrat in the 4th century BC. Finely carved reliefs round the outside illustrate the main activities of such a man. They have nothing to do with Alexander the Great.

We then commenced a third, which appeared to get on all right, and the workmen were allowed to go on with an occasional inspection. I was summoned down urgently one morning to the place, and on descending found that our shaft had no earth on two of its sides, from the rock upwards to the foundations of the corner, which were sticking out over a great void quite as large as the shaft itself. The soil we were working through had been very wet on this side (there had been some old shaft, I suppose), and the stuff had gradually all come down in the shape of mud into the gallery the men were working in, without being observed by them, and had been carried up. It was of vital importance to our work that there should be no subsidence of any old wall, and so the only thing to be done was to fill this place up as fast as we could. Accordingly the fellahin were bundled out, and Sergeant Birtles and I proceeded to tamp up the branch galleries, while every thud of earth let down to us shook small pieces from the foundations, which rattled over our heads with an ominous noise. But as long as we were in these galleries we were comparatively safe, for had the smash come we should probably have been only shut in, and might have starved on until we were dug out; but when they were tamped up, and we were in the shaft itself, it was a very ugly job, for we had to break open the side of the shaft and throw earth and stones into the cavity, while each basketful thrown in, though helping to fill it up, made the trembling foundations more and more unsafe; and all the time, through the opening we had made, stones and rubbish kept flying in upon us from above, taking away our breath, blowing out the light, and giving us an idea how something larger would come down. We were battling against time; gradually we found ourselves mounting up the 30 feet, until after five hours of it we were able safely to underpin the old wall, and feel that we had once more stolen a march upon accidents. . . .

The galleries were originally either 3 feet square, or 4 feet 6 inches in height and 3 feet wide. We found, however, by experience, that the best height for our workmen was from 3 feet 4 inches to 3 feet 8 inches, and the width from 2 feet 8 inches to 2 feet 10 inches." Until more refined methods of excavation could be devised, outstanding discoveries were more likely to be made by men of genius and enthusiasm with little resort to digging.

Warren was not the first man to excavate on any scale in the Holy Land. This distinction belongs to the French scholar Ernest Renan, whose *Vie de Jésus* (1863), the first life of Christ to present a vivid and accurate picture of the land in which he had lived, was one of the most hotly debated books of the century. Three years before its publication Renan had been commissioned by the French government to go to Syria in quest of ancient Phoenician monuments, sites and inscriptions. In a single year of intense activity from October 1860, he directed four campaigns, each based on a single center: Arvad, Byblos, Tyre and Sidon. In so far as time and primitive research techniques allowed he gathered a vast amount of information on standing monuments, rock-cut cemeteries and surviving visible inscriptions, all admirably published with little delay in *Mission de Phénicie* in 1864.

In 1867 a pupil of Renan's, Clermont-Ganneau (1846–1923), was appointed to the French consulate in Jerusalem. Almost his earliest achievement was to secure a squeeze of the now celebrated inscription of Mesha, King of Moab – the "Moabite Stone" – later broken up by local Arabs. Clermont-Ganneau, however, was able to secure the fragments for the Louvre. In 1871 he found a Greek inscription, reused in the walls of a school near the Haram esh-Sherif, site of the Temple in Jerusalem. It warned Gentiles that they entered the inner courts at the peril of their lives (Acts 21:28). In 1873 to 1874 the Palestine Exploration Fund commissioned Clermont-Ganneau to undertake archaeological investigations during which he found an ancient Jewish necropolis at Jaffa, important Hebrew and Greek bilingual inscriptions at Gezer, and numerous inscribed ossuaries and rock-cut tombs near Jerusalem. Later he obtained a squeeze of Hezekiah's inscription in his rock-cut water tunnel at Jerusalem before it was cut out and sent to the Imperial Ottoman Museum in Constantinople.

It was in every way the golden age of spectacular discoveries and uninhibited digging, similar to the pioneer work of Schliemann in Greece and at Troy. In March 1887, an American missionary, William K. Eddy, wrote a fascinating letter to the recently founded *American Journal of Archaeology* about current finds at Sidon that he had been privileged to inspect for himself before Turkish officials took them over:

"It has long been known that the plain and the hills about ancient Sidon are full of interesting antiquities. The pots filled with 8,000 coins of Philip and Alexander, the sarcophagus of Ashmunazer with its Phoenician inscription, and other finds, have aroused general interest in the subject of hid treasure. At present all excavations are conducted by laborers who quarry for stones. The building-stones that they sell nearly repay them for their work, while any antiquities found in the rubbish and ruined buildings or in unopened tombs make the work remunerative. No systematic exploration has been conducted since the French occupation of 1860, when the necropolis south of the city was excavated. Two years ago hundreds of tombs were discovered and opened at the foot of the hills east of the city. . . . Lately, some workmen, while they were digging in an open field about a mile to the northeast of Sidon, came upon a shaft, about twenty feet square, sunk in the sandstone."

Eddy then describes his visit to the rock-cut chambers leading off this shaft that contained, among others, four magnificent carved sarcophagi, now called respectively the "Alexander," "Weepers," "Lycian" and "Satrap," and the anthropoid coffin of King Tabnit of Sidon, all now in the Archaeological Museum at Istanbul:

"As I walked about this sarcophagus [i.e. the 'Alexander'], the surprises which met my eye rendered it difficult to make mental notes. That I was fortunate in seeing what I did is evident, for from that hour no European has been allowed to enter the excavations. Anything like measurements, notes, or photographs, was wholly out of the question. . . . Only one tomb has been found as yet unrifled, and that contained decayed wood or decayed mummy-remains, a vase of alabaster 10 inches high, a gold ring with stone, and a gold chain weighing over 100 grammes; also a gold frontlet of small size."

Archaeologists and historians. On two occasions, between 1890 and 1910, excavators of genius came to Palestine – W. M. F. Petrie (1853–1942), and George Reisner (1867–1942). Both had experience of digging in Egypt and appreciated the special nature of Palestine's ancient sites and the way they should be excavated. But before they could establish and develop their archaeological methods on the spot they had to leave Palestine.

The true significance of the numerous tells all over Palestine and Syria was only slowly realized. Pioneer topographers like Robinson took most of those in the Jordan valley to be natural hillocks. Even when Warren had revealed by cuttings that they were artificial, largely made up of mud-brick, he seems to have assumed that this was merely a platform upon which buildings had once been set. One of his soundings at Jericho came within feet of discovering the great Neolithic stone tower revealed almost a century later by Dr Kenyon's excavations. It was not until 1890, when Flinders Petrie studied the mound of Tell el-Hesi for the Palestine Exploration Fund, that their true nature and archaeological potential was fully revealed. In a lecture to the Fund, Petrie used the history of London to explain a tell's growth and how its history might be reconstructed from the excavation and analysis of the sequence of levels revealed. He went on.

"Only instead of needing to cut a deep hole to the bottom [ie of Tell el-Hesi] a fine section was already prepared through the 60 feet depth of the tell by the wearing away of the stream on one side.

The first difficulty that we meet is that there are no coins and no inscriptions to serve to date any of the levels. How then can we read history in a place if there is not a single written document? How can we settle here what the date of anything is, if not a single name or date remains? This is the business of archaeology. Everything is a document to the archaeologist. His business is to know all the varieties of the products of past ages, and the date of each of them. When our knowledge is thus developed, every-

Typical archaeological sections cut through city mounds, or tells, at different periods. 1. Petrie's excavation of Tell el-Hesi in 1890. Walls are shown in cross section, a layer of ashes lies over a stone stratum, and a glacis (fortification bank) is indicated at left. 2. Part of Reisner's excavations at Samaria (1924). Walls are shown in sequence (a. Ahab level, Israel b. Hellenistic c. Roman) but with no indication of their relation to occupation levels. 3. Kathleen Kenyon's main trench cutting at Jericho (1952–1957) is a more sophisticated job, showing a. pre-pottery Neolithic b. Neolithic c. Bronze Age and d. Iron Age levels and walls in complex relationship.

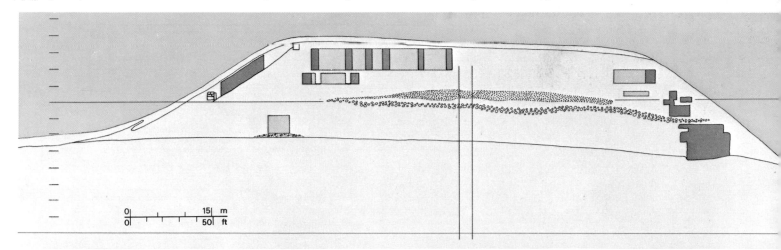

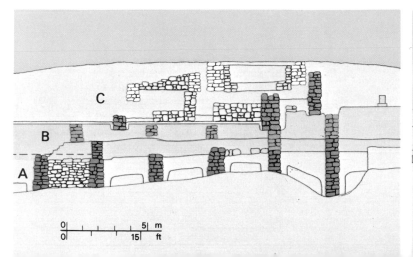

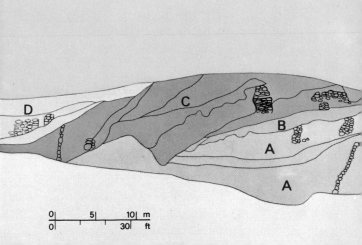

View across the top of the mound at Jericho some time after the end of Dame Kathleen Kenyon's excavations.

thing teems with information. Nothing is so poor or so trivial as not to have a story to tell us. The tools, the potsherds, the very stones and bricks of the wall cry out, if we have the power of understanding them.

But how are we to proceed in a country where we know nothing as yet of the age of its products? It is like an inscription in an unknown language: for that we have to wait for a bilingual tablet, and so begin to read the unknown from the known. Thus in the same way we must wait till we find objects from other countries of known age, intermixed with those as yet unclassified, in order to spell out the archaeology of a fresh country. This interpretation of the archaeology of Palestine was the special attraction to me for working there. The materials of known age proved but scanty in my work; a few pieces of pottery were all I had to rely on. To anyone unfamiliar with such evidences this might seem a slender basis for the mapping out of a history; yet I had full confidence in it."

In this, time has proved Petrie right, though his methods now seem crude. Perceptive and novel as was his understanding of the basic anatomy of a Palestinian tell, and the manner in which its history might broadly be established through a pottery sequence, his concept of debris excavation was elementary. He had worked at Hesi from a ready-made section cut through the mound by the erosion of a stream and was thus, in his all too brief encounter with a tell, not confronted with the complexities he would have found in cutting trenches down from the top. F. J. Bliss, his American successor at Hesi (who later excavated four tells in the Shephelah), though not unaware of the successive levels of debris, treated them arbitrarily as absolute horizontal bands, happily disregarding their structural eccentricities. At Sandahan, one of the Shephelah tells (the Hellenistic city of Marissa) the original plan was to uncover the whole site level by level, but mercifully only the first, Hellenistic, city was cleared.

Bliss's collaborator, R. A. S. Macalister, later excavated the tell of Gezer between 1902 and 1909 and the three volumes he published on this work may be taken as an outstanding example of the pioneer phase of tell excavation. He worked there on his own, save for his untrained laborers, who cut into the site strip by strip, the debris from succeeding strips being dumped back into those cut earlier. The published architectural plans of eight "strata" in the city's history are in reality composite, each made up of buildings from several different levels. No record is given to identify which area, let alone which trench, each object came from. Artifacts are simply classified into arbitrarily-named phases, covering centuries in some cases. Subsequent excavations have confirmed that Macalister's sequence for the Iron Age was distorted by a gap in occupation that he failed to notice. In three ways his methods contrast strikingly with those used 60 years later. Now considerable emphasis is laid on adequate supervision by trained staff, on the meticulous recording of changes in the vertical stratigraphy of the tell, and the direct relation of all finds to the layers from which they came.

Reisner's excavations at Samaria-Sebaste from 1909 to 1910 mark the emergence of modern methods, though they were to be long in bearing fruit. His emphasis on adequate training and staffing, on the close supervision of work in progress, on detailed and accurate recording of finds, including the systematic use of photography, would not in themselves have transformed Palestinian archaeology. What did prepare the way for major change was his exceptionally clear insight into the nature of a Palestinian tell, for by chance he had chosen a singularly complicated example. He immediately realized that, though his German contemporaries might show great skill as architects and surveyors of the buildings they found, they could never hope to date and phase their construction correctly, or for that matter the objects found in them, without careful detection and separation of the layers of debris in and around them. It is rather difficult to establish quite how much of the excellent theory Reisner expounded in his final report, not published until 1924, was applied in practice, the more so as his collaborator, Fisher, reverted very much to the German architectural tradition when digging elsewhere later. Reisner's brief career in Palestine shows, if demonstration was really needed, that no textbook of method, however good, is any substitute for the continuing presence of the master in the field teaching his junior assistants, who will be his successors.

It is impossible to indicate briefly the acute insights Reisner revealed in his final report, *Harvard Excavations at Samaria*, for not only does he consider every kind of debris in detail, but also the agents, natural and human, which affect their character. One brief extract must serve to show how much more sophisticated than Petrie's was his definition of tell structure:

"The hill [i.e. of Samaria], as we approached it, presented a mass of broken horizontal and vertical strata, and some time elapsed before we recognized the significance of all its features. When it became clear that regular horizontal strata were not to be expected, the plan was adopted of clearing . . . until we found a floor-level either actually existing or indicated by the foot of a superstructure wall on the surface of a different kind of debris. Then we cleared along this level. At first, puzzled by the filled holes . . . these filled holes were completely cleared in connection with higher stratum from which the filling had come. Finally, with a knowledge of our deposits which made it possible to recognize almost instantly the character and age of the debris, we were able to proceed with greater consistency."

Almost a quarter of a century later, also at Samaria, Kathleen Kenyon introduced fresh and radical refinements of method when a member of a Joint Expedition under Crowfoot from 1931 to 1935. Dr Kenyon's approach derived from the techniques developed and expounded in England by Mortimer Wheeler for, as she argued, "almost identical methods can be applied in the East, though the difficulties are undoubtedly much greater, both from the succession of strata and the difficulty of getting enough intelligent workmen." Part of Dr Kenyon's fuller exposition of the problems, in an article published in 1939, presents an interesting comparison with Reisner's earlier discussion. She writes:

"Throughout all periods in the history of a site like Samaria, builders have found it easier to pull down and dig up the walls of their predecessors in order to obtain stone, than to quarry new blocks. The result is that many walls are represented only by the holes out of which their foundations have been grubbed. Fortunately these robber trenches can always be identified, as they are inevitably filled by material differing from the undisturbed floors on either side. . . .

Such then, is the problem with which an excavator of a site such as Samaria is faced. It is quite clear that to go straight ahead and clear out all the soil would destroy all the evidence. It would be useless to record the absolute depth of the objects, since in different parts of the site this has a different significance, and it may well have arrived in its position by a foundation trench or a robber trench cutting through the earlier levels. It is necessary, therefore, to examine and correlate all the layers of soil, particularly in relation to the walls. Therefore, the worst possible thing to do is to clear along the face of a wall, as its relation to the layers is thus destroyed. It is necessary to cut a section at right angles to each wall, in order to decide which layers are earlier, contemporary and so on. The next stage is to secure sections across the whole area, linking it all together. The method of digging therefore is to start by cutting trenches across the area in order to identify the floors, foundation trenches and robber trenches. When the meaning of a layer has been established and complete records have been made, by planning, photographing, and drawing sections, it can then be removed, care of course being taken to keep separate material from the foundation

J. B. Pritchard's excavations at Tell es-Sa'idiyeh in Jordan.

trenches and robber trenches. . . . For the purposes of identification later, it is of course necessary that full notes should be kept as to where everything comes from. . . . When the season's work is over, the excavator thus has a complete record of the site. He has plans of walls which he can prove are contemporary by their association with the same floors. He has pottery and objects from various levels, with measured sections to prove to which of the various building periods they belong, and he has photographs. He is therefore able to classify his material, and to date the unknown by association with the known. Most of the dating of Palestinian objects is based on association with objects imported from Egypt and elsewhere." The tradition extending from Petrie through Reisner is very clear in this presentation, though the emphasis is different.

Meanwhile at the smaller, historically less significant site of Tell Beit Mirsim, occupied over a much longer period of time, W. F. Albright was conducting a series of excavations between 1926 and 1932 which for the first time set the archaeology of Palestine in an adequate and reliable framework. Albright used the methods of work advised by Reisner, but transformed them through his attention to detail, outstandingly so in his analysis of the pottery sequence, and his already very wide knowledge of the relevant archaeological and historical literature. It is fascinating to observe through his reports how his mastery of the site developed season by season until at the close he could rapidly, and accurately, recognize the pottery forms and fabrics distinctive of each major period of occupation on the tell. But he clearly perceived the dangers of the Reisner method in the hands of a careless or insufficiently informed excavator: "Of course, this method is only sound when applied with adequate knowledge of pottery and comparative archaeology, otherwise it may conceal thoroughly unsound execution and interpretation."

Whether intended or not, Albright's words here are a fair comment on a number of exceedingly ambitious contemporary excavations in Palestine. At Megiddo for instance, excavated between 1925 and 1939, the initial plan envisaged removing the whole tell stratum by stratum. Even had this proved feasible, prohibitive expense fortunately prevented it, leaving plenty of the tell for future excavators to dig by more sophisticated techniques in later years. Nor was the work helped by changes in the supervisory staff, as each had to adjust afresh to the rigors of the work. In peeling off the debris of the tell in successive layers of uniform depth, grave pits or tomb shafts went unnoticed, so that finds from the actual graves when reached were recorded with those often earlier objects found in the soil about them, not with the material from the higher level from which they had been sunk in antiquity. In other words pottery groups, perhaps separated by hundreds of years, were hopelessly mixed up. In the same way any disturbance, the robbing out of walls or the cutting of rubbish pits, or any inconsistency in levels due to terracing or natural declines, was overlooked, with inevitable confusion in the subsequent chronological attribution of buildings and finds. As the results of these excavations were published in a relatively raw state, the reports may now be used as a basis for revision in the light of subsequent discoveries elsewhere; but even then inconsistencies remain, only to be solved by further digging. This is, naturally, impossible where previous excavators had totally stripped an area, illustrating the need for equal care in excavation and publication. Archaeology is destruction and the excavator's report the only record of what he has removed to reach earlier levels.

Since World War II, though the number of excavations in Palestine and Syria has enormously increased, field techniques have been refined, rather than fundamentally altered in the constant quest for ever more foolproof methods for retrieving all possible information from the soil. The primary change has been in the use of much larger supervisory teams, numbering among them not only archaeologists, surveyors and architects, but also geographers, zoologists, botanists, and many other natural scientists. The so-called Wheeler-Kenyon methods have been widely adopted and improved, not least by Dr Kenyon herself in excavations at Jericho and Jerusalem. In two ways particularly American excavators have sought to refine this approach. There is first a greater emphasis on teamwork, with mutually critical cooperation both in fieldwork and publication, and secondly a more elaborate system of recording and studying such basic evidence as pottery. Great indeed is the contrast between the expeditions of Macalister to Gezer and that of G. E. Wright to Shechem half a century later. In the words of one member, L. E. Toombs:

"The critical judgement of half a dozen persons all intimately involved in the excavation and a number of note-book sections are thus combined to produce a result which is likely to be far more accurate than the interpretation of any single individual."

The approach may change, the methods improve and the range of interpretation grow, but each generation of excavators stands, as it were, on the shoulders of the one that went before, and all are united in a single quest – a better understanding of the ancient history of Palestine and Syria.

Hazor: A Canaanite city

Tell el-Kedah, ancient Hazor, is one of the largest and most impressive archaeological sites in the Syro-Palestinian region, with a mound occupying 32 acres and a large outer enclosure or lower city of 175 acres. In 1928 the British archaeologist John Garstang made trial excavations there, but it was an Israeli expedition under Professor Yadin between 1956–8 and 1968–70 that revealed striking archaeological confirmation of the scattered historical information on Hazor's importance, found in ancient texts. The city is mentioned early in the 2nd millennium BC in the Egyptian "Execration Texts," in the 18th century BC letters from Mari, when it took an active part in the vital tin trade, and in the Tell el-Amarna letters of the 14th century BC when its ruler, though a vassal of the pharaoh, was called "king."

Joshua defeated an alliance of Canaanite kings led by Hazor's ruler. The city is mentioned in the wars of Deborah, was strongly fortified by Solomon, and was destroyed by the Assyrians in 732 BC.

Excavations showed that the "enclosure" was a lower city with its own fortifications founded in the 18th century BC, destroyed in the 16th (perhaps by Egyptian armies) and later restored. It was particularly prosperous in the 14th century BC, with important temples and fortifications like those of other major Canaanite cities. Settlement on the mound or upper city shown below began in the 3rd millennium BC, and during the 2nd ran parallel with the lower city. For much of the Iron Age it served primarily as a fortified acropolis with administrative buildings and storerooms.

Above: a full aerial view of Tell el-Kedah, ancient Hazor, looking north, with the main mound or upper city in the foreground and the massive enclosure of the lower city beyond. It is an outstanding example of an ancient Near Eastern city site, with mounds representing the remains of almost two thousand years in the history of a site whose strategic frontier position gave it a vital role in international trade and politics.

Below: an aerial view with the main mound of the upper city extending across the center, its height well emphasized by the shadows. The excavations of the citadel in area B may be seen clearly at its western end; Iron Age storerooms in the center. In the foreground is the southern end of the lower city with excavations in area C cutting through its ramparts. Here at the foot of the rampart was found the "stelae temple" illustrated on a following plate.

Left: bronze inlay plaque of a Canaanite from the "Orthostats Temple," about 1450 BC.

Reconstruction of part of the upper city in the time of Jeroboam II (c. 786–746 BC). At this time buildings in the area were changed from public administrative purposes to more residential and commercial use, including houses, shops and workshops. They are among the best built structures of the Israelite period at Hazor, testifying, as do the fine objects found in them, to the prosperity of Hazor's citizens at this time.

Reconstruction of the buildings contemporary with the Assyrian occupation after the sack of Hazor in 732 BC, when a citadel was built at one end of the upper city occupying the whole of its western bluff. Its form and position indicate that at some time between about 700 and 550 BC it served as an isolated fort for the occupying Assyrian, Babylonian, and perhaps eventually Persian troops controlling this strategic area.

Above: excavation trench cut through the fine mudbrick wall of the upper city (built in the 18th century BC) to show its structure.

Top: aerial view of excavations at the end of 1958 in area A at the northeast end of the upper city, showing the Solomonic gateway and casemate wall below a pillared storeroom of Ahab's time, in turn below a courtyard building of about the time of Jeroboam II (c. 786–746 BC).

Right: looking down into the water-system designed to ensure water supplies for the upper city in time of siege. It was cut in the earlier 9th century BC when Aramaean and Assyrian threats to Israel had become menacing.

Above: the "Orthostats Temple," looking from the porch towards the Holy of Holies; a typical Late Canaanite temple found at the end of the lower city furthest from the main mound. It had three main rooms set one behind the other exactly as did Solomon's Temple in Jerusalem. At the far end was the Holy of Holies with two pillars, wall benches and ritual fittings; then a Middle Hall with side rooms and two free-standing pillars flanking its entrance much as the pillars "Jachin" and "Boaz" did in Solomon's Temple; then a porch. The name of the temple derives from the well-dressed basalt slabs lining the lower walls inside the Holy of Holies and the porch.

Below: a big orthostat carved with a crouching lion in low relief; probably carved in the 15th century BC to line the right hand side of the entrance. Similar lions were found at Tell Atshana (Alalakh) in Syria. It had been carefully buried, perhaps when the temple was reconstructed in the 13th century BC.

Left: adjacent to the "stelae temple" were several large buildings in one of which was the potter's workshop, shown here, with his wheel (top right in two pieces) and a fine clay mask.

Below: this relatively small clay mask from the potter's workshop, with neither open nostrils nor open mouth, may have been fitted to a statue's face or hung on a temple wall as a votive.

In excavating the Middle Bronze Age rampart surrounding the lower city a small shrine of the late Canaanite period was found cut into it. In a broad hall there was a niche in the western wall containing small stelae and a statue. There were also benches along the walls for offerings. Symbols on the stelae and statue: full and crescent moons, suggest that this temple was dedicated to a moon god and his consort.

A seated male statue, only 18 cm high, found in the final
burnt level of the Canaanite tripartite "Orthostats Temple."
The chair on which the figure sits is clearly reproduced. The
head had been broken off in the final destruction at the end of
the Canaanite period and was found close by in a deep layer
of ashes. A rather similar statue was found elsewhere in the
Canaanite lower city. Since the man wears no identifying
headdress or emblem on his chest, he is more likely to be a
human being (perhaps even the ruler of Hazor) than a god.
The statue would have been set in the temple as a permanent
token of worship by the donor.

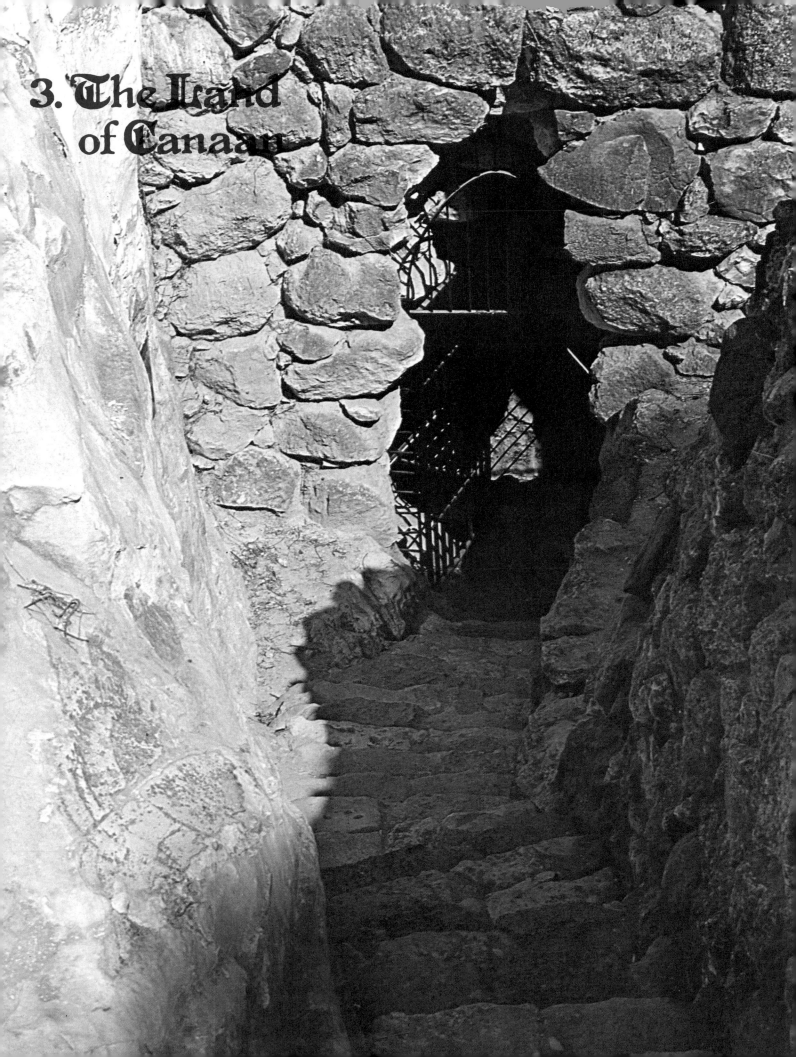

3. The Land of Canaan

Nomads and townsmen. Towards the end of the 3rd millennium BC documents from Egypt and Mesopotamia reveal that many parts of the Near East were troubled by one of those sporadic eruptions of nomadic peoples into the centers of urban settlement recurrent in the region's history. Even in fully historic times it is difficult to identify the mainsprings of such movements. It is particularly so when archaeological and written evidence is both sparse and uneven. The fine balance always existing between inhabitants of the marginal areas along the fringes of the great Arabian desert and their prosperous neighbors settled in more naturally favored areas needs only to be upset at one point, perhaps by minor climatic changes leading to drought and famine, for a whole chain reaction to be set off. Rulers in Mesopotamia from at least as early as 2300 BC tried to stem the flow by force of arms, even by building great walls; but people known to them as "Amurru(m)," modern "Amorites," slowly merged into Mesopotamian society at many points, recognizable by their distinctive personal names. Within a few centuries of 2000 BC Amorite names in surviving texts from cities like Mari, Alalakh and Ugarit show their penetration deep into Syria as well.

Though less exposed, for its land bridge with Asia is very narrow, Egypt did not escape similar intrusions. In the declining years of the Old Kingdom, towards about 2200 BC, with the central authority greatly weakened by internal dissensions, Semitic peoples penetrated across Sinai into the Delta in increasing numbers. In an ancient Egyptian text in which the dead King Khety III is depicted writing instructions for his son Merikare, the natural contrast between Egypt and Palestine is neatly described and the will-o'-the-wisp character of the intruders noted. In Wilson's translation part of it runs:

"Lo, the wretched Asiatic – it goes ill with the place where he is, afflicted with water [i.e. rain], difficult from many trees, the ways thereof painful because of the mountains. He does not dwell in a single place (but) his legs *are made to go astray*. He has been fighting (ever) since the time of Horus, (but) he does not conquer, nor yet can he be conquered."

For Palestine, where there are no local written records, the impact of nomadic intruders in the centuries just before 2000 BC is clearly illustrated in the archaeological record. After a long period of settled urban life – archaeologically the Early Bronze Age – excavated tells show a marked break in the continuity of settlement, regularly accompanied by signs of destruction, followed in some cases by temporary, in others by more permanent absence of walled settlements and well-built houses. This has been variously designated by archaeologists as the Middle Bronze Age I, or Early Bronze to Middle Bronze period. The latter name better denotes its essentially transitional character. In the meanwhile what evidence there is for human occupation is confined to temporary encampments, sometimes in caves or crudely-built dwellings. By way of contrast con-

Stone stela of the Middle Bronze Age from Ras Shamra (Ugarit), showing Baal in his guise as a weather-god. The small figure on a pedestal in front of him may be a goddess related to him.

siderable attention was paid to the cutting of remarkably diverse rock tombs, or the building of tumuli, well furnished with pottery, copper weapons and simple jewelry. The lack of homogeneity in the material culture of Palestine at this time emphasizes the varied character of its creators. Although neither the course nor the origin of these nomadic intrusions may yet be exactly charted, the equipment they brought to Palestine is most nearly matched earlier in eastern Syria. Whether they were all, or even in part, Amorite, as has commonly been argued, is still an open question. At this time both the Negev and Transjordan also supported considerable populations.

The slow return to urban life in Palestine after 2000 BC was also stimulated from Syria, where generally there had been no such radical break. Here, as in Mesopotamia, the newcomers had often been peacefully assimilated. This new phase, known to archaeologists as the full Middle Bronze Age, may most conveniently be labelled "Canaanite," as these people are first referred to in the 18th century BC in a document from Mari in Syria. But, since it is used

Left: fragment of chalky limestone inscribed in Egyptian hieratic by a scribe under tuition about 1200 BC. It relates the famous story of Sinuhe, a high Egyptian official exiled to Palestine and Syria centuries earlier.

Above: map of Canaan until about 1200 BC. The exact geographical limits of Canaan are hard to establish and are most unlikely ever to have been fixed in any but the most general way, since Canaan was a community of loosely linked city-states.

p. 41: entrance to the water system at ancient Megiddo, constructed to ensure a supply of water in times of siege.

The head of a man sculpted in stone, which was found in a shrine adjoining the Palace of Yarimlim at Tell Atshana, and dates from the 18th century BC. The identity of the sitter has not been firmly established, but it may even be the king himself.

in the Old Testament to describe the major element in the population of Palestine west of the Jordan (Num. 34:2–12) at the entry of the Israelites to the area in the later 13th century, it is the best available generic term for the culture of Palestine, and much of Syria, in the 2nd millennium BC. Its original meaning is still debated. Theories that Canaan was named after the crimson dye industry or after its vigorous merchant community, to cite but the most common explanations, do not bear close examination. Indeed it is probable that *Kn'n*, a word of uncertain origin, was the area's original name and that the name of the dye was derived from it, not the reverse.

Canaanite cities. The state of Palestine and Syria in the crucial transitional period is uniquely portrayed in a fascinating Egyptian text recounting the exile there of a high-ranking Egyptian official, Sinuhe, during the reign of the pharaoh Sesostris I in the 20th century BC. Sinuhe's wanderings took him through a society primarily semi-nomadic, with only a few scattered towns. In the region of southern Syria, where he settled, agriculture and herding, supplemented from olive groves and orchards, provided the necessities, while conflicts over rights of pasture and

water were apparently common. The local prince entrusted to Sinuhe both a district and a tribe, reflecting again the bedouin nature of the people. Nothing in this account indicates Egyptian control of Palestine, though it shows that travel between the two was relatively easy and that Egyptians were resident at local courts.

Again from Egypt, about a century later, come a series of texts, inscribed on bowls and figurines used in magical rites to curse the pharaoh's enemies ("Execration Texts"), that list the names of Semitic princes, Amorites among them, ruling in Syria and Palestine. Significantly, in the earlier group, from about 1870 BC (the 12th Dynasty), certain areas are ruled by a number of chiefs, while in the later, from about 1800 BC (13th Dynasty), virtually all the towns and city states listed, embracing Palestine and Syria, have a single prince. This is valuable confirmation of an urban revival in the 19th century BC evident from archaeological excavations. It was the beginning of one of the most prosperous periods in the history of ancient Palestine that was eventually to have profound effects on Egypt.

Cities were reestablished, some independent, some loosely confederated, perhaps even at first unwalled, but soon with simple fortifications. At Megiddo, for instance, a city with salient and recess fortifications grew up again around the age-old shrines and "high place." Later, walls were set upon massive earthern ramparts revetted with plastered slopes or cyclopean masonry footings, witness as much to increased wealth as to internal town rivalries. Populous towns have been excavated at such widely separated sites as Ras Shamra and Tell Atshana in Syria, Hazor, Taanach and Megiddo, Shechem, Jericho and Gezer in Palestine. The most important of all, like Carchemish, Qatna and Hazor, grew so large in the 18th century BC that great areas with formidable ramparts had to be added to the original towns, which then became the upper city housing the ruler's palace and its ancillary buildings. In the Negev and Transjordan, however, the prevailing way of life remained nomadic until the 13th century BC.

Excavations, always very partial on such large sites, have only revealed bits of such towns, but sufficient to establish the general character of their walls and gateways, temples, administrative buildings, patrician and common houses (a contrast particularly marked by the end of the period), and shops and storehouses. Architectural distinction is rare. So far the only palace attributable to this period is that in the city of Alalakh in Syria. Here in the early 18th century BC, King Yarimlim, vassal to a more powerful local ruler, had a palace rising on three terraces above the town. Basalt blocks formed the foundations, timber and mudbrick the walls. Rooms at the northern end served ceremonial purposes, others less well built across a courtyard to the south were the domestic quarters, some with painted plaster walls. A well-sculpted man's head, perhaps a king's, came from an adjacent shrine and is one of the rare pieces of

Right: baked-clay stand (restored) for use in a temple at Bethshan near the end of the Bronze Age. It appears to represent a three-storeyed house with a man and a woman at the upper windows, a snake at the lower. Their cult significance is unknown.

Far right: finely made gold axehead from Byblos, of the 18th century BC, when her trading activity, particularly with Egypt, brought the city great wealth.

and animal bones point to sacrifices. Clay figurines of doves were common, but not so important as figurines of women, cast on the spot in copper or bronze and silver. Late in the period, about 1600 BC, a distinctive form of "fortified" temple appears which, on the sites where they have so far been excavated – Shechem, Megiddo and Hazor – were to survive for over 400 years in modified form. The Shechem temple, perhaps dedicated to Baal-berith, had massive walls enclosing a rectangular shrine with a double row of columns. Towers, perhaps supporting sacrificial altars, flanked a narrow entrance porch. In a courtyard before the temple stood an altar and two upright stones (*massebot*). The thick walls and towers suggest a building of more than one story, whose form may be guessed at from a series of baked clay models found in a later temple at Beth-shan.

The now famous "High Place" at Gezer also belongs to the end of the Middle Bronze Age. It was first excavated in 1902 by Macalister and reexamined in 1968. It consisted of a row of ten monoliths, some over nine feet high, set on a north-south axis, in a large square. A huge stone block, a basin or socket for another monolith, lay to the west. A low wall surrounded these installations with an extensive plastered area on the perimeter. The monoliths were all set up at the same time. This has long been thought to be one of those Canaanite "high places," later denounced by the prophets of Israel, with its stone uprights representing the goddess Asherah. But more recently it has been explained, on the analogy of a ceremony at Gilgal recounted in Joshua (4:1 ff.), that this was the scene of a ceremony for renewing a covenant uniting ten city states in a league.

Large and well-equipped rock-cut graves offer glimpses of household equipment not so well preserved in tells.

monumental stone sculpture from this region in the 2nd millennium BC. The palace archive room yielded a valuable collection of inscribed clay tablets that reveal something both of contemporary political history and of the city's social structure, with its autocratic ruler, its freemen, semi-free dependents owing services and dues in kind to the palace, and slaves, usually prisoners-of-war or debtors.

Of temples Palestine has more to show, though forms varied and there is little certainty about the deities worshiped in them. An isolated shrine at Nahariyah, within yards of the Mediterranean, was perhaps dedicated to Asherah of the Sea. Its plan was modified a number of times, growing larger and more substantial. Within a mound (bamah) of piled stones there were traces of the libations poured over it and the cult vessels used; hearths

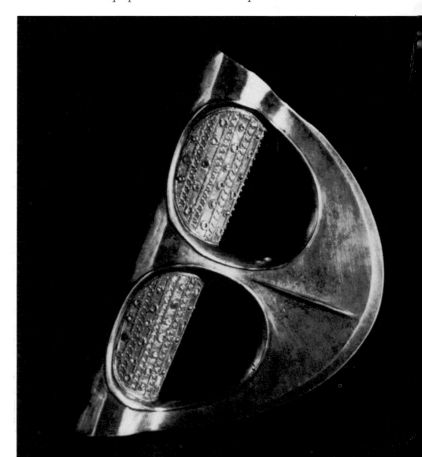

Pottery, for which the wheel was now extensively used, was inventive in form and often of fine fabric, the surface red, brown or cream, and richly burnished. A distinctive painted ware has affinities far afield in Syria. Copper, now alloyed with tin, which came to great cities like Hazor from Mari on the Euphrates, was used for a growing range of well made tools and weapons. In the minor arts Egyptian influence was particularly conspicuous, notably in the manufacture of wooden furniture, remarkably well preserved in a series of tombs cut into rock at Jericho, alabaster vessels copied in local stones, faience vessels and figurines, amulets, scarabs and jewelry of gold and semi-precious stones.

Undoubtedly the most significant and enduring contribution of the Canaanite Middle Bronze Age to civilization was the invention by unknown scribes of a simple alphabetic script. In 1905 Petrie's excavations at Serabit el-Khadim in Sinai revealed several short inscriptions in an unknown pictographic script carved by Semites working in the local turquoise mines for the Egyptians. Deciphered partially by Gardiner in 1918, more fully by Albright in 1948, it was shown to have arisen under the direct influence of literate Egyptians, though the texts were mainly supplications to the chief gods of the Semitic laborers. A growing number of related inscriptions, all very short, show that by about 1600 BC this script was sporadically used in such cities as Lachish and Shechem to write the local language. It then consisted of 27 letters, all pictographic, their stance depending on the direction of writing, which was still flexible. Each sign represented a consonant plus any vowel; an abstraction and simplification not achieved earlier and essentially an alphabetic system of writing. Now for the first time in theory at least, literacy was put within the reach of many more people. But for centuries international diplomatic correspondence was to be conducted in Akkadian, the language of Mesopotamia, written on clay tablets in the infinitely more complex cuneiform script.

Egypt at this time valued Palestine as a source of agricultural supplies, primarily cattle. Egyptian officials, whose statuettes, seals and seal-impressions have been recovered in excavations, were stationed in key Palestinian cities, presumably with military detachments, to ensure the regular flow of this trade. The cities in question lay either on the coastal road, like Megiddo, Gezer and Tell el-Ajjul, or like Byblos, Beirut and Ugarit on the coast or, as at Qatna, at sensitive points in Syria. Only in rare cases did the pharaoh intervene with his armies. Sesostris III campaigned in Syria and the Shechem region.

Egyptian relations with the Syrian cities in particular were generally more complex. The finest artifacts of Syrian origin to have survived from this period were included in a treasure of silver vessels, seals and amulets in bronze chests presented by the pharaoh Amenemmes II to the temple of Monthu at et-Tod, south of Luxor in Egypt. The traffic in such luxury goods was reciprocal, for pots of obsidian, caskets of ivory, ebony and gold, pectorals of gold and precious stones, mirrors and scarabs, many inscribed with the names of the pharaohs Amenemmes III and IV have been found in the royal tombs at Byblos. But Byblos, where for the moment archaeological evidence is richest, may have been a special case. This was the port through which Egypt received indispensable supplies of timber from the Lebanese mountain slopes. The city's rulers wrote their names in cartouches, like the pharaohs,

Left: the mosque at Hebron built on the traditional site of Abraham's burial.

Above: tiny sandstone sphinx from Serabit el-Khadim in Sinai with an early alphabetic inscription.

Large mound of stones in the Middle Bronze Age temple area at Megiddo. These stones are generally thought to be the base for an altar (*bamah*).

but described themselves as governors in a manner suggesting that they acknowledged some kind of subservient allegiance to the Egyptian throne.

Biblical patriarchs. It is into the Middle Bronze Age that the Biblical patriarchs are to be fitted. According to the Biblical account, the Patriarchs and their tribes came peacefully from the east at a time when towns were reviving and when there was free passage between Palestine and Egypt. This would best suit the situation as revealed by archaeology for the 19th to 18th centuries BC. In a way

difficult to reconstruct with any exactitude from scattered literary and archaeological evidence, they were a group within the wide range of semi-nomadic Semitic tribes who commanded the principal lines of communication, including the desert routes, from Mesopotamia to Syria and thence into Palestine and Egypt. The geographical background of the first 11 chapters of Genesis, it is to be noted, is predominantly Mesopotamian, not Palestinian. The beast of burden of these tribes was the ass, as the camel had not yet been domesticated in this area.

With the appearance of Abraham in chapter 12 a narrative with clear historical content identifies two of the places associated with the Patriarchs as Ur of the Chaldees, most probably the city in southern Iraq (Mesopotamia) excavated by Sir Leonard Woolley, and Harran in Syria. Archaeology endorses these links. Though the theological inspiration is distinct, there is much in common between the mythological tradition of Mesopotamia, with its accounts of antediluvian kings and heroes, of a Golden Age and a Flood, and parallel passages in Genesis. The great mud-brick temple towers of Mesopotamia, the ziggurats, could alone have inspired the Tower of Babel (i.e. Babylon). The names of the Patriarchs, whether or not they really were historical figures, are not only very ancient, but occur in Mesopotamian texts of the earlier 2nd millennium BC.

Tablets from the city of Nuzi in eastern Iraq, written in the 15th century BC but certainly reflecting a much older tradition, explain much that is obscure in the Old Testament account of Patriarchal customs in marriage, adoption, inheritance and land tenure. They show, for instance, Rachel's purpose in stealing the images of her father's

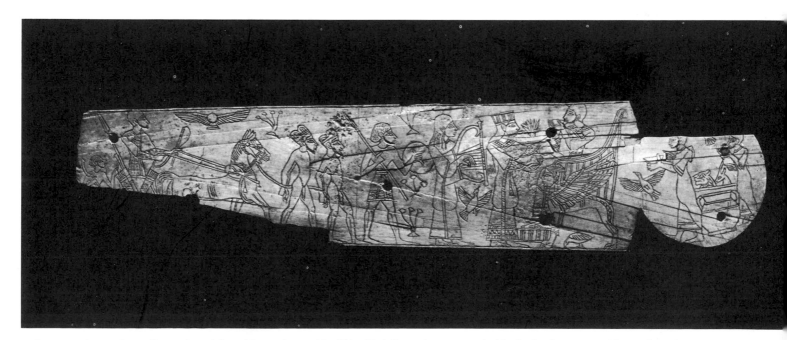

13th century ivory plaque from a hoard found in a palace at Megiddo. To left, a prince returns in his chariot from war with two bound captives and a foot soldier; to right, the prince is shown enthroned, drinking, with his wife offering him a lotus and a towel, lyre-player behind. Egyptian art clearly underlies this scene, but it has a distinctive Canaanite character.

Multicolored faience plaque showing an Asiatic prisoner from Medinet Habu in Egypt, about 1200 BC.

household gods and sitting on them so that Laban's search proved fruitless (Gen. 31). At Nuzi, when there was doubt about an inheritance, possession of the family gods was taken as evidence for right of inheritance.

Nuzi had a predominantly Hurrian-speaking population. The Hurrians were one of the most widely diffused groups in the ancient Near East. Originating in the area of Lake Van in Turkey, they had entered northern Iraq in the 3rd millennium BC and in the next thousand years were established with varying intensity in Turkey, Syria and into central Palestine. Their presence is revealed by traces of their distinctive language, with Caucasian affinities, and personal names in the archives of cuneiform tablets found at places like Mari and Alalakh in Syria. Their major

political accomplishment was the establishment of a kingdom, under the rule of the Indo-European Mitannian aristocracy, in the middle of the 2nd millennium BC in the vicinity of Harran in eastern Syria. Their military successes at this time were achieved by great mastery of the light horse-drawn chariot which had become progressively more common in the Near East after about 1800 BC, and the use of the composite bow, a very powerful weapon skilfully made of strips of horn and various woods. The deep penetrating power of arrows fired from such bows stimulated the development of bronze scale-armor both for men and horses. So far the Hurrians may not certainly be recognized in Palestine before about 1500 BC, though by then already long established in Syria. Thereafter their presence is known from Egyptian diplomatic archives and rare cuneiform tablets from cities in Palestine itself. Such terms as "Horite" and "Hivite," possibly even "Jebusite," in the Old Testament refer to Hurrians.

During the 17th century BC, when the central government in Egypt was weak, Asiatics infiltrating into the Delta from Palestine slowly established a political supremacy, exercising authority over much of the country. Burials with typical Palestinian equipment have been found at sites in the Delta like Inchas and Tell el Daba'a. The leaders of these people were known to the Egyptians as Hikau-Khoswet: Princes of Foreign Countries (Modern Hyksos). In a manner not yet fully determined the Hyksos drew their power from the by now prosperous city states of Palestine; but their name may not be used, as was once customary, as an ethnic or cultural term. Many practices and artifacts once called "Hyksos" are now seen as products of the much wider Canaanite civilization, such as glacis fortifications (banks on which attackers were exposed to assault), the burial or funerary sacrifice of animals of the horse family, specific types of scarab-seals, and the production of a dark-colored pottery with punctured designs known as "Tell el Yahudiyeh" ware, usually juglets for unguents or perfume.

Throughout their rule in Egypt the Hyksos were based in the Delta and it may well be that the historical elements in the Biblical story of Joseph refer to this period. In the second half of the 17th century BC local Egyptian rulers at Thebes, away to the south, slowly established an independent army and prepared to expel their Asiatic overlords. This was not accomplished rapidly. Started by Kamose, the war was brought to a satisfactory conclusion by Ahmosis, founder of the 18th Dynasty. The only surviving record of this crucial struggle was inscribed by a naval officer, bearing the pharaoh's name, on the walls of his tomb at el-Kab. Wilson translates part of it:

"Thereupon I was appointed to the ship 'Appearing in Memphis.' Then there was fighting on the water in the canal Pa-Djedku of Avaris [the Hyksos capital] . . . then Avaris was despoiled . . . then Sharuhen was besieged for three years. Then his majesty despoiled it."

Sharuhen has been identified with Tell el-Farah (south)

excavated by Petrie in 1928 to 1930. Whether Egyptian forces pursued the Hyksos into Palestine beyond Sharuhen is far from clear, as the appearance of cyclopean fortifications at sites in the hill country, and destruction levels at places like Jericho and Shechem about this time, may well be the result of internal rivalries as much as foreign threats.

The expulsion of the Hyksos from Egypt, broadly dated about 1550 BC, is taken by archaeologists to mark the beginning of the Late Bronze Age, assumed to last for over three centuries in Palestine until the invasions of the "Peoples of the Sea" and the Israelites. At first Middle Bronze Age traditions of architecture and craftsmanship persisted. The most striking new feature in the archaeological record is ceramic evidence for Palestine's growing involvement in east Mediterranean trade: a peaceful prelude to her subsequent embroilment in international politics and war. Cypriot pottery increased in quantity on Palestinian sites; a new and distinctive ware decorated in red and black paint with birds and fishes, more rarely cattle and goats, in geometric frames, has been found not only in Cyprus, where it may have been made, but throughout Palestine and into Syria, Egypt and even the Sudan. Its wide distribution is to be accounted for by its intrinsic charm and whatever may have been traded in it – a constant mystery in the study of ancient pottery. To the period about 1550 to 1480 BC belong some unusually fine groups of gold jewelry concealed in hoards at Tell el-Ajjul. Among them are gold pendants showing the face and pudendum of a female, and eight-pointed stars, commonly associated with the worship of the goddess Astarte.

International power politics. The political history of the period from about 1480 to 1220 BC may best be separated from archaeological evidence for later Canaanite civilization. Now for the first time Syria and Palestine were closely involved in the growing political rivalries of the great powers about them: the Egyptians, determined to avoid another foreign domination; the Mitanni across the Euphrates in northern Mesopotamia; and the Hittites of Turkey. It may be noted in passing that the word "Hittite" is used in the Bible either to denote Syria or Syrian rulers, or to describe a local people with Semitic names who have no relation to the historical Hittites of Turkey. From Egyptian written records, supplemented sporadically from other sources, notably the Hittite royal archives, it now becomes possible to speak more often of historical events, involving known places and personalities.

Egyptian intervention in Palestine and Syria in the century or so after the expulsion of the Hyksos was sporadic and of little consequence. The situation was transformed by the emergence of a pharaoh whose military genius matched his energy. In about 1468 BC, months after achieving authority independent of his redoubtable relative Queen Hatshepsut, Tuthmosis III marched against a hostile confederation of rulers in Syria, under the leadership of the prince of Qadesh, supported by

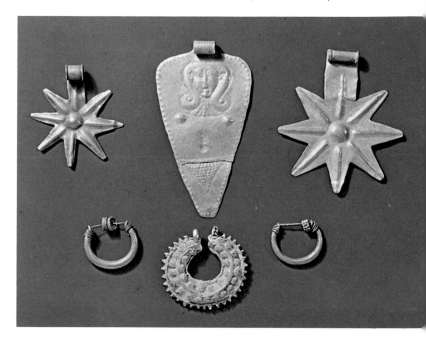

Gold jewelry, made about 1500 BC, from Tell el-Ajjul, where it was found in graves and hoarded in jars. The central pendant bears the face of a fertility goddess, probably Astarte.

the Mitanni. He met and routed them at Megiddo. Archaeological evidence shows that Megiddo was destroyed and remained uninhabited for much of the 15th century BC. On the pylons of the Temple of Amon at Karnak in Egypt Tuthmosis listed the 119 districts, embracing the vital route from Egypt to Syria, that acknowledged his tutelage; within a few years he was to add the names of 270 towns captured in northern Syria. In his 8th campaign, about 1457 BC, he finally reached the Kingdom of Mitanni and its king fled before him. The rulers of the Hittites, of Assyria and Babylonia propitiously sent him rich gifts and pledges. But as his successors rapidly discovered, such an empire required a tireless ruler to hold it together. Amenophis II conducted a number of campaigns to offset Mitannian intrigues; Tuthmosis IV sustained his heritage both by force of arms and eventual marriage to a Mitannian princess. At his death the heroic phase of Egyptian intervention in western Asia was for the moment over. Remaining rulers of the 18th Dynasty depended largely on diplomacy and marital ties. Slowly their hold over Syria and Palestine disintegrated.

In 1887 a unique series of clay tablets from the Egyptian foreign ministry archives of the earlier 14th century BC were found by chance at Tell el-Amarna in central Egypt, capital of the "heretic" pharaoh Akhenaten (Amenophis IV). These and others discovered later reveal much, both about the state of Palestine and southern Syria at this time and the nature of Egyptian rule there. Though dating to a time when Egyptian control was on the wane, they are close enough to the time of Tuthmosis III to give some idea of the system he envisaged. This archive, as extant, contains about 150 letters relevant to Palestine, written in internat-

White stone seated statue of Idrimi of Alalakh inscribed with his autobiography. *Below*: a plan of his palace.

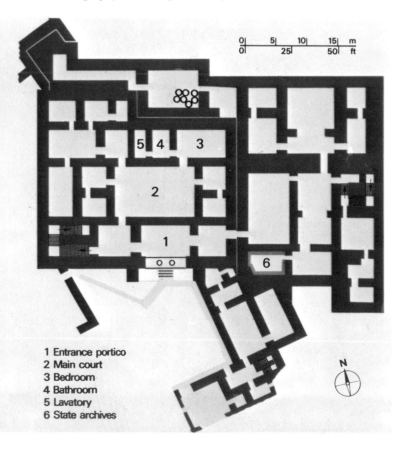

1 Entrance portico
2 Main court
3 Bedroom
4 Bathroom
5 Lavatory
6 State archives

ional Akkadian in the cuneiform script, but liberally sprinkled with local Canaanite grammar and vocabulary by Canaanite, more rarely Egyptian, scribes. This evidence may be supplemented by rare texts from Palestine itself and more vividly from the reliefs and inscriptions in tombs of Egyptian officials, who had served in Asia or had had to receive foreign envoys and their tribute.

Palestine was divided among a network of city states varying greatly in size, each with its own ruler, who had taken vows of allegiance to the pharaoh and had been formally installed as a vassal; kings among themselves, they were generally addressed as the "man of X" by the pharaoh. Abdu-Heba, prince of Jerusalem, for instance, writes, in Albright's translation:

"Behold, as for me, (it was) not my father and not my mother (who) set me in this place; the arm of the mighty king brought me into the house of my father. Why should I commit transgression against the king, my lord." Considerable freedom was allowed these vassals so long as they fulfilled their obligations to send troops when required for Egyptian campaigns into Syria, to garrison vital cities on the main routes thither from Egypt, and to levy, collect and deliver annual taxes and impositions. If pledges of good conduct were thought necessary, a vassal's sons were taken as hostages to be educated at the pharaoh's court or daughters absorbed into his harem. At the time of the "Amarna Letters" there were three main Egyptian administrative provinces: two in Syria, and one in Palestine with its capital at Gaza.

As so often in subsequent imperial administrations, the pharaoh had commissioners, usually Egyptian but occasionally, to judge by their names, local men, directly responsible to him. These men regulated day-to-day business between the pharaoh and vassals or adjudicated in cases of conflict between vassals. Temples and estates in Palestine were also at times designated the property of the crown or of major temples in Egypt. In short Egypt's primary aim was to keep her vassals from rebellion while extracting the maximum revenue, largely in kind. The detailed disposition of Egyptian garrisons is unknown, but Megiddo was a base to begin with, later Beth-Shan, both in the strategically vital plain of Esdraelon. Excavations in both towns have yielded ample evidence of an Egyptian presence. Garrisons were relatively small, depending on chariotry and archers for speed and impact. The whole system, save perhaps along the primary lines of communication, was not particularly resilient. The vigorous rivalries and machinations of the vassals, especially under a weak or disinterested pharaoh, might easily subvert the Egyptian authority in Palestine, as Hittite intrigue largely did in Syria in the early 14th century.

A single letter may be selected to illustrate the situation. Here, late in the reign of Amenophis III, Lab'ayu, ruler of Shechem, embroiled with the ruler of Gezer, more loyal and faithful to Egypt, protests his innocence to the pharaoh; in Albright's translation:

Left: stone stela of the Egyptian pharaoh Sethos I (c. 1305–1290 BC) erected at Bethshan to record his triumphs in Palestine and Syria. This city, crucial to Egyptian control of the west to east land-route in northern Canaan, long had an Egyptian garrison.

Right: painted pottery jar of the 15th century BC from Tell Atshana (ancient Alalakh) in Syria. The distinctive style of the bird and geometric designs painted on such pottery has been associated with the Mitanni, overlords of much of Syria at this time.

"I have heard the words which the king wrote to me, and who am I that the king should lose his land because of me? Behold, I am a faithful servant to the king, and I have not rebelled and I have not sinned, and I do not withhold my tribute, and I do not refuse the requests of my commissioner. Now they wickedly slander me, but let the king, my lord, not impute rebellion to me! Further, my crime is namely that I entered Gezer and said publicly: 'Shall the king take my property, and not likewise the property of Milkilu [prince of Gezer]?' I know the deeds which Milkilu has done against me. Further the king wrote concerning my son. I did not know that my son associates with 'Apiru and I have verily delivered him into the hand of Addaya. . . ."

The letter also serves to bring to our attention the *Apiru*, whose exact relation to the Biblical Hebrews remains a matter for lively debate. The *Habiru/Hapiru* are mentioned in all important archives of cuneiform tablets throughout the Near East in the 2nd millennium BC. The matter is greatly complicated by the fact that in some cases the Hapiru seem to be a social class, in others an ethnic group. Whenever they appear they are generally foreigners. They are either household servants, mercenaries or marauders, and are rarely settled in communities. In the Old Testament "Hebrew" is primarily used by foreigners, or by Hebrews when speaking of themselves to foreigners.

It is most likely that the Biblical Hebrews were part of the people known elsewhere as Hapiru, but not necessarily identical with any specific group yet encountered in other Near Eastern texts.

Some idea of city life in a north Syrian state, in this case under Mitannian rule in the 15th century BC, may be gleaned from finds in and about a palace excavated in level IV at Tell Atshana (ancient Alalakh) in the Amuq plain. A crude, white stone statue preserved in a temple until the final destruction of the city around 1200 BC, and then piously buried, portrays a King Idrimi, vassal to the Mitannian King Parattarna, seated on his throne. His adventurous career is described in an inscription carved all over the figure. Told in the first person, though written by a named scribe, it recounts how the royal family was forced into exile by popular revolt, how Idrimi went to Canaan, where he lived among semi-nomadic Hapiru, how he then slowly reasserted his authority at Alalakh with Mitannian help, regained his throne for 30 years and built a palace. This is almost certainly the so-called "Palace of Niqmepa" uncovered by Woolley's excavations. When this building was finally destroyed, perhaps by the Hittites, some attempt was made to save the archives of cuneiform tablets, some of which were found scattered in the outer courtyard and through the rooms leading to it from a small inner archive room. Some of these documents

One of the two main city temples of Ras Shamra (Ugarit), set side by side on the highest part of the mound. This one was dedicated to Baal and the other to Dagon. They are typical Canaanite temples in layout, foreshadowing Solomon's Temple in Jerusalem.

reveal details of the international law and custom operating between the various local states under Mitannian overlordship. Others deal with the law of the community, with commerce and agriculture, but none with the city's religious life.

Energetic Egyptian military control of Palestine was revived by the rulers of the 19th Dynasty. The campaigns of Sethos I are, for this period, remarkably well documented by reliefs on the outside north wall of the great Hypostyle Hall at Karnak in Egypt and by commemorative stelae set up in Palestine. The Karnak inscriptions show his main objectives to have been the bedouin in Sinai and southern Palestine, people in the hilly region of central Palestine and southern Syria, and the Hittites in central and northern Syria. Two stelae set up at Beth-Shan give details of a campaign in the Jordan valley and against the Hapiru; on the coast Acre and Tyre were taken and in Tyre at least another stela set up. He later fought deep into Syria, but never brought matters to a head with the Hittites. This was left to his son, Ramesses II who, in his fifth campaign, engaged the Hittite king in battle at Qadesh in Syria. It remains one of the best known battles of antiquity thanks to the pharaoh's detailed record; in fact it seems to have been a Pyrrhic victory for him. The frontier dividing the spheres of Hittite and Egyptian influence in Syria remained much where it had been a century earlier. There it was to stay until totally unexpected pressures shattered the aspirations of both great powers within the next century.

Ugarit, Bronze Age city in Syria. One archaeological site above all others at present offers a microcosm of developed urban civilization in the Late Bronze Age. Ras Shamra, the ancient city of Ugarit, lies about seven miles north of Latakia in Syria. A considerable area of the city mound has been explored and some work done on the remains of a port nearby at Minet el-Beidha on the Mediterranean. From private houses and public buildings have come a vast number of inscribed clay tablets dealing with the city's social structure, its foreign relations, its commerce, its legal and administrative system, and above all its religious life. Many of these texts were written in a previously unknown language and an alphabetic cuneiform script. As this writing was composed of a limited number of signs and the division of words was marked by a special sign, initial decipherment was rapid. Of the 30 signs used, 27 are the usual Semitic type expressing a consonant plus any vowel, while three, exceptional in a Semitic system, express 'a, 'i, 'u respectively. This basically alphabetic script was almost certainly invented originally by a single scribe, using the cuneiform script of Mesopotamia as a medium for writing his own local language, "Ugaritic," which was akin to Phoenician and Hebrew, and also for writing Hurrian. Diplomatic correspondence is written as customary in international Akkadian and in the conventional cuneiform script.

In the 14th and 13th centuries BC the city was dominated by a huge palace covering about 2.5 acres. The original building, very like the palace at Alalakh, was gradually extended around a series of courtyards to provide for an ever more extensive and powerful administration. Numerous rooms have been cleared, some with upper stories, eight porticoed entrance staircases, and a large walled garden with flowerbeds and a pavilion. Every aspect of kingship, public and private, was exercised here. There were ceremonial reception rooms, council chambers, private apartments and shrines for a monarch who was supreme judge, administrator, general and high priest. His archives were arranged with care. The department for the fiscal business of provincial regions occupied apartments by the main west entrance, while correspondence about dues from the various classes in city and palace went to the eastern archives near the entrance from the city. A central

Ivory box-lid carved with a scene in Mycenean Greek style from
Minet el-Beida, the port of Ugarit; 13th century BC.

A 13th century BC bronze statuette of a seated figure covered with sheet gold, from Megiddo. It is commonly assumed that such figures represent Canaanite gods, perhaps in this case Baal or El, deposited as votive offerings in public and private shrines to invoke the god's favor. Though a considerable number have survived these must be only a fraction of the original production. The figures themselves are never inscribed, though bases on which they were set may have been.

archive handled legal matters in which the king was directly involved, such as the conveyancing of property, royal gifts and feudal investitures. The south archive was the foreign ministry, dealing with the city's Hittite overlord, his viceroy at Carchemish to the east on the Euphrates, and lesser local rulers in Syria. Commerce was handled in a smaller palatial building to the south. The main palace also had, in addition to the usual domestic services for so extended a household, workshops for the manufacture and repair of fittings and furnishings, notably those decorated with carved ivory. There was even a royal burial chamber, underground, with three fine, corbeled vaults.

Immediately adjacent to the palace on the south and east were the comfortable villas of the aristocracy and senior civil servants, all aping the style of their master's residence. Each had sophisticated architectural fittings and drainage, richly equipped burial vaults, in some cases even private libraries and archives. The homes of the poorer classes clustered about narrow streets to the north and northwest. Set somewhat apart, around a square to the south, was the craftsmen's quarter. A large building on one side housed a library of Babylonian astrological and literary texts. The whole city was defended by a massive wall with a postern gate of distinctively Hittite type. In the port down by the sea the richer merchants had finely appointed houses, with burial vaults, as well as stores and counting houses.

The wealth and influence of Ugarit, built on a long fertile stretch of coast, depended on its position at a vital junction of land and sea routes between the Aegean world and the lands further east. Ships could sail easily to Cyprus and Turkey, beyond to Crete, and southwards to Palestine and Egypt. Overland caravans brought westwards the products of the East. Agricultural goods like grain, olive oil, wine and wood, with the fine metal and ivory work made at Ugarit, and local textiles, often dyed a rich purple, formed the backbone of the city's export trade. The king himself was fully involved in trade, with his own caravans. Taxes in silver were imposed on immovable property as well as on goods in transit. The population of the city and port was as cosmopolitan as her commerce and diplomacy. Tablets, the most reliable source, reveal the presence of a significant Hurrian-speaking minority, of Cypriots, Hittites and Egyptians, men from Tyre and Byblos, from Mesopotamia and Palestine. Resident Mycenaean (Greek) and Cretan merchants have been inferred from rich collections of their distinctive pottery. Dictionary tablets offer vocabularies in Hurrian, Sumerian and Akkadian, apart from Ugaritic.

Social ties were predominantly feudal within the local population. The king granted land and certain privileges in return for services, which were tied to the land, not to the individual holding it. The more ancient military aristocracy of the Hurrians was now a landed nobility. The largest class was the peasantry working their own land or

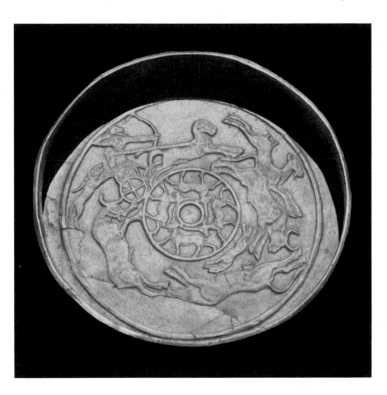

14th century gold plate with a raised outer rim from Ras Shamra (Ugarit) decorated in *repoussé* and depicting a scene of hunting by chariot.

the land of the aristocracy, as freemen, but bound by certain obligations to the crown, and subject to many taxes in kind. From them the army was recruited, with auxiliary mercenaries. At the head of the whole social pyramid stood the king and his council of notables.

From the later 16th century Ugarit, like the coastal towns of Palestine, had been largely under Egyptian influence. The city is mentioned in the "Amarna Letters," but in Akhenaten's reign suffered a major disaster, thought by the excavator to be an earthquake, that destroyed part of the palace and town. Soon afterwards Ugarit was drawn into the Hittite orbit, though there is no reason to think commercial links with Egypt were broken; indeed such contact did something to stabilize relations between the Great Powers. Political texts from Ugarit yield much information about Hittite government in Syria. This initially political relationship, generally just and fair, was to have enduring cultural effects on Syria, where elements of Hittite civilization, known as "Neo-Hittite," survived long into the 1st millennium BC after the fall of the Hittite Empire.

The religious texts from Ugarit are still unique. They offer the best extra-Biblical evidence for the cults and cult-practices of a major city which, if not strictly Canaanite, was closely akin to it. Canaanite religion is, for obvious reasons, largely ignored by Old Testament authors, and temple excavations and deity statues are no substitute for textual evidence in seeking to understand a religion. It ought, however, to be said at once that even these Ugaritic texts are still open to a great variety of possible interpretations and the beliefs they describe were never universal over a large area. Each region and major city in Palestine and Syria had its own favorite·gods and goddesses, each with their own individual rituals and sacred stories. What the texts from Ugarit so richly offer is a vivid glimpse of the main deities and more important festivals, rites and sacrifices of one such major city.

Most of the large mythological tablets came, not surprisingly, from the high priest's residence between the two main city temples, to Baal and to Dagon, on the highest part of the tell. The temples are substantial rectangular buildings. Both have an innermost "Holy of Holies" for the deity statues, an inner hall or court, and an open court, with a great altar where the public, or at least a privileged part of it, would have been able to participate in religious festivities. Both temples probably had towers, upon which sacrifices were offered. The high priest's palace was a magnificent place; under one floor was a great hoard of bronze tools and weapons presented to the high priest by a metalsmith.

The gods and goddesses of Ugarit were numerous, all conceived in human form and subject to human passions. Gods were born, died and were reborn, married and begat children. The supreme deity was El ("God"), creator of men and father of the gods, with a wife Asherah, Lady of the Sea. In extant texts this senior pair are eclipsed by the stormy couple Baal and his virgin sister Anath, a goddess of love and war, who is on occasion exceedingly violent. Baal was associated, in a filial relationship, not only with El, but also with Dagon (Hadad) the great Semitic god of storm, bringer of rain and fertility, a warrior god particularly associated with cities like Mari on the Euphrates. Among the many minor deities Astarte, a lesser counterpart of Anath, is best known. The mythology has a strong urban bias: gods fight for the title of king and the possession of a palace. The basic themes include the cosmic myth of a struggle against original chaos, in which Baal conquered Yam, beloved of El, the personification of sea and fertility. The seasonal alternation of fertility and sterility is represented in the beneficial stay of Baal on earth and his descent to the kingdom of the dead, or by cycles of seven-year periods when Mot, the enemy of Baal, god of dryness and death, threatens to shrivel up the abundance brought by Baal.

Although no single Late Bronze Age site in Palestine can match the fascination of Ras Shamra, scattered finds increasingly throw light on religion and culture there. A simple shrine, known through three successive phases, built in a slight ditch at the base of the great Middle Bronze Age ramp at Tell ed-Duweir (Lachish), yielded a jar inscribed in the Canaanite script as a dedication to the shrine of Elat ("Goddess"). And one of the most interesting of the Late Bronze Age shrines at Hazor was actually cut into the Middle Bronze Age rampart. Small as it was, the surviving fittings are unusually interesting. A basalt seated statue of a man holding a cup was set beside a row of ten stone stelae varying from 22 to 65 centimeters in height. Only one was carved with a relief, representing two raised arms with hands outstretched to a disk and crescent, perhaps denoting a moon god. Also associated with this shrine were a silver-plated bronze standard and a small baked clay mask of a man with open eye sockets, but no apertures for the mouth or nostrils. On the standard, probably once held in the hand of a stone statue, is a crescent and a stylized snake above a woman holding snakes in her uplifted hands.

That Palestine also had richly equipped palatial dwellings, at least in its major cities, is revealed by a hybrid collection of ivory fragments found in the treasury of such a building at Megiddo, destroyed in the second half of the 12th century. There is only one datable object, a model pencase bearing the name of the Egyptian pharaoh Ramesses III, but some of the objects deposited were made as much as a century earlier. An elaborately decorated plaque is distinctively Hittite in subject as in style; some fragmentary floral designs, two plaques beautifully carved with recumbent griffins and a comb carved with a lion attacking a goat are no less certainly from Mycenaean workshops located in Cyprus or somewhere in the Aegean itself. Many other pieces, though probably made locally, show marked Egyptian influence, such as the gods Bes and Anubis, or the human-headed sphinx. Scenes of chariots, of banquets and the reception of prisoners and booty use Egyptian formulas but render them in a local "Canaanite" manner.

The eclipse of Canaanite civilization. In the later 13th and 12th centuries BC the so-called "Peoples of the Sea" from the west, and Israelites and Aramaeans from the east, entered Syria and Palestine, destroyed the Canaanite supremacy there, and inaugurated a long period known to archaeologists as the Early Iron Age, which reached down to the establishment of the great Achaemenid Persian Empire.

In the 5th year of his reign, about 1220 BC, the Egyptian ruler Merneptah, son and successor of Ramesses II, repulsed an invasion of Libyans allied with certain "Foreigners, or Peoples, of the Sea," named as Akawasha, Tursha, Lukku, Sherden and Sheklesh. The invaders are represented as coming with their families and household goods. Some of these people are known from earlier texts. The "Amarna Letters" contain references, if rightly interpreted, to Lukku pirates, to Sherden in and about Byblos; also to another such people, the Danuna, in some relation to Tyre. At the battle of Qadesh Ramesses II was supported by Sherden, the Hittites by Lukku. Yet still their origins are obscure, though they are generally considered to have included elements from the Aegean, perhaps as a result of the breakup of the great Mycenaean Empire after

12th century BC baked-clay coffin (restored) from Bethshan, in the Egyptian style associated with the "Sea Peoples."

the Trojan War. The sparse surviving records do no more than indicate groups of people, variably composed, who in a number of waves over an extended period, created havoc in the settled areas of Turkey and the eastern Mediterranean.

The Lukku may be associated with the later province of Lycia in Turkey, the Danuna with Cilicia and the Amuq plain of Syria, the Akawasha, perhaps, with the Mycenaean Greeks, or "Achaians." But what truth may be allowed to theories linking the Sherden to Sardinia, the Sheklesh to Sicily, remains a very open question. Two other such peoples, the Tjekker and Philistines (Pelest), do not appear in Egyptian records until the second major assault of the Sea Peoples in the reign of Ramesses III. This naval conflict, in which Egypt was again victorious, is vividly depicted on the walls of the pharaoh's mortuary temple at Medinet Habu in Egypt, but the accompanying inscription is so bombastic as to be ambiguous. It is debated whether the struggle took place on the Syrian coast or in the Delta and southern Palestine. After it the Pelest (Philistines) settled along the coast of Palestine.

After their victories both pharaohs employed contingents of Sea Peoples as mercenaries to garrison towns in Palestine. A variety of baked-clay mummiform coffins have long been associated with these garrison troops. The form, and the features modeled on the lids, clearly show Egyptian inspiration. Once exclusively identified as "Philistine," it is now clear that their occupants might be any among the Sea Peoples, or even native born Egyptians. In a 13th-century cemetery at Deir el-Baleh in the Gaza (Philistine) region the equipment is typically Egyptian, while later at Beth-Shan there is no trace of the distinctive decorated "Philistine" pottery with such coffins.

Although there is yet no evidence outside the Old Testament for the Israelites' stay in Egypt, or for the Exodus, the context of these narratives is sufficient to provide them both with reasonably certain historical settings. Early in his reign the pharaoh Ramesses II undertook extensive restorations and rebuildings at Pithom and Ramesses, two cities in the Delta where the captive Israelites served (Exodus 1:11). On a stela erected by the pharaoh Merneptah in his fifth year to commemorate victories, Israel is mentioned for the first time in an extra-Biblical text. Significantly it is written with the determinative sign for a people rather than a country. This has been taken to show that the Israelites were already in Canaan, but not yet settled there. Thus the Exodus and wanderings may be dated very broadly about 1250 to 1225 BC. Archaeological survey and excavation has also shown that early in this century, after an interval, some kind of settled urban life returned to Edom, Moab and Ammon. Since these kingdoms feature in the Biblical

account this provides additional confirmation for such a dating. A much later date is unlikely in terms of present information.

The Israelite conquest. Two factors still greatly complicate any attempt to provide a coherent historical account of the Israelite conquest of Canaan. The narrative in the Bible is a mosaic, assembled and edited from a variety of sources long after the event. These blend sagas and legends, devised either to explain why places have certain names or why certain religious practices arose, with stories from which ancient and reliable historical traditions must be carefully separated by textual criticism. Archaeology has no way of remedying these historical deficiencies, for the most distinctive trait of the Israelites, their religion, is archaeologically invisible. Moreover, it has so far proved impossible to credit them with any distinctive artifact through which the course of their conquest might be certainly charted. What archaeological evidence there is must be used cautiously, as negative evidence from this source is no ground for rejecting any part of the literary tradition. Destruction levels have been found on a number of sites named in the Biblical record of Joshua's campaigns, but in no case can the destruction be definitely attributed to the Israelites.

In the destruction level at Tell ed-Duweir (Lachish), for instance, there was a broken pottery bowl, its inside surface used by an Egyptian tax collector to record in ink wheat deliveries from local farms in the fourth year of a pharaoh whose name is lost. Epigraphically it is most likely to be Merneptah. But then, even were we able to decide whether the destruction was the work of Egyptian armies. or Sea

The site of Shiloh as it appears today with two unfinished churches started in the 1930s on the site of ruined Byzantine churches. This was the first major religious center for Israelites after the invasion.

Peoples or Israelites, we might still be troubled by a scarab of the later pharaoh Ramesses III associated with the same archaeological level. Then again, of Joshua's most spectacular triumph, the capture of Jericho, archaeology has so far offered no evidence. But as the upper levels of the tell covering this very ancient city were very much eroded, all trace of 13th-century settlement might have disappeared long before the excavators got there.

Again at Ai (Josh. 8:1–29) archaeology has failed to reveal a city which might have been taken by the Israelites. In the 12th century there was only an unwalled village of less than three acres. It has been suggested that the Biblical account is merely a later explanation of conspicuous earlier ruins at Ai, or a transposition of events at a neighboring site of another name. At Hazor the archaeological evidence would appear to be more direct and vivid. This city was destroyed when a distinctive Mycenaean Greek pottery was still current, in the later 13th century. The subsequent occupation, in the 12th century, is very primitive in contrast to the great Canaanite city. Silos, hearths, tent and hut footings bear witness to semi-nomadic inhabitants using simple pottery, found also on a number of similar settlements in Galilee that may indeed be "Israelite."

For the conquest as a whole, bearing all these cautions in mind, only a summary of events may be offered. The arrival of the Israelites in Canaan was at first partly a slow infiltration into regions sparsely inhabited, and partly accommodation with existing inhabitants that varied, from area to area, from one Israelite tribe to another. Accepting the Biblical narrative, if the Exodus is placed at about 1250 BC, followed by a generation of wandering, then Joshua's crucial crossing of the Jordan and entry into Canaan would fall in the last decade or so of the same century. At each stage of the conquest thereafter came sporadic conflicts, only some of which have survived in the official record. In the earliest phase the Israelite sanctuary at the oaks of Moreh near Shechem was established as a vital center for tribes coming into the conquered hill country, and there were campaigns in the north against a confederation led by "Jabin the king of Canaan who reigned at Hazor."

By the middle of the 12th century some kind of equilibrium had been reached. Israelites were established in the hills and in Transjordan, but were unable to overcome a number of strongly fortified Canaanite cities, like Beth-Shan, Taanach and Megiddo. These only fell with the final passing of Egyptian authority, towards the end of the 12th century. For the Israelites there followed a time of retrenchment. Struggles were internal, or with invaders from the desert regions – "whenever Israel sowed seed, Midian would march up with Amalek and the sons of the East" (Judges 6:3). Society was tribal, with no capital and no central government. A confederation of 12 tribes was united by their common allegiance to the covenant with Yahweh, its laws and rites, and focused on the Ark of the Covenant at Shiloh, though worship at other places was not excluded. In times of peril leaders were elected, known as "Judges," to lead their tribes in war. Conflicts were scattered and sporadic, engaging small bands whose victory depended on the enterprise of individual leaders.

Infinitely more important for the future was the gradual development at this time of the very special Israelite religion. Here again the Old Testament account must be carefully sifted to extract the material in it that goes back to this formative stage. This leaves little doubt that already by the time of the Judges the major themes of Israelite theology were well established. The cult was distinguished from other ancient Near Eastern religions in a number of striking ways. First, and fundamentally, it was based not on theological abstractions, but on the memory of an historical event of great moment, when Yahweh (Jehovah) had chosen the Israelites as his people and had brought them from captivity and slavery in Egypt, through Sinai, to the promised land. Their rites commemorated and strengthened this covenant, or pact, with Yahweh. Thus they worshiped one God, in marked contrast to all their neighbors, and condemned all others. Their cult celebrations laid great emphasis on personal purification and expiation, making the individual deeply aware of his sins in the sight of God. Of this God, who could not be seen, no images might be made: again totally unlike other contemporary religions, as indeed was a complete absence of close association between the deity and natural phenomena. Most other gods of this time were identified with aspects of nature and lacked any clear moral character. Yahweh, though all-powerful over nature, was removed above and beyond it, exercising a supreme moral authority. The great novelty of all this will be clearly apparent by comparison with the concise review of Canaanite religion given earlier.

Meanwhile in Syria another intrusive people, later to play a vital part in the history of Israel, were rapidly establishing themselves. Like so many of the peoples who came out of the Arabian desert to settle in Syria and Mesopotamia, the Aramaeans emerge into history without a discernible past. Towards the end of the reign of the Assyrian king Tiglath-Pileser I (c. 1116–1078 BC) the first wave of Aramaean invaders struck Assyria; about the same time Babylon was affected. Complex traditions in the Bible, which may project a later situation back into the Patriarchal period, indicate some close relationship between the Aramaeans and Israel's ancestors: "My father was a wandering Aramaean" (Deut. 26:5). It may be that the Aramaeans, who inhabited a very similar area initially, were descendants of the Amorites or a closely related group. When, under David, they emerged into the clear light of Biblical history they were already a formidable power in Syria and Transjordan, controlling the crucial network of international trade routes which focused on Damascus. It must be assumed that it was sometime in the 12th century that they first gained a hold in central Syria, profiting from the political vacuum left there by the eclipse of the Hittites and Egyptians.

Pottery: A key to the past

VISUAL STORY

Major stages in the history of human settlement in Palestine from about 7000 BC may be defined according to the shapes and decoration of pottery. Archaeologists have built up a knowledge of these changing forms and decoration so that newly discovered sites may be rapidly dated through pottery found on the surface, and each level in a mound similarly attributed. Attention is now turning to the scientific study of methods of manufacture and the chemical composition of pottery, to define more accurately the times and places of production and the scope of trade in pottery. These two jugs, that on the right made in Cyprus (perhaps to transport opium in solution) and that on the left a copy of a Cypriot pot made in Palestine in the 13th century BC, reveal how pottery most obviously reflects trade contacts.

Left: large painted jar from a tomb at Ras Shamra (Ugarit), c. 1650–1550 BC. The painted decoration is similar to a bichrome painted ware found in Palestine, c. 1550–1470 BC. Some of it may have been made in Cyprus. It is common on sites dating from the beginning of the Late Bronze Age after the expulsion of the Hyksos from Egypt had caused changes in Palestinian society.

Below left: painted jug of fine cream ware from northwest Syria, c. 2000–1900 BC. Through coastal trading, pottery of this kind traveled south to the Lebanon and north Palestine. Here it was imitated, but in pottery that was less finely made and less skilfully decorated.

Below: model wagon in buff pottery from Hammam in Syria, c. 2200 BC. Without such rare models these vehicles would be virtually unknown to us. Actual examples of wagons, made of wood, survive only in exceptional frozen or waterlogged conditions. Covered wagons are mentioned in the 15th century BC autobiography of King Idrimi of Alalakh, and may have been used by the Patriarchs.

Right: two jars of the pottery typical of the nomadic Amorite intruders into Palestine about 2200–2000 BC, from a tomb at Jericho. Though well made, the pottery fabric is often brittle and not well fired. The bodies of the vessels were handmade and the rims turned on a slow wheel. Both in form and decoration they contrast sharply with pottery made earlier and later in Palestinian cities.

Right: a biconical jug with a rather crudely painted decoration in red. This jug was taken from a tomb at Tell el-Far'ah (South) and dates from approximately 1400–1350 BC. The shape in which it has been made and the style in which it has been decorated are both fairly common to pottery used in Palestine at the time of the "Amarna Letters."

Below: pedestal vase, piriform juglet and bowl from a tomb at Jericho, c. 1750–1700 BC. The vase well illustrates the elegance of the best pottery of one of the most prosperous periods in Palestine's history. The juglet is related to the "Tell el-Yahudiyeh" juglets containing oil, which were traded over a wide area. At this period the potter's wheel was increasingly used in Palestine.

Left: a large bowl with three folded feet, which was taken from a tomb at Jericho and dates from approximately 1850–1800 BC. Its sharply angled side and the shape of its feet suggest that it is a copy of an identical bowl made out of sheet copper or bronze, as were many of the bowls of this period. The decoration in red and blue has been crudely applied over the thick white slip coating the rough surface.

Left: Cypriot vessel in the shape of a bull, from the 15th century palace of Idrimi at Tell Atshana (ancient Alalakh) in Syria. A luxury object suitable for a royal palace, it illustrates the wide commercial connections of Cyprus at this time. It may have carried a fine oil or cosmetic.

Below left: plain bowl from Tell ed-Duweir (ancient Lachish) inscribed in the Egyptian hieratic script. It carries a record of wheat production in the fourth year of a pharaoh whose name is lost (probably Merenptah, c. 1230 BC). Found in a destruction level which it helps to date, it gives no indication who the conquerors were.

Bottom left: pilgrim flask of a type made in the Greek world c. 1450–1350 BC, imported into Palestine and copied there. The right-hand vessel is a copy, and both are from Tell el-Ajjul.

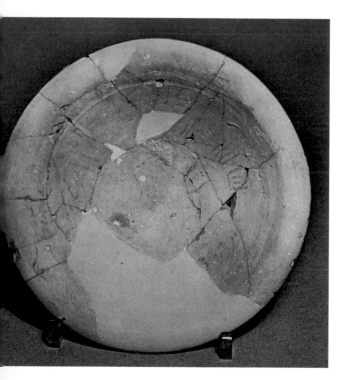

Left: a juglet, mug and bowl from a tomb at Tell ed-Duweir, c. 900 BC to 750 BC. They are typical examples of common household pottery in Judah at the time of the divided monarchy. The mug shape is new to Palestine, and has been said to derive from the Philistine's taste for beer drinking.

Below: jug, juglets and painted chalice from a tomb at Tell el-Far'ah (South), c. 950–800 BC. The chalice is one of the few common Iron Age pottery forms decorated with paint. Their entire surface is sometimes covered with elaborate floral and geometric decoration, particularly in southern Palestine. More commonly pottery of this period is distinguished by a finely polished red or black surface

Right: a stirrup-jar made somewhere in the Greek world and found at Tell el-Ajjul, and the Philistine version of the same kind of vessel, c. 1150 BC. The form remains the same, but the type of decoraton is very different.

Left: two spindle bottles of red lustrous ware from Tell Atshana, c. 1500–1450 BC. These distinctively shaped vessels have been found throughout the Levant and into Egypt, showing how popular was the unknown substance traded in them.

Above left: a finely burnished juglet in the form of a pomegranate from Jerusalem c. 700 BC. Delicate modeled vessels such as this are rare and may have been luxury unguent vessels especially made for use in shrines and rich men's houses.

Above: a jug from Jerusalem c. 700 BC which illustrates very well the fine appearance that could be achieved by burnishing. A slip (generally red at this time) was applied to the surface of the vessel, and when the pottery was leather hard it was polished with a smooth, rounded stone or bone to a lustrous finish – in this case freehand.

Left: two burnished bowls from Jerusalem, c. 700 BC. They had been concealed in a cave after use in a shrine, so that they would not be profaned by further, secular, use. They exhibit the ring-burnishing so characteristic of Iron Age bowls in Palestine. In this case a potter's wheel has been used to obtain the regularly burnished lines.

4. The Phoenicians

The city states of Phoenicia (c. 1200–330 BC). After the upheavals of the 12th century that saw the invasions of the "Peoples of the Sea" from the west, the Israelites and Aramaeans from the east, the only area in which Canaanite cultural and political traditions survived together was in the narrow strip of land known today as the Lebanon. With their land supremacy severely curtailed, the inhabitants of this region increasingly turned seawards to become among the greatest sailors and traders of any age.

Though we now refer to them as "Phoenicians," following the Greek translation of Canaanites, their contemporaries usually called them collectively "Sidonians." In the 5th century BC the great Greek historian Herodotus scattered through his *Histories* a series of complimentary observations on the Phoenicians, recording the excellence of their ships, their skill in mining, and in digging a canal for Xerxes across the Athos peninsula in northern Greece, their enterprise in sailing around Africa and their colonization of parts of Greece, to which they also brought the alphabet. Pomponius Mela, a Spaniard, writing five centuries later, was no less generous:

"The Phoenicians were a clever race, who prospered in war and peace. They excelled in writing and literature, and in other arts, in seamanship, in naval warfare, and in ruling an empire."

Sadly these testimonials of ancient authors have yet to be matched in the archaeological record. Research in the most promising places, notably the mother-cities of Tyre and Sidon, and their greatest colony, Carthage, is hampered either by later accumulations of debris reaching to modern times or by the ruins of great Roman cities. A clergyman, writing of the Lebanon in 1870, graphically describes the results of such intensive occupation and the relentless demands of each succeeding generation of builders:

"The stones of Sidon, Tyre and Sarepta have been carried recently to Acre, Beirut and Joppa by boat in immense quantities, and after being cut afresh, and much reduced in size, are placed in buildings, which, in turn, will fall to ruin in a hundred years, when the same process will be repeated until they are found no more."

A century of intermittent excavation, much of it no more than treasure hunting, particularly at Sidon, has revealed something of the larger cities from the time of the Persian Empire, but virtually nothing before then. Even at Byblos, where whole sections of the Bronze Age city have been excavated, the Phoenician town lies under the modern village. At Sarepta alone, and then only very recently, has work started with modern methods on an unencumbered site.

Nor is the situation remedied by the survival of ancient Phoenician documents. Save for short, relatively uninformative, funerary and dedicatory monumental inscriptions, none has survived. The nearest we can come to

original Phoenician histories is through Josephus, a Jewish historian writing in the 1st century AD, who briefly cites them. About the same time Philo of Byblos (c. 64 to 141 AD) wrote an account of Phoenician religion in his *Phoenician History* that he claimed was based on the earlier work of a certain Sanchoniathon, a priest born at Byblos, perhaps in the 6th century BC or earlier. Until the discovery of the Ras Shamra texts this claim was doubted; but with the earlier evidence now available the reality of Sanchoniathon is accepted. Even so Philo's work survives only in extracts later assembled by Eusebius (c. 260 to 339 AD), Bishop of Caesarea in Palestine. Phoenician history must then be reconstructed from scattered references in the Old Testament, in the Assyrian royal records and in the writings of classical authors. Inevitably the result is very uneven, with an overemphasis on the foreign relations of the Phoenician cities and very little real knowledge of their internal history. It is ironic indeed that the people who taught the West to write should have left such a meager written legacy themselves.

The independence and self-sufficiency of the Phoenician coastal cities existed from as early as their history may be traced. In the 14th-century "Amarna Letters" the existence of active city states at Tyre, Sidon and Byblos, each with their own rulers and political ambitions, and of Arvad with its fleet, are well documented. An Egyptian school exercise of the later 13th century, the Papyrus Anastasi I, names again the great commercial cities, incidentally revealing the very real interest Egypt had in them. Wilson translates the relevant part as follows:

"Pray, instruct me about Beirut, about Sidon and Sarepta. Where is the stream of Litani? What is Uzu [the land city of Tyre] like? They say another town is in the sea, named Tyre-the-port. Water is taken (to) it by the boats, and it is richer in fish than sand."

In the *Legend of King Keret* among the Ras Shamra texts the distressed monarch vows at shrines in Tyre and Sidon.

The fate of the Phoenician cities during the invasions of the "Peoples of the Sea" is by no means clear. Certain classical sources suggest that Tyre was then destroyed and later refounded from Sidon. But if they suffered at all in the earlier 12th century, it was a temporary eclipse. The best witness to their continuing activity and independence around 1100 BC is an account left by one Wen-Amon, an official of the Temple of Amon at Karnak in Egypt, sent to Byblos to buy timber for the god's ceremonial barge. No longer is he treated with the deference and respect such an official would automatically have received as little as a century or so earlier. Inadequately supplied with money or credentials, he is bullied and pushed from pillar to post by the Phoenicians. At one point Zakar-Baal, prince of Byblos, admonishes him (Wilson's translation):

"Aren't there twenty ships here in my harbor which regularly trade with Ne-su-Ba-neb-Ded [ruler of the Egyptian Delta]? As to this Sidon, the other place which you passed, aren't there fifty more ships there which trade

---

p.65: baked clay figurine of a pregnant woman from a Phoenician cemetery at Akhziv in Israel, 500–300 BC.

Aerial view of the island city of Tyre in the Lebanon, now joined to the mainland by a neck of land which originated in the huge mole built by Alexander the Great's engineers, when he besieged the city for seven months before taking it.

with Werket-El?" The latter is presumably an Asiatic merchant, resident in Egypt, trading with Sidon.

About the same time as Wen-Amon's report, the Phoenician cities received a reminder that their commercial wealth tempted powerful predatory monarchs to the east. On a foundation tablet commemorating the rebuilding of the Anu-Adad Temple at Ashur the Assyrian King Tiglath-Pileser I recorded (Oppenheim's translation):

"I went to the Lebanon. I cut (there) timber of cedar for the Temple of Anu and Adad, the great gods, my lords, and carried (them to Ashur). I crossed over in ships (belonging) to Arvad, from Arvad which is on the seashore, to the town of Samuri which (lies) in Amurru (a distance of) 3 double-miles overland." The absence of Tyre from this list may corroborate the legend that it was destroyed.

There is some evidence that in his struggles with the Philistines David was aided by an alliance with Abibaal, and later his son Hiram, Kings of Tyre. The Phoenicians stood to benefit from a curtailing of Philistine maritime activity. In the mid-10th century Hiram undertook an extensive building program in the city, enlarging the island fortress and its harbors. According to Josephus:

"He raised a bank called the wide place, and dedicated the golden pillar which is in the temple of Zeus [i.e. Baal-shamen]. He also went and cut timber from the mountain called *Libános*, for the roof of temples; and when he had pulled down the ancient temples, he built both the temple of Heracles [i.e. Melkart] and that of Astarte."

Hiram's alliance with Solomon is discussed elsewhere, but Josephus has recorded, in two rather contradictory accounts, an interesting commentary on Solomon's legendary wisdom that may be quoted here if only to show that there are two sides to every story. In one version Solomon is never foxed, but in another, the Phoenician account, the emphasis is different:

"It is said that Solomon . . . sent riddles to Hiram and asked for others from him, on the understanding that the one who failed to solve them should pay a sum of money to him who succeeded. Hiram agreed and being unable to guess the riddles, spent a large part of his wealth on the fine. Afterwards they were solved by a certain Abdemun of Tyre, who propounded others. Solomon, failing to solve these, paid back Hiram more than he had received." Ancient, like modern, diplomacy is rarely so whimsical.

In the 9th century Ahab, King of Israel, was married to Jezebel, daughter of Ethbaal, King of the Sidonians; a

Silver shekel of Sidon showing a Phoenician galley.

fateful alliance which had far-reaching effects on the history of Israel. According to Josephus this Phoenician monarch founded the cities of Botrys (Batroun) in Phoenicia and Auza in Libya.

Menace from the East. But by now the shadow of Assyrian imperialism was creeping ever close to Phoenicia. In 876 BC Assur-nasir-pal II took tribute from the kings of Tyre, Sidon, Byblos and Arvad. His son, Shalmaneser III, met a coalition formed by the rulers of Hama, Damascus, Israel and Arvad in battle at Qarqar on the river Orontes in Syria that for some years restrained Assyrian activity in the west. When the Assyrian king returned four years later he marched through Phoenicia, setting up a monument at Mount Carmel in the south, on the boundary between Israel and Phoenicia, and carving a victory stela on the rock at the mouth of the Dog River (Nahr el-Kalb), near Byblos. Tribute from the region was represented in the royal palaces at home in Assyria on such monuments as the "Black Obelisk" from Nimrud and the Bronze Gates at Balawat. In the late 9th century King Adad-Nirari III of Assyria took Damascus, and the Phoenician cities sent him tribute to forestall any intentions he might have had against them. Then for about half a century Assyria was pre-occupied with home affairs.

With the reign of Tiglath-Pileser III (c. 745 to 723 BC) began a period of over a century marked by progressively more stringent Assyrian demands. At first, as before, sporadic levies of tribute were made, though early in the reign of Sargon II (c. 721 to 705 BC) a revolt in Arvad was crushed. Under Sennacherib (c. 704 to 681 BC), after a coalition of Phoenician and Syrian cities was put down in 701 to 700 BC, annual tribute began to be imposed. During this campaign the acute rivalries of the main Phoenician cities were painfully revealed when some of them provided the Assyrians with a fleet that for five years unsuccessfully besieged Tyre. It was only in Esarhaddon's reign (c. 680 to 669 BC), when the Phoenician cities became inextricably involved in anti-Assyrian politics, that their position sharply deteriorated.

In 677 to 676 Sidon, allied with rebel kings in south-eastern Turkey, was sacked, its ruler executed and its people deported to Assyria. The city's possessions were reorganized under an Assyrian governor and some of its cities given to the King of Tyre, at this time loyal to Assyria. Parts of his treaty with the Assyrian King Esarhaddon survive; it was clearly too onerous to last. In 671, in support of the Egyptian pharaoh Tarhaqa, Tyre revolted; as a consequence supplies to the city were cut off and tribute imposed. Phoenicia was by now a series of small Assyrian provinces governed from Simyra in the north, from a new foundation at Sidon (Kar-Esarhaddon) and from Ushu, the land city of Tyre, in the south. Only Arvad, Byblos and island Tyre retained some vestiges of independence.

In his first two campaigns against Egypt Ashurbanipal (c. 668 to 627 BC) seems to have felt able to ignore Tyre, but on his third campaign the Assyrian king besieged the city, forcing its ruler, still the King Ba'il who had earlier supported Egypt, to submit. In Oppenheim's translation:

"In my third campaign I marched against Ba'il, King of Tyre, who lives (on an island) amidst the sea, because he did not heed my royal order, did not listen to my personal commands. I surrounded him with redoubts, seized his communications on sea and land. I (thus) intercepted and made scarce their food supply and forced them to submit to my yoke. He brought his own daughter and the daughters of his brothers before me to do menial services. At the same time, he brought his son Iahimilki who had not (yet) crossed the sea to greet me as (my) slave. I received from him his daughter and the daughters of his brothers with their great dowries. I had mercy upon him and returned to him the son, the offspring of his loins." Arvad was also subjugated. On returning from his Arabian campaign Ashurbanipal massacred the inhabitants of mainland Tyre (c. 639 to 637 BC), who had defaulted in their annual tribute.

This was the end of tight Assyrian control, for its Empire slowly began to disintegrate. In the following interval, before the arrival of new masters from Meso-potamia, the Phoenician cities enjoyed that great prosperity, associated particularly with Tyre, which was cursed by Ezekiel (27:1–9). The prophet imagined Tyre as a great ship, symbol of her commercial prosperity, describing both the range of the city's trading contacts and its political preeminence among Phoenician cities:

"Tyre, you used to say: I am a ship perfect in beauty. Your frontiers stretched far out to sea; those who built you made you perfect in beauty.

Cypress from Senir [Mt Hermon] they used for all your planking. They took cedar from Lebanon to make your mast.

From the tallest oaks of Bashan they made your oars.

They built your deck of cedar inlaid with ivory from the Kittim [ie of the whole Levant] isles.

Embroidered linen of Egypt was used for your sail and for your flag.

Purple and scarlet from the Elishah islands formed your deck-tent. Men from Sidon and from Arvad were your oarsmen. Your sages, Tyre, were aboard serving as sailors.

The elders and craftsmen of Gebal [Byblos] were there to caulk your seams.''

After the fall of the Assyrian capital, Nineveh, in 612 BC and the defeat of an Egyptian army at Carchemish in 605 BC, Syria and Phoenicia lay open to the Babylonians, now heirs to the Assyrian supremacy. But Nebuchadnezzar II did not in fact intervene until a revolt was organized in support of Egypt. For 13 years (c. 585 to 572 BC) Tyre, provisioned from the sea, withstood a Babylonian siege, vividly described in Ezekiel 29:18–19:

"Son of man, Nebuchadnezzar King of Babylon mobilized his army for a great expedition against Tyre. Their heads have all gone bald, their shoulders are all chafed [through wearing helmets and carrying arms for so long], but even so he has derived no profit from the expedition mounted against Tyre either for himself or for his army." Though Ezekiel was no doubt right, records of ration issues for captives, preserved on clay tablets found at Babylon, reveal that, even if he did not storm the island city, he finally received its nominal submission, sending royal and noble hostages back to Babylon.

19th century drawings of a sculptured relief (now lost) from the palace of King Sennacherib at Nineveh in Iraq, showing King Luli of Tyre and Sidon fleeing by sea from Tyre in 701 BC after an Assyrian attack. It illustrates both the traditional rounded shape of Phoenician merchant ships, with oars and masts for sails, and their warships with rams.

Phoenicia, like so much of the Babylonian Empire, passed peacefully to the Persians under Cyrus in 538 BC. Its cities were enrolled in the fifth satrapy (or province) with their own rulers, supervised by officials of the imperial administration. Thus – well treated and free to expand their trade in return for regularly-paid taxes – the Phoenician cities long remained loyal to Persia. Their fleets provided indispensable support for the Persian attacks on Greece. To judge from buildings found at Sidon – its harbor works, the palace of a Persian king or satrap in the Persepolitan style, the rebuilt Temple of Eshmun on a hill outside the city, and fortifications at various other places along the coast – Phoenicia at this time enjoyed unparalleled material prosperity. Diodorus records 100 ships at anchor in Sidon's harbor in the mid-4th century BC. Tyre controlled the coast from Sarepta to Mount Carmel and Ascalon; Arvad extended landwards; Sidon in about 450 BC received Dor and Joppa in the south; Tyre, Sidon and Arvad in collaboration founded Tripoli.

In the 4th century, with the central administration of the Persian Empire weakening, the Phoenician cities were seduced into the Greek camp. In 392 BC they submitted to Evagoras, King of Salamis, a major Greek-speaking state in Cyprus; in 362 BC the King of Sidon, notoriously pro-Greek, welcomed an Egyptian army in revolt against Artaxerxes II. With the collapse of the satraps' revolt the

The Ishtar Gate of Babylon, decorated with sacred beasts in polychrome glazed tiles, as reconstructed in a Berlin Museum.

Phoenician cities returned temporarily to the Persian fold, but, in 347 to 345 BC, Tennes, King of Sidon, rebelled. Now, however, the empire was ruled by the ruthless and dynamic Artaxerxes III who burned Sidon, slaughtering over 40,000 people. Tennes, who tried to save himself at the last minute by treacherously handing over his city, was also put to death. Such action deterred further revolts. Sidon was rebuilt, but commercial and political leadership passed to Tyre.

Tyre's supremacy this time was to be brief. Alexander the Great decided, after his victory over the Persians at the Battle of Issus in 333 BC, that it was vital to control the Phoenician seaports and their fleets in order to protect his rear as he advanced deeper into Asia against the retreating Persian king. Sidon and Byblos received him submissively. Tyre dithered, then refused to surrender her island-city. But Alexander was not a man to be baulked, and there ensued one of the world's most famous sieges which permanently modified the city's topography. During a seven-month blockade Alexander's engineers built a great mole from the mainland to the island along which, by a clever diversionary use of seapower, his army eventually stormed the island-city of Tyre.

Quintius Curtius, writing a history of Alexander in the 2nd century AD, completed his account of this siege with a summary of Tyre's history that may provide a preface to a more general consideration of Phoenician culture and achievement.

"Tyre was taken in the seventh month after the beginning of the siege, a city worthy of note in the memory of later times both for its ancient origin and its frequent changes of fortune. Founded by Agenor [in Greek mythology father of Europa, mother of Minos, thus linking Phoenicia and Crete], it long held under its sway not only the neighboring part of the sea, but whatever portion of it its fleets could reach. Also, if one wishes to believe report, this people was the first either to teach, or to learn, the art of writing. At any rate, its colonies were distributed over almost the whole world: Carthage in Africa; Thebes in Boeotia, Gades [Cadiz], on the Ocean."

Little is known either of Phoenician government or of the internal politics of the individual cities. It will have been apparent from this brief review of their history that the cities were staunchly independent, rarely given to any kind of cooperation. Each had a monarchy, hereditary as far as it is possible to judge. The king and queen also acted as chief priest and priestess. Yehimilk of Byblos describes himself as "a just king and a righteous king towards the holy gods of Byblos." Each king had a council of elders. Ezekiel refers to those at Byblos, while Esarhaddon mentions at Tyre "the ancients of your land in council." In Tyre they could take decisions in the king's absence and at Sidon, where they seem to have numbered one hundred, they could act against the king if they thought fit. Briefly under the Assyrian governors all local authorities were subject to them. Esarhaddon told the king of Tyre that: "Any letter I send you you shall not open without the governor. If the governor is not there you shall await him and then open it." By at least the Persian period the councils of elders, largely merchants, began to attain to fuller authority and in some cases superseded the monarchs. At Tyre, from the Babylonian period, a dual magistracy (judges) exercised extensive executive powers.

Cults and cult practices. The religious beliefs and practices of the Phoenicians in the 1st millennium BC directly descended from those of the Canaanites, vividly – if partially – portrayed in the Ras Shamra texts. As evidence for cults and cult practices obtained from the cities themselves is very sparse until after Alexander's conquest, modern surveys of Phoenician religion depend heavily on information provided by Classical authors, on scattered monumental inscriptions, largely from North Africa, and on comparisons with the earlier Ugaritic texts. This has its dangers. Greeks and Romans, writing much later, naturally interpreted what they saw – and that was more often colonial Carthaginian than original Phoenician – in their own terms. Dedicatory inscriptions and sacrificial texts are brief and cryptic, and when they come from the western Mediterranean may well reflect conditions very different from those in the homeland cities. In Phoenicia each city had its own pantheon of gods that was never static; new gods were introduced and old ones assumed fresh identities or new roles. Ugaritic prototypes, some at least half a millennium earlier, may be a very unreliable guide in such circumstances.

The pantheon of Tyre in the early 7th century BC was recorded among the customary oaths at the end of the treaty between the city's ruler and Esarhaddon, King of Assyria. At the head stood three Baals: Baal-shamem, "Lord of Heaven"; Baal-malage, "Lord of Fishing"; and Baal-saphon, "Lord of Storm." They are followed by Melkart, chief god of Tyre and Carthage, Eshmun of Sidon, and Astarte. Melkart, identified by the Greeks with Hercules, was a solar deity with marine attributes. Eshmun, who came to supersede Melkart at Carthage, was an earthy deity presiding over health and healing. Astarte was a many-sided goddess as at Ugarit, primarily of fertility and motherhood. Among numerous other deities shared by the Phoenician cities and not mentioned in this treaty are a number also familiar from the Ras Shamra texts: Reshef, god of lightning and fire, Dagon of fertility; personifications of qualities like Sydyk (justice) and Misor (righteousness); or of skills like Chusor, patron of craftsmanship.

Flexible and fluid as the system was, a triad of gods common to all the cities suggests that the very complex Greek explanations of Phoenician religion in terms of their own gods, Kronos, Aphrodite and Adonis, are essentially correct. First and foremost stood the supreme male god, protective deity of the city, with his wife or female companion, symbolizing fertility, and then a young male god, normally son of the goddess, who was a symbol of nature's

Enlarged view of a tiny sheet gold pendant of a worshiper, probably from Cyprus. The pendant has two suspension loops on the back. It is made in the Phoenician style and dates from the 6th century BC. This figure may contain (as do other such amulets) a magical charm inscribed on a tiny piece of sheet gold or silver.

course through the annual cycle. Believed to die with Nature at the onset of winter, he rose again with the spring.

All cities had monumental shrines to the main deities; in addition there were many sanctuaries outside in the hills, near the water, or trees and rocks that were venerated. Some of these were the well-known "high places," open air sanctuaries with altars and symbolic pillars or conical stones (betyls). The close relationship between Solomon's Temple and Phoenician shrines is clear from the Bible. In Phoenicia it is only the later versions of such temples that have so far been explored. Of these the Hellenistic temple of Eshmun at Sidon and that at Umm el-Amed, 12 miles south of Tyre, are the most important. Within the main temple enclosures there were many small chapels, each with their own altars and cult statues, often dedicated by private donors. Each temple had a great establishment of priests, officials and servants. The most important festival was that in honor of the young god Adonis, whose funeral was reenacted with offerings and banquets.

Numerous votive statuettes were made of deities in clay, stone and metal. A 5th or early 4th century shipwreck, recently explored, about half a mile off the coast of Israel north of Acre, was carrying a cargo of pottery and mold-made baked clay figurines, marked in some cases with a dolphin, or a raised right arm, or the symbol of the goddess Tanit. The existence of an export trade in such figurines is as surprising as the presence in homeland Phoenicia of Tanit, a fertility goddess, long thought to belong exclusively to Carthage and the western colonies.

Ever since 1862 when Gustave Flaubert, in a dramatic chapter entitled "Moloch" in his novel *Salammbo*, called attention to child sacrifices at Carthage, they have been the best known aspect of Phoenician religion. Flaubert's description is based on an account by Diodorus Siculus (c. 40 BC) of a particular moment of crisis at Carthage. In 310 BC, when the city was threatened, its inhabitants attributed their peril to the anger of the god Kronos – to

Above: stone funerary stela of Baaljaton, a high priest of Tyre in the 3rd or 2nd century BC.

Below: black basalt Egyptian style coffin with Phoenician inscription for Eshmunazar II of Sidon, 5th century BC.

Polychrome glass perfume bottles widely made and traded through Phoenician influence, 500–300 BC.

whom recently they had sacrificed only sick children or children bought for the purpose. This time in atonement they sacrificed 200 children from noble families. The child was placed in the hands of a huge bronze statue of Kronos from which it rolled into the flames. In the sanctuary of Tanit at Carthage urns have been found containing the burnt bones of lambs and goats, but more often of children. Inscriptions from the city contain the expressions: "offerings of lamb/offering of man." The crucial word *molk* in this context refers not to a god Moloch, but to a specific sacrificial offering. The name Moloch is associated with *mlk*, to rule, and may be just an alternative title for well-known Phoenician deities like Melkart, not a separate god.

In the western colonies such child sacrifices were undoubtedly routine; the same may not have been true of the homeland. They were certainly practiced there, but probably only at times of extreme crisis, personal or national. Indeed they were briefly introduced into Palestine. The requisite sacrificial precincts, now known to archaeologists in North Africa, Sardinia and Sicily as *topheth* ("roaster"), are named after the place near Jerusalem where such sacrifices took place: "He [King Josiah] desecrated the furnace in the Valley of Ben-hinnom, so that no one could make his son or daughter pass through fire in honor of Molech" (2 Kings 23:10).

Phoenician burials were primarily inhumations in rock-cut tombs; for royalty and nobility fine stone sarcophagi were provided. The earliest, and most famous, of a series of human-shaped stone coffins, usually with just a face and mummiform body on the lid, are two imported from Egypt to be inscribed in Phoenician in the 5th century BC, intended to hold the bodies of King Tabnit of Sidon and his son Eshmunazar II. They established a long-popular fashion both in Phoenicia and the western colonies. In the same rock-cut complex at Sidon four chest-like, magnificently decorated stone sarcophagi in the Greek manner were found, probably made in Asia Minor for aristocrats of the later Persian Empire. Cremation was also favored in

Left: 8th century BC ivory plaque made for inlaying into a piece of wooden furniture found in an Assyrian palace at Nimrud in Iraq. The Egyptianizing character of the design is typical of Phoenician art. Although the row of uraeus-snakes, winged disk and flanking men in double-crowns are distinctively Egyptian, the jug held by the man on the left is a typically Phoenician vessel.

Right: 8th century ivory inlay plaque from Nimrud in Iraq, showing a girl playing a lyre. Her clothes and the way in which her hair (or wig) is curled are in the Egyptian fashion, but the manner of carving the ivory may indicate a place of manufacture in Syria rather than Phoenicia.

Phoenicia. Most burials were well equipped with vessels for food and drink, personal ornaments and cosmetic articles.

Craftsmen and traders. Though confined for space, the Phoenician hinterland was very fertile, producing vines, olives, dates and figs in valleys and on lower mountain slopes, and higher up the renowned cedar and cypress forests. Phoenicia imported linen from Egypt, grain, honey and balm from Palestine, horses and mules from southeast Turkey, metals and semi-precious stones through Arabia and Mesopotamia from Iran and beyond, wool from Syria, and sheep from the bedouin of Arabia. From the western Mediterranean, Spain and Sardinia came silver, iron, lead and tin. Out of the African hinterland came ivory, slaves, gold, silver, apes and peacocks. The *Odyssey* recounts a number of incidents of Phoenician piracy and the kidnapping of men, women and children for selling into slavery: "Phoenicians, men famed for their ships, greedy knaves, bringing countless trinkets in their black ship" (Book XV 403–404).

But the Phoenicians were by no means just carriers, transporting raw materials or manufactured goods produced by the labor of others. They were craftsmen of great skill, particularly famous as metalsmiths, weavers and dyers, carpenters and cabinet-makers, quarrymen and masons. It is not to be expected that much would have survived of their work in perishable materials like linen and wood; but it is regrettable that evidence for their skill with metals (especially their decorated bowls) and carved ivory (largely decorated plaques for inlays in furniture) still comes entirely from outside Phoenicia, from Assyria and Palestine, from Cyprus, Greece and her islands, and from Italy. Isolating original Phoenician work from these countries is difficult, as they had their own craftsmen capable of copying or modifying fashionable Phoenician products.

The hallmark of Phoenician art is assumed to be, with good reason, dependence on Egyptian inspiration in decoration and design; more particularly the use of Egyptian themes and motifs in a non-Egyptian manner, reflecting the hands of men not trained in the formal conventions of Egyptian art. This characteristic is hardly surprising when Canaanite art is recalled or the very strong links between Byblos and Egypt for over 2,000 years before the peak of Phoenician prosperity. In the report of Wen-Amon, about 1100 BC, the ruler of Byblos indeed remarks, in Wilson's translation:

Left: 7th century silver-gilt Phoenician bowl decorated with *repoussé* and lightly chased designs.

Above: 7th century silver Phoenician bowl, more clearly Egyptian in style.

"See Amun created thunder in heaven when he gave Baal his kingdom. For when Baal founded all lands, he founded them after first founding Egypt whence thou comest; for craftsmanship issued from it to reach the region where I am, and instruction issued from it to reach the region where I am."

Ivory is listed among tribute received by Assyrian kings from Syria and Phoenicia. It was used for small objects, but more commonly for inlay and overlay plaques on wooden beds, couches, stools, etc. Indeed some pieces found in excavations at Nimrud in Iraq bear Phoenician letters scratched on the back to assist the cabinetmaker with assembling the finished article. From Ur in southern Iraq comes a plain, rectangular, ivory, cosmetic box-lid with an inscription in Phoenician: "This box Amat-Baal, daughter of Patisi, slave girl . . . presents to Astarte." Such indirect clues and a strong preference for Egyptian motifs in their designs have led scholars to identify as specifically "Phoenician" carved ivory plaques, all detached from their original settings, found in palaces at Arslan Tash in Syria, Samaria in Palestine and Nimrud in Iraq. Many were originally embellished with inlaid colored glasses, frits, or semiprecious stones, as well as gold-leaf.

None of these finds provides evidence from which it is possible to write a history of Phoenician ivory carving, for all were found in destruction debris that does no more than provide an upper limit for the time of their manufacture. Some belong to the 9th, some to the 8th century BC. Not only in style but also in the choice of motifs Egyptian inspiration is striking: the child Horus on the lotus flower, human-headed, winged sphinxes, floral designs involving the lotus and papyrus flowers, imitation hieroglyphic inscriptions, and human figures in Egyptian-style wigs and costumes, carrying royal Egyptian scepters. Whether these themes represent specific Phoenician religious myths in Egyptian guise has yet to be decided. Since they were so popular far beyond the area where such inspiration would have been meaningful, much of their appeal was clearly intrinsic in their rich designs and fine craftsmanship.

Even more widely distributed are a series of shallow silver, silvergilt and bronze bowls whose inner surface is chased or incised with patterns set within concentric borders. The *Iliad* speaks of a silver bowl – "far the finest in the world; Phoenicians brought it over the cloudy sea . . ." The *Odyssey* mentions a gold-lipped silver bowl given as a gift by the King of Sidon. Layard found a concentration of such bronze bowls in the royal palace at Nimrud in

Iraq, but examples are also known from Cyprus, Crete, Greece and Etruria. They are by no means so homogeneous in style and technique as the ivories. Though Egyptian influence is again pervasive, it is more often blended, or overshadowed, by markedly Assyrian or Syrian motifs. The designs are a remarkable hotchpotch of subjects, some entirely decorative, others which seem by their juxtaposition to be telling a story. At one extreme is a fine silver bowl from a tomb at Praeneste in Italy; it is predominantly Egyptian but inscribed with the owner's name in Phoenician. From Cyprus, at a slightly later date, come examples in which local Greek influences make themselves very apparent. Some of these bowls may come from "Phoenician" workshops in Cyprus, where in the 7th-century royal cemetery at Salamis elaborate metal trappings for chariots and chariot-horses are "Egyptianizing" in style.

the designs often bear traces of Egyptian inspiration.

The Phoenicians may also have been important glass-makers. Although Pliny was certainly wrong in attributing to them the invention of glass, they played a vital role in its dissemination. In the 9th and 8th centuries BC there was a renaissance in glassmaking, after a period of eclipse, with two main centers of production: one in Iraq, the other in Phoenicia. At this time, and until the invention of glass-blowing in the 1st century BC, quantities of small poly-chrome glass vessels were made by winding strands of molten glass around a core, made of straw and a binding agent, in the shape of the vessel desired (the so-called sand-core method). The shapes varied from period to period, generally copying small unguent and perfume flasks of pottery and stone. Such vessels are found all over the Mediterranean and into the Black Sea area. It is unlikely

Above: aerial view (1974) of the recently excavated Phoenician temple at Kition in Cyprus.

Above right: 7th century earrings from the Lebanon; a Phoenician product widely traded and copied in the Mediterranean.

Phoenician metalworking was far more varied than these surviving vestiges might indicate. Our best clue to this lies in the description of Solomon's Temple in the Book of Kings:

"King Solomon sent for Hiram of Tyre; he was the son of a widow of the tribe of Naphtali but his father had been a Tyrian, a bronzeworker. He was a highly intelligent craftsman, skilled in all types of bronzework. . . . He cast two bronze pillars. . . . He made the "Sea" of cast metal. . . . He made ten stands of bronze. . . . He made ten bronze basins. . . . Hiram made the ash containers, the scoops and the sprinkling bowls. . . . He made them by the process of sand castings, in the Jordan area between Succoth and Zarethan." Fine jewelry, in gold and silver, with excellent granulated and repoussé decoration, was produced in many Phoenician cities at home and abroad. Here again

that all come from workshops in Phoenicia: there were probably subsidiary factories in Cyprus, on Rhodes and elsewhere.

Phoenicia, famed as it was for fine textiles, has always been even more renowned for the purple dyes that colored them. To this day large heaps of broken shells, of *murex brandaris, murex trunculus* and *cardium* (cockle), originally used as bait, mark certain parts of the Lebanese coast. Pliny has left a concise description of the process which brought the Phoenicians so much wealth and fame. Part of it reads, in Rackham's translation:

"The vein [in the fish's throat] . . . is removed, and to this salt has to be added, about a pint for every hundred pounds; three days is the proper time for it to be steeped . . . and it should be heated in a leaden pot, and with 50 lbs. of dye to every six gallons of water kept at a uniform and moderate temperature by a pipe brought from a furnace some way off . . . after about nine days the cauldron is strained and a fleece that has been washed clean is dipped for a trial, and the liquid is heated up until fair confidence is achieved. A ruddy color is inferior to a blackish one. The fleece is allowed to soak for five hours and after it has been carded is dipped again, until it soaks up all the juice. The whelk [bucinum = Purpura haemastoma] by itself is not approved of, as it does not make a fast dye; it is blended in a moderate degree with sea purple [murex] and it gives to its excessively dark hue that hard and brilliant scarlet which is in demand; when their forces are thus mingled, the one is enlivened, or deadened as the case may be, by the other. The total amount of dye-stuffs required for 1,000 lbs. of fleece is 200 lbs. of whelk and 111 lbs. of sea purple; so is produced that remarkable amethyst colour. For Tyrian

purple the wool is first soaked with sea purple for a preliminary pale dressing, and then completely transformed with whelk dye. Its highest glory consists in the colour of congealed blood, blackish at first glance but gleaming when held up to the light." (*Natural History*, 9:LXII.) It was inevitable that such enterprise, both as manufacturers and as traders, would lead the Phoenicians ever further westwards.

Phoenicians overseas. For centuries before the assaults of the "Sea Peoples" in the later 13th century the coastal cities of Syria and the Lebanon had maintained lively commercial contacts with Cyprus and beyond. Whether, as seems more than likely, there had been resident Asiatic merchants in Cyprus has yet to be determined. By the 10th century at least Phoenicians were settled at Kition, which was to remain their main colony in Cyprus. At this time (according to one interpretation of an enigmatic comment in the writings of Josephus) Hiram, King of Tyre, conducted a punitive expedition against settlers at Kition who were withholding their taxes. From Kition may also come a 9th-century funerary inscription, the earliest Phoenician inscription reported from Cyprus. At the time of the second Hiram of Tyre, in the later 8th century, a governor of "Qart Hadasht" (possibly Kition) dedicated some bronze bowls to "Baal of the Lebanon." By 800 BC the Phoenicians had built a fine temple at Kition, on the site of earlier shrines, rectangular in shape and divided up internally with four parallel rows of seven columns. It has yielded a wealth of pottery and small finds, many distinctive of Phoenician settlements all over the Mediterranean.

How far Phoenician settlement, as distinct from intensive trading contacts, extended beyond Kition at this time is still uncertain. The sum of epigraphic evidence suggests that Phoenician political authority, closely controlled at first by the mainland mother-cities, was only sporadically extended further. Most often it was just a matter of

As seafarers and explorers, the Phoenicians extended their influence throughout the Mediterranean.

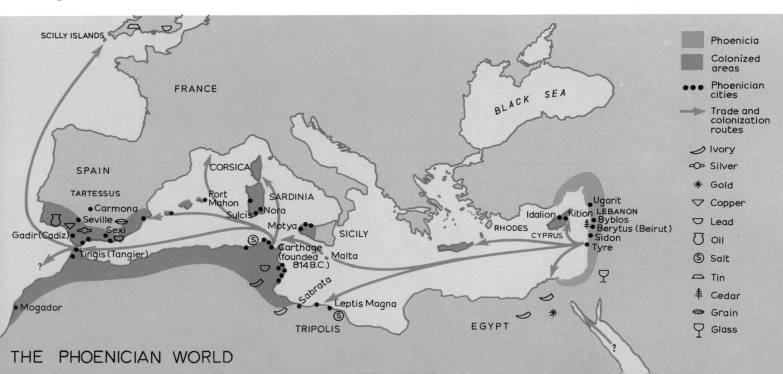

THE PHOENICIAN WORLD

Multicolored glass amulets worn as necklaces, widely made and traded under Phoenician influence in the 5th and 4th centuries BC.

Phoenician merchants mixing freely with the Greek-speaking population, greatly stimulating their part in east Mediterranean commerce. Although there is plenty of evidence from Cyprus for strong Phoenician influence in art and religion, this need not presuppose extensive colonization. From the later 6th century, under Persian rule, the authority of the Phoenicians in Cyprus certainly spread widely, since the Persians favored them in opposition to the local Greek kingdoms. Kings of Kition with distinctively Phoenician names now extended their rule over cities like Idalion and Tamassos. At Lapithos coins were minted bearing the ruler's name in Phoenician letters, while numerous Phoenician inscriptions from this period mirror their increasing activity.

Phoenician penetration of the Aegean and Greece has proved even more difficult to identify archaeologically, though classical authors held it to be important. Herodotus credited them with settlements in Thera, Kythera, Thasos and Boeotia. So far archaeology has failed to substantiate the claim. On the island of Rhodes literary tradition and archaeological findings blend more happily. Here there is evidence to show that by the later 8th century BC Phoenicians were settled as participants in the manufacture and trade of unguents and the pots to contain them. The best known aspect of this industry is the production, in faience and frit, of charming little vessels, some in human and animal form, as well as amulets and scarab-seals in an "Egyptianizing" style. As in the transmission of the alphabet, it is not yet possible to say whether the many objects made in the east that traveled west to Greece in the later 8th and 7th centuries BC were carried in Greek or Phoenician merchant ships, or in an amicable combination of both.

Greek and Roman historians were also in no doubt that Phoenician colonists had been active in the west Mediterranean from the later 12th century BC, long before the Greek incursions there. Traditionally, Cadiz in Spain and Utica in Africa, north of Carthage, were founded in 1110 and 1101 BC respectively, while some authors placed the Phoenicians' North African colonies even earlier. So far there is no clear archaeological evidence for a substantial Phoenician presence at any site in this region before the 8th century BC. This contradiction, which has given rise to a lively and continuing debate, is more apparent than real. There is no reason why Phoenicians should not have sailed regularly into the western Mediterranean, making occasional and transitory landfalls as circumstance required, or even formed tiny minorities among the local seaboard communities long before distinctive architecture and artifacts proclaimed their presence. Had it not been for an abundance of contemporary inscribed clay tablets, for example, archaeologists would never have recognized a famous Assyrian colony of the early 2nd millennium BC at Kültepe in southeast Turkey. The material culture of the colonists was that of their hosts.

Phoenician maritime activity along the Libyan and Tunisian coast is likely to have begun with irregular calls at sheltered anchorages, followed by intermittently occupied trading posts in the 8th century, at sites like Leptis Magna, Oea and Sabratha, then in the next century by full settlements. The traditional date for the founding of Carthage, the most famous of all Phoenician colonies, is 814 BC. As yet the earliest datable pottery with Greek affinities coming from the site, found within the precinct of the goddess Tanit – who may well have protected the settlement of the earliest colonists – cannot be dated before about 730 BC. A small circular gold pendant from the "Tomb of Tadamil," bearing a dedication that is the earliest Phoenician inscription from Africa, also belongs to approximately this period. In Sicily, despite the opinion of the Greek historian Thucydides to the contrary, Greek penetration was contemporary with the earliest Phoenician settlements, if it did not actually precede them. A Phoenician colony was established at Motya by about 720 BC, with a Phoenician presence in Malta soon afterwards. Both these enterprises may have owed more to Carthage than to the Phoenician mother-cities. With firm bases at Carthage and Motya, controlling both sides of a narrow point in the Sicilian channel, the Phoenicians were in a strong position to exploit advantages in the western Mediterranean earned earlier by their commercial enterprises.

The most recent translation of the famous 9th-century Phoenician inscription from Nora in Sardinia shows that it records a victory by Phoenician forces over native tribesmen at Tarshish, a refinery town in Sardinia, perhaps even Nora itself, at the time of King Pummay of Tyre (c. 821 to 785 BC). This may well have been an expedition sent specifically to protect mining interests. Pummay is the Pygmalion of Greek legend. This raises interesting new possibilities. Not only does it confirm the extent of Tyre's western enterprise by the late 9th century; it also gives additional support to the traditional date for the foundation of Carthage, in the seventh year of King Pygmalion, 814 BC. By the very late 8th century there was at least one sacrificial center (topheth) on Sardinia, at Sulcis, and wider colonization was undertaken in the following decades. Sometime in the middle of the 7th century Carthage established a colony on Ibiza, though it is likely that Phoenicians had earlier made use of the fine harbor at Port Mahon (Mago) on Minorca. Carthaginians in the 7th and 6th centuries took the initiative in settling communities down the Atlantic coast of Morocco from Tangier to Mogador.

If southwest Spain really was the Biblical "Tarshish," as many scholars have argued, then Phoenician commercial contacts there, if no more, might really extend back as far as the traditional date for the founding of Cadiz at the end of the 12th century BC. By the later 8th and early 7th century Phoenician colonial activity is clearly marked by a series of trading stations along the southern coast of Spain from Villaricos to Cadiz, almost wherever suitable anchorage offered. A rich cemetery near Almunecar (classical Sexi) contained, apart from Phoenician and Greek types of pottery, large Egyptian alabaster vases bearing inscriptions of the pharaohs Sheshonk II (c. 890 BC), Osorkon II (c. 874 to 850 BC), and Takeloth II (c. 850 to 825 BC), used as cinerary urns. The associated Greek pottery clearly indicates that the graves were of the early 7th, not the 9th century. Similar jars were found in the ruins of the palace of Assur-nasir-pal II at Assur in Iraq, one with a local inscription saying that it was part of King Esarhaddon's booty from his campaign against King Abdimilkuti of Sidon in 677 BC. It is tempting to associate the arrival of such jars in Spain with Phoenician refugees from this Assyrian onslaught. Indeed, it has been suggested that it was such Assyrian pressures on the whole economic basis of homeland Phoenician society in the early and mid-7th century that intensified their colonial activity in the western Mediterranean.

Westwards beyond Cadiz Phoenicians sailed inland up the deep and broad Guadalquiver river, strongly influencing the material culture of local settlements like those at Seville and Carmona. But the real focus of Phoenician interest was further west still in the rich mining area of Rio Tinto (the red river), inland from Huelva. Here, at

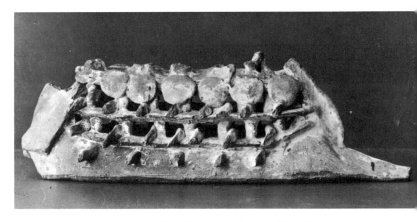

Above: 5th or 4th century model of a Phoenician warship with three banks of oars and a ram, from Armant in Egypt.

Below: model of a Phoenician merchant ship from Amathus in Cyprus, showing rowers' benches and cabins.

Silver double shekel of Sidon showing a warship with prow
figurehead and the Persian king (or Baal) in a chariot, c. 350 BC.

Mount Solomon, where the river rises, ancient slag heaps
still bear witness to long exploitation of the local metal
ores, especially silver. Recent research has revealed buildings with vestiges of metalworking, accompanied by
pottery of the 8th to 7th centuries BC, more distinctively
Phoenico-Palestinian than the earliest pottery from sites
like Carthage and Utica.

Harbors, shipping and exploration. The development
of underwater archaeology in recent years has greatly
aided the study of Phoenician maritime activity. Although
it has long been realized that Phoenician sailors favored
certain readily recognizable anchorages at home and
abroad throughout the Mediterranean, it was often very
hard, if not impossible, to date these harbors accurately.
Nothing was known of ships save from illustrations that
offered little in the way of accurate detail. Slowly the
position is changing. Harbors have been carefully surveyed and new dating evidence proposed. A ship which
may be Canaanite was excavated in 1960. It was wrecked
off Cape Gelidonya in southern Turkey about 1200 BC,
and carried a cargo of metal ingots and scrap. A Phoenician
ship wrecked off Acre has already been cited, and the wreck
of what may be a Carthaginian warship is under investigation off Motya in Sicily.

The earliest harbor works on the exposed coast of
Phoenicia were cut, not built, out of rocky outcrops,
offshore reefs running parallel with the coast, or islands,
as variously illustrated by the harbors of Sidon, Tyre and
Arvad. Only after techniques for building walls under
water had been perfected, perhaps not until the middle of
the 1st millennium BC, did it become possible to create
compact harbors, as at Sidon in the 5th century. Initially
rock masses were cut to make a quay on the sheltered
landward side, leaving a wall of rock, if necessary artificially
heightened by building, on the weather side. Such vital
fittings as sluices, warehouses, mooring bitts and other
installations were also rock-cut. All major harbors tended
only to be on islands large enough to be inhabited, as at
Tyre and Arvad. Elsewhere bulky cargo ships lay offshore,
loading and unloading by lighter. For this, outer auxiliary

harbors might be created on offshore reefs as at Sidon and
Machroud, nearly two miles south of Arvad Island, opposite the 9th-century settlement at Tabbat el-Hammam on
the main Syrian coast. As ancient ships could probably not
have sailed against the wind, their sailors may often have
been forced to seek anchorage at points, like offshore
shallows or even dangerous rocks, now obsolete and
marked only by heavy stone anchors long since submerged.

The ancient Greeks readily acknowledged the Phoenician mastery of the arts of sailing and navigation. Particularly they learned from them a better way of determining
north by the Lesser Bear instead of the Great Wain or the
Plow. Phoenician sailors were more enterprising than
some modern accounts would allow. They almost certainly did not travel only by day, hugging the coastline.
Sailors today in the Mediterranean are often forced to sail
at night in craft comparable to those of the Phoenicians
and vary their courses as circumstances dictate.

Like all great naval peoples the Phoenicians were masters
of shipbuilding to a variety of designs, producing warships,
merchantmen, fishing boats and other, smaller craft. A
baked clay model from Byblos, about 1500 to 1200 BC,
represents a cargo ship of rounded shape with perfect
symmetry, the keel projecting at bow and stern. At each
end there is a platform with railings around it. Such are
the ships of the "Peoples of the Sea" shown on Egyptian
reliefs, though they have animals' or birds' heads carved on
bow and stern. This basic tradition was to persist throughout. Such boats are represented in a relief from King Sennacherib's palace at Nineveh in Iraq of the fleet of Luli,
King of Tyre and Sidon, about 701 BC. This shows various
ships that may be grouped into two hybrid types. Both
could be sailed and masts lowered as required, both have
upper decks carried on stanchions (supports) and protected by rows of shields, and both are propelled by two
ranks of oars on each side. But while one has the traditional
rounded shape of the merchantman, the other has a warship's ram. No pictorial evidence has survived for the next
two centuries, but with the regular minting of coins by the
Phoenician cities in the 4th century BC galleys became the
favorite motif at Arvad, Byblos and Sidon; after Alexander's reign other cities followed suit.

Of these, Sidon has the most varied and informative
range, showing a trireme, with its three superimposed
rows of oars, the characteristic ship of the period. In
Phoenicia it had developed directly from ships like King
Luli's, differing only in the addition of another row of oars
and an eye-shaped forecastle. As the Phoenician galley had
a wide hull, it was possible to accommodate the third row
of oars without using an outrigger for one rank, as was
necessary on the narrower Greek trireme. To judge from
coin illustrations, and a fine terracotta model from Armant
in Egypt, the rowers sat in oblique rows of three, each
slightly higher than the other, from the ship's side inwards.
It has been estimated that these Phoenician galleys were
about 120 feet long with 174 rowers, three rows of 29 oars

Above: late 4th century Phoenician funerary inscription found at Larnaca in Cyprus by Pococke in 1738.

Below: inscribed limestone coffin of Ahiram of Byblos, dated 1250–1000 BC – the major monument of Late Canaanite art.

on each side. They are well-evoked in Plutarch's description of the Battle of Salamis, "with their towering sterns and lofty decks" so vulnerable to fresh breezes and choppy seas, as Themistocles shrewdly realized in directing the strategy of his less vulnerable, smaller Greek triremes. The continuous upper deck allowed a Phoenician trireme to carry, according to Herodotus, 30 Persians, Medes and other troops in addition to her normal crew.

The Phoenician galleys were ornamented for religious, not aesthetic reasons, with an ensign near the stern consisting of a staff bearing a globe and crescent to denote Astarte, stern draperies and figure heads. Herodotus writes of figureheads called *pataikos*, the pigmy with animal head, feather crown, bandy legs and raised arms like the very popular Egyptian god Bes. Sometimes the figure was helmeted and armed. More conventional figureheads – lions, horses and other beasts – were also popular.

Phoenician voyages westwards through the Mediter-

ranean have already been discussed in talking of colonization and trade, but this was not the only area of Phoenician maritime activity. Hiram, King of Tyre, "sent men of his, sailors who knew the sea, to serve with Solomon's men. They went to Ophir and from there they brought back four hundred and twenty talents of gold" (I Kings, 9:27–8). The exact location of Ophir is unknown, but it probably lay in western Arabia on the sea route to India rather than in India itself. A sherd of pottery found on the surface at Tell Qasile near Tel Aviv, probably of the 8th century BC, bears an inscription, with 30 written in the Phoenician manner, "(G)old (of) Ophir. (Belonging) to Beth-horon/ 30 sh(equels)." It was from the Red Sea also that the expedition of Phoenician sailors sent out by the Egyptian pharaoh Necho, about 600 BC, sailed southwards to circumnavigate Africa. Herodotus relates that:

"[E]very autumn [they] put in where they were on the African coast, sowed a patch of ground, and waited for

next year's harvest. Then, having got in their grain, they put to sea again, and after two full years rounded the Pillars of Hercules in the course of the third and returned to Egypt. These men made a statement which I do not myself believe, though others may, [indeed they do, and accept it as indication that the Phoenicians really did undertake this voyage] to the effect that as they sailed on a westerly course round the southern end of Africa, they had the sun on their right: to northward of them. This is how Africa was first discovered to be surrounded by sea." (IV.42).

Two of the most famous voyages associated with the Phoenicians were made from Carthage. Both took place in the later 5th century BC. Himilco, whose voyage is only known from the record of a Roman geographical textbook, sailed across the Bay of Biscay to Brittany and to Cornwall, seeking the tin mined there. Hanno set up an account of his voyage in the temple of Baal Hammon at Carthage, now only preserved in an inaccurate and often inconsistent Greek translation. He sailed around the west coast of Africa at least as far as Sierra Leone, possibly well into the Gulf of Guinea.

The Phoenicians' greatest legacy: the alphabet. The alphabetic script developed in Canaan in the 2nd millennium BC had assumed the form now known as "Phoenician" in the 11th century. At this time linear letter forms replaced pictographs completely, the number of signs stabilized at 22, as did the stance in which they were written, and sentences ran from right to left. Only the consonants were written, as common in Semitic languages, the reader supplying the vowels. One of the earliest linear, as distinct from pictographic Phoenician inscriptions is a brief phrase or so on a bronze spatula from Byblos, now dated in the 11th century. Far more important are two lines of text, probably cut about 1100 BC along the lid of an earlier decorated stone sarcophagus reused for the burial of Ahiram, King of Byblos, invoking the customary curses on anyone who disturbed the burial. Thereafter there is a long succession of Phoenician inscriptions extending down to a Sidonian inscription from the Piraeus in Greece dated 96 BC. Virtually all are stereotyped funerary or dedicatory texts giving little more than the names of gods and people.

But there is one striking exception. The most remarkable of all Phoenician texts is that at Karatepe, set in a relatively lonely and remote valley among the Taurus mountains southwest of Marash in Turkey. Here in a small fortress the local ruler, Azitawadda, most likely in the later 8th century BC, set up a statue, and in the gateways a series of decorated stone slabs, with an autobiographical inscription in the local hieroglyphic script. Rather surprisingly this was also given in Phoenician, reflecting, as did Sidon's alliance with rulers of the region in 677 to 676 BC, the strength of Phoenician penetration of the region. Clearly Phoenician merchants in the local community were significant enough to merit royal inscriptions in their own tongue. Among the carved scenes were some directly inspired by Phoenician art.

The date and place of the adoption of an alphabetic script by the Greeks continues to be debated, though none would now question the ancient tradition that Phoenicia was the ultimate source. A minority of scholars believe that Phoenician merchants had already carried it to outlying Greek islands, like Crete and Thera, by soon after 1100 BC. The majority are more cautious. For them a steadily increasing number of Greek alphabetic inscriptions from the later 8th century, and none before, suggests a median date for adoption of an alphabet about 750 BC. This would also fit well with the view that it was the late 9th-century Phoenician administrative script that most nearly matches the earliest Greek letter forms. Significantly this was the time of Pummay, King of Tyre, who as Pygmalion made more impact on Greek tradition than any other Phoenician king.

The earliest known Greek alphabetic inscriptions, dated to about 720 BC, come from the most distant Greek colony of the time, Pithekoussai on the island of Ischia, near Naples in Italy. A certain academic partisanship enters into discussions of how the alphabet traveled and where in the Greek world it first took root. Some would allow Phoenicians the initiative and Crete the priority; Odysseus, it may be noted, left Crete in a boat manned by Phoenicians. Others, remembering that Greeks from Euboea and elsewhere were residing at ports like al Mina and Tell Soukas on the Syrian coast from at least 800 BC, give the initiative to Greek merchants, who would have then transmitted their newly-acquired writing skills, very useful in commerce, rapidly westwards to places as distant as Ischia. Whatever its future history, the Phoenicians had placed at the disposal of the Greeks, and those who inherited their cultural legacy, a supremely efficient working tool indispensable to the development of general literacy.

As writing involves writing materials, it is no coincidence that the Greek word for book [*bublos* (papyrus)/*biblion* (book)] is thought to derive from the name of the Phoenician city of Byblos. Large quantities of papyrus, rolls of which for centuries formed the nearest approximation to the modern book, were transhipped from this port. The Report of Wen-Amon tells how "500 (rolls) of finished papyrus" were among goods sent from Egypt to the prince of Byblos in exchange for timber.

The history of Palestine, to which we now return, was at many points linked to that of Phoenicia, not least through the Canaanite tradition. On many occasions when political considerations drew the two regions together the Canaanite minority still in Palestine and Phoenician contacts did much to modify and develop the artistic, even the religious, life of Israel and Judah.

Solomon's Temple

Apart from the pyramids, no building of the ancient world is as well known as Solomon's Temple in Jerusalem, even though not a stone of it has yet been found. So ruthless was Herod the Great's reconstruction of the Temple, that it is most unlikely that anything much remains within the huge stone platform his masons created. Building began in the fourth year of Solomon's reign and finished in the eleventh. The Temple was designed and built by masons from Phoenicia, and largely arranged by David, who had brought the "Ark of the Covenant" to Jerusalem and acquired the site, north of Ophel, on which to build a temple fit to house it. By correlating the Biblical description (1 Kings: 6) with information obtained through excavation in a number of countries in the Levant, it is today possible to reconstruct Solomon's Temple and adjacent royal palace with considerably more accuracy than fifty years ago.

Above: this modern drawing unites current opinions on the outside appearance of the Solomonic Temple – a much smaller, simpler and more austere building than traditional reconstructions have proposed. It follows closely the form of earlier Canaanite temples, as at Hazor. The two free-standing bronze columns at the entrance, named "Jachin" and "Boaz," were made by the Phoenician smith Hiram in the Jordan valley. Similar columns appear on terracotta model shrines from Cyprus. Dressed stones direct from the quarry were used for the walls. No archaeological evidence so far allows for an accurate reconstruction of the three arcades, each slightly broader than the one below, set on the outside of all but the entrance wall.

Right: the inside walls of the Temple were lined with cedar wood, richly carved and covered with gold. Within the "Holy of Holies" and among motifs elsewhere were represented the mysterious creatures called "cherubim." Since the Old Testament tells us that the craftsmen here were Phoenicians, it is now assumed that excellent parallels for the Temple's interior decoration (though on a much smaller scale) are to be found among the numerous carved ivory plaques of Phoenician manufacture in Assyrian palaces at Nimrud in Iraq. Among them are illustrations of hybrid monsters with the body of a lion and the head, (often shown full-face as here) of a man or woman wearing an Egyptian-style wig. Such it seems is the nearest approximation we yet have to the appearance of the "cherubim."

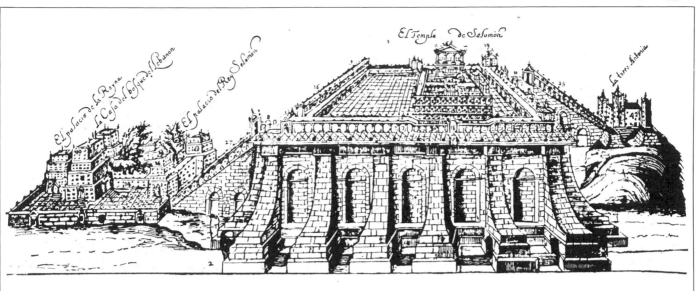

Above: early reconstructions of Solomon's Temple, before the days of serious archaeological research, rest entirely on imaginative interpretations of the Old Testament description, commonly using the fashionable architectural styles of the time of writing. This 1641 attempt uses a Roman architectural style and, in contrast with many more fantastic versions, is notable for the relative accuracy of the topography. Modern scholars would be more likely to site the palace (on the left here) onto the platform north of the Temple.

Below: this 19th-century reconstruction, published by the French scholars Perrot and Chipiez, represents a later stage in the Temple's history, but it is one of the first serious attempts to make use of archaeological evidence. The architectural style and the careful details of the masonry owe much to the researches of the French scholar Renan in the Lebanon. Bolder than most modern attempts, this one may well catch the atmosphere better than they do, even though in isolated details the latter are more accurate.

Above: one of the best archaeological parallels for the ground plan, and possible relation between palace and temple, of Solomon's scheme, is provided by near contemporary remains at Tell Tayanat in Syria.

Right: the Old Testament describes clearly the ground plan of Solomon's Temple. It is very close to that of many earlier Canaanite temples excavated in Palestine and Syria.

Below left: closest in time and place to Solomon's Temple is a shrine excavated at Tell Arad in Israel. This altar for burnt offerings was found in its courtyard.

Below right: the "Holy of Holies" in the Arad Temple is smaller than the main chamber, but retained many of its simple furnishings.

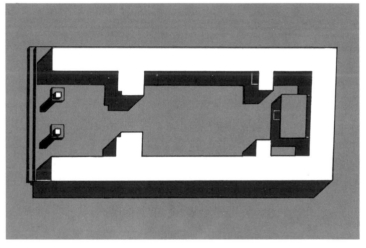

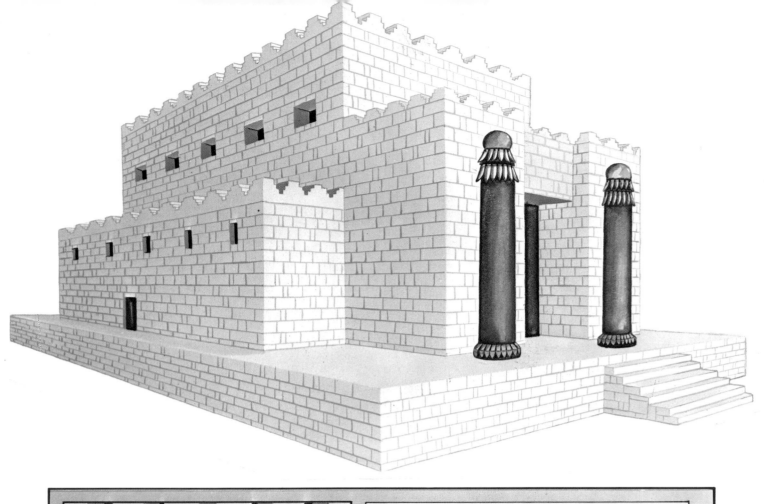

Any attempt to provide a series of architectural drawings designed to illustrate the plan and elevations of Solomon's Temple must rest on the detailed, if not always explicit, description of the building found in the Bible in I Kings 6. This is the work of a well-informed author, but not, of course, an architectural blueprint. The tripartite internal division and its basic dimensions are given in cubits, as are many details of the interior fittings and decoration. But even if anything exactly like this building had been excavated (and it has not) it would be difficult to establish the appearance of anything above foundation level. Dr Busink's reconstructions here are all that is at present possible without unwarranted speculation.

Right: few of the cedars for which the mountain slopes of Lebanon (Phoenicia) were renowned in antiquity are to be seen there today. They were ruthlessly exploited for too long. As Hiram, King of Tyre, told Solomon, "In this matter of timber, both cedar and pine, I will do all you wish. My men shall bring down the logs from Lebanon to the sea and I will make them up into rafts to be floated to the place you appoint."

Far right: as part of his palace buildings adjacent to the Temple at Jerusalem Solomon had constructed the "House of the Forest of Lebanon." It was built, as its name indicates, with four rows of cedar columns, fifteen to a row, with a beamed roof of cedar set on them. Its function is not clear, but it seems to have been a large council or reception hall not unlike the columned halls later so common at Persepolis (see final Visual Story).

Ivory plaques to *left* and *below*. I Kings 6 records that "the cedar inside the house (ie the Temple) was carved with open flowers and gourds." As with the cherubim, these floral ornaments were almost certainly similar to those used on a smaller scale by Phoenician craftsmen carving ivory plaques to be inlaid in wooden furniture. These are two typical examples from Assyrian palaces at Nimrud in Iraq.

Right: miniature versions of the bronze trolleys cast by the Phoenician smith Hiram for the Temple are known two or three centuries earlier in Cyprus. The example shown here is an almost exact parallel to Hiram's . . . "they had panels set in frames; on these panels were portrayed lions, oxen and cherubim, and similarly on the frames . . . Each trolley had four bronze wheels with axles of bronze."

Far right: this small stone altar from Megiddo, with horns at each corner of the cavity on top in which incense was burnt, is typical of many used in the domestic shrines of the Iron Age in Palestine. No doubt those in Solomon's Temple were of similar design but grander and of more splendid materials.

Above: modern model of Herod's Temple. After many vicissitudes Solomon's Temple was finally sacked by the Babylonians and its treasures taken away to Babylon. It was restored about 515 BC and then completely rebuilt by Herod the Great in the 1st century BC, using the Greco-Roman style he so much admired. Little remains of earlier work, for Herod's plans were so ambitious that his greatly enlarged platform for the Temple engulfed what it did not destroy. This temple was sacked by the Romans in 70 AD.

Right: stone altar from Palmyra (Biblical Tadmor) in Syria. In part its inscription reads, "in the month of September of the year 396 (85 AD), this *hamman* and this altar were made and offered. . . ." This is a vital clue to the correct translation and identification of the Biblical *hamman* (2 Chronicles 34:4) as an incense-altar, as shown between the two men in the sculptured relief here. It was items such as this that went into the Temple in Jerusalem at times of pagan worship under the Divided Monarchy.

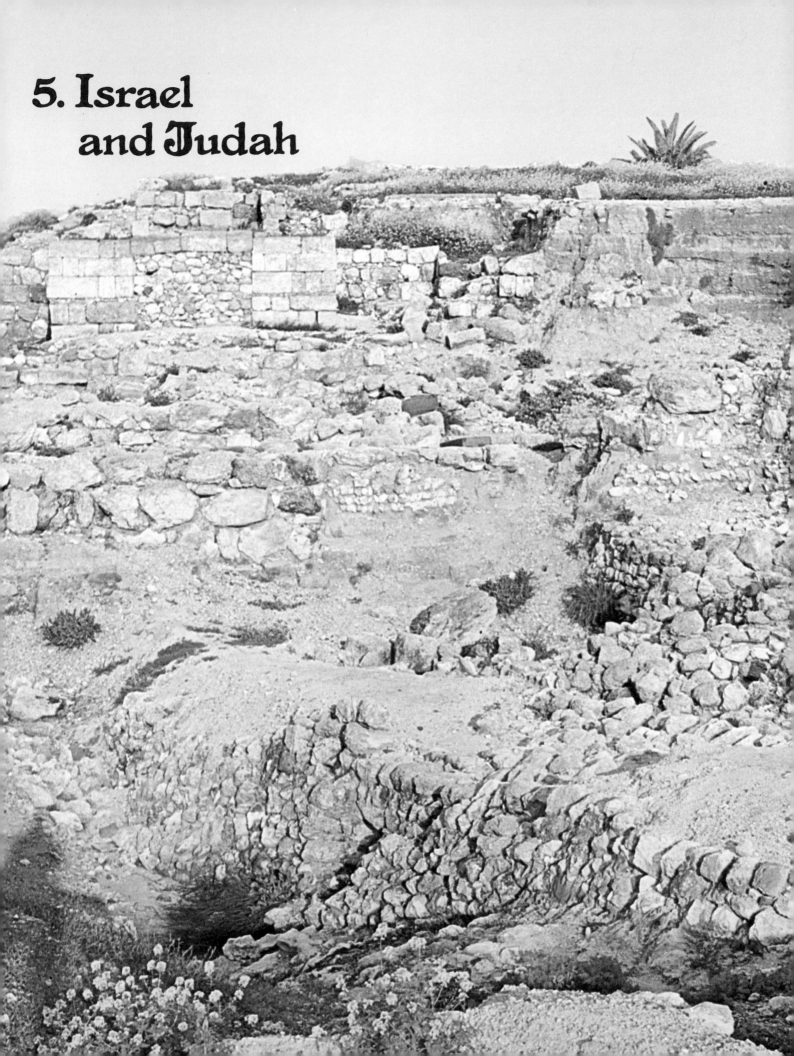

5. Israel and Judah

The Philistines. The Philistines, one group among the many "Peoples of the Sea," settled much of the coastal plain of Palestine from south of Gaza to south of Joppa in the early 12th century BC, initially as Egyptian vassals. Of their five principal cities, Gaza, Ashkelon and Ashdod have been definitely located, but exactly where Gath and Ekron lay has yet to be reliably established. In their area of settlement a distinctive type of painted pottery is concentrated, which has a slip in different shades of white decorated with one or two-color designs. Both shapes and designs reflect the cultural influences, Mycenaean Greek, Egyptian and Cypriot, which touched the Philistines as they moved eastwards in the 13th century from somewhere in the Aegean or western Turkey. This ware ceased to be made after the 11th century, though imitations are current later. The first regular use of iron for the manufacture of tools and weapons was introduced into Palestine by the Philistines, who exercised a monopoly over metalworking when they dominated the Israelites (1 Sam. 13:19–22).

Of Philistine language and literature nothing is known. Their religion is equally obscure, as the only deities attributed to them in the Bible bear Semitic names. In Israel they were known for their practice of divination and soothsaying. A recently excavated temple in a Philistine town at Tell Qasile, on the north bank of the Yarkon river about a mile upstream, has a plan not yet exactly matched in Palestine. Entering a small antechamber lined with plaster benches the worshiper turned right into the main hall of the shrine, again with wall benches and with the roof supported by two cedarwood columns set on stone bases along the central axis. A partition wall divided off a small rear storeroom. Against it was set a small platform, approached by steps, that served as an altar. Cult vessels were found here and in the storeroom, including a bird-shaped bowl, a lionshaped rhyton and various stands. Animal sacrifices were offered in an outside court and pits were dug there to conceal used cult vessels and protect them from profanation; one such vessel was made in the shape of a woman or goddess. To judge from a later inscribed ostrakon found on the surface, the god worshiped here may have been Horon.

The Philistines differed most markedly from their Semitic neighbors by being uncircumcised; but beyond that, knowledge of their social structure and customs is sparse. At first, each of their five main towns seems to have been ruled by a five-man council, but these later became monarchies with the same kind of social hierarchy as in the earlier Canaanite cities. This, and the sturdy independence of the Philistine cities, survived down into the Hellenistic period, though after about 1000 BC their material culture is in no way different from that of Judah and Israel.

Saul, David and Solomon (c. 1020 to 922 BC). The challenge presented to the tribes of Israel by the Philistines led eventually to the creation of a monarchy, thereby opening up one of the most significant periods in the

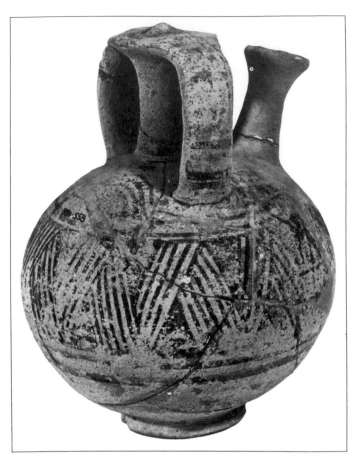

p. 91: American excavations at Megiddo in the 1930s as preserved. *Above:* a Philistine stirrup-jar (restored) from Tell el-Farʿah (South) about 1150 BC, in Mycenaean Greek style.

history of Palestine. Events remarkable enough in themselves are made more so by the Biblical account of them. Now for the first time contemporary, or near contemporary records are available from Palestine itself. In some instances they have the clarity and richness of detail of an eyewitness account (see II Sam. 9–20 or I Kings 1–2). No other period in the history of ancient Palestine is so well known, no individual so vividly depicted as David, both the man and the king. Much of Solomon's reign is recounted in actual excerpts, or paraphrases, of official documents. By contrast, the archaeological record is singularly meager. For Saul there is a fortress at Tell el Ful (Gibeah), for David virtually nothing, and even for that energetic builder Solomon, little more than the foundations of his military installations in certain key cities. Were the achievements of the period to be judged by the surviving remnants of its material culture alone, the tale would be a dreary one.

Only a shadowy account, derived mainly from folk tales, survives of the incipient animosity of the Philistines and the Israelites that culminated in Israel's defeat around 1050 BC when the Ark, specially brought to the battlefield from Shiloh, was captured. The shrine of the Israelite tribal league at Shiloh was destroyed, Philistine garrisons imposed and Israel's metal (armaments) industry rigorously controlled. The Ark was finally taken to Kirjath-jearim, where it remained until David moved it to Jerusalem a generation later. What little leadership Israel now had was provided by Samuel, in all but name the last of the "judges," nurturing the remnants of ancient tribal traditions and aspirations until the emergence of Saul. So alien was monarchy to the Israelite spirit that its exact origins are far from clear in the surviving account, which may well suffer from the prejudices of later editors embittered by the institution's subsequent history.

Saul, victorious over the Ammonites, was popularly acclaimed ruler at the ancient tribal center of Gilgal – a choice endorsed by Samuel, though he lived to regret it. A signal victory over the Philistines at the pass of Michmash, in which Saul's son Jonathan excelled himself, stabilized Saul's claims as an effective military leader. Saul, forced by circumstances to remain more of a soldier than an administrator or legislator, ruled over an area broadly extending in the north to Mount Hermon, in the east into Gilead, south to Beersheba, and confined in the west by Philistia and Phoenicia. His monarchy lacked most of the traditional trappings. His base at Gibeah, just north of Jerusalem, was a solidly built fortress at the center of a village. It stood about 15 meters (49 feet) square, with projecting corner towers. At least part of the superstructure in the first phase, destroyed in the 12th century, was of timber; that of Saul's time was little more sophisticated.

The Bible vividly depicts Saul's character: a man of fine appearance, modest, energetic and courageous, but emotionally unstable, increasingly so under the mounting pressure of events. Quarrels with Samuel, who finally sought to revoke his kingship, and the ever more popular David, bosom friend of his son Jonathan, husband to his daughter Michal, provoked Saul into a disastrous attack on the priestly family of Shiloh, then established at Nob near Jerusalem. He also broke off his daughter's marriage and began a running feud with David that diverted his attentions from Israel's real foe, the Philistines. David, eventually tiring of a bandit's precarious existence, took service with the Philistine king of Gath, who established his new vassal in the Negev, from where David astutely pursued a double role, apparently loyal to his new master, but maintaining his hold over the imagination of his own people. A Philistine invasion and military triumph over Saul at Mount Gilboa, where the wounded king took his own life, brought matters to a head.

Abner, chief of Saul's army, fled from the battlefield and crowned Eshbaal, one of Saul's surviving sons, as king at a new capital, Mahanaim, across the Jordan. Still under Philistine auspices David, like Saul before him, was popularly acclaimed king and anointed at Hebron in Judah. For the first time the fateful division of kingdoms, north and south, emerged; but only momentarily. For David the truly heroic period of his life had now begun.

Shechem, an important Canaanite city on the main road from Jerusalem to the north, which retained special status under Israel.

He exploited a quarrel between Eshbaal and Abner, who went over to David, to concentrate in his hands rule of Israel and Judah. He seized the Jebusite capital at Jerusalem, thus eliminating a foreign wedge between the tribes of north and south, while securing a well-placed capital in neutral territory that was, by right of conquest, royal property. Excavation has shown that the walled city he took, extending to about 11 acres, occupied the rocky ridge of Ophel extended by enormous stone terraces, built like a honeycomb filled with rubble – perhaps the Old Testament *Millo* ("filling"). The Philistines' military power was reduced to insignificance and their borders contracted to the outskirts of Gath, Ekron and Ashdod. Canaanite cities remaining independent in the Shephelah, in Sharon and the northern valleys were captured and in some cases became royal estates. In the north the Aramaeans were defeated and a garrison placed in Damascus. In the south Edom was overrun and a port secured on the Red Sea. Not only had David taken Israel to a pinnacle of authority, he had created for her a totally fresh political role.

This creation was something particularly his own, quite independent of the tribal confederacy he had initially controlled; indeed that was now but part of a realm which comprised Canaanite enclaves, conquered and tributary kingdoms, some with Israelite governors, and vassal provinces in various ways acknowledging David's hegemony. In such circumstances concentration of power in the monarch's hands was a foregone conclusion. David's bureaucracy followed Egyptian models, possibly at second-hand through the pattern of Canaanite government; a census laid the foundations for systematic levy of taxes and military reorganization; division into districts under governors facilitated royal control over traditionally tribal rights, stimulating deep resentment against the monarchy in certain quarters.

David's religious policy was sensitive and farsighted. He transferred the Ark to Jerusalem and made detailed arrangements for a temple to house it there, shrewdly associating it with the crown as an institution of state. He was responsible for the plans and inventory of temple furnishings; he collected materials for the building and gold ingots for its sacred furniture; he assembled the workmen and fixed the classes and functions of the clergy. Above all he secured the site on a rocky massif north of Ophel. These plans only came to maturity under Solomon. Opposition to David's policies and uncertainty over the succession filled his declining years with violence and rebellion, led first by his son Absalom, then by Sheba ben Bichri at the head of the Israelite tribes, alienated by what they saw as David's indulgence towards Judah. In the event, over-precipitate action by Adonijah, David's eldest son, forced his father to approve the immediate anointment of his younger son Solomon as heir apparent, supported significantly by the leaders of the priesthood and army.

Solomon was as different from his father as were the circumstances of their reigns. The new king was neither by instinct nor necessity a military leader; he was an administrator called upon to maintain, not to expand, a realm already too varied for enduring stability. Foreign affairs presented few problems, as the Assyrians were quiet and the Egyptians amenable. Under the Pharaoh Siamun Egyptian forces, perhaps encouraged by David's

The actual territory of the United Kingdom of Israel and Judah did not extend beyond the borders of Palestine.

defeat of the Philistines, attacked cities on the coastal plain, whose commercial aspirations had long conflicted with those of the Delta towns and ports. The Canaanite city of Gezer was taken and then given to Solomon as dowry when he married one of the pharaoh's daughters; in itself symbolic of the change in relations between the rulers of Egypt and Palestine. No longer was Egypt the aloof overlord. The passage of Siamun's army may be reflected in destruction levels excavated at Ashdod and Gezer, while a scarab seal bearing his name was found at Tell el Far'ah (South). More significant for Solomon than his Egyptian alliance was maintenance of a treaty with Hiram, King of Tyre, inherited from his father. It led to important commercial and industrial, as well as artistic cooperation.

At home Solomon's reign saw the final creation of a dynastic state, the growth of urban communities and the emergence of a social structure akin to that of the earlier Canaanite city states. Chariotry was developed, on the Canaanite model, as an essential, decisive military force; previously the Israelites had depended on foot soldiers. New administrative districts were created in part to reduce tribal boundaries further and to integrate the former Canaanite cities, but primarily to provide the provisions and forced labor required to support the expanding court and standing army. Royal commercial monopolies exploited not only the many existing caravan routes from Arabia, epitomized by the visit of the Queen of Sheba (modern Yemen), but also stimulated Red Sea trade, with the help of Phoenician sailors, and a lively commerce in chariots from Egypt and horses from Cilicia, in southeast Turkey.

It is no accident that in the folklore of the Near East Solomon is renowned, not as in the West for his wisdom, but as the creator of buildings magnificent in style and enormous in proportions. Military policy dictated the creation of strong points in such cities as Hazor, facing the Aramaeans in Syria, at Megiddo guarding the crucial east-west road, at Gezer on the eastern edge of the plain, and at Tamar in the south near Edom. Excavations at Hazor, Megiddo and Gezer have revealed defensive systems and gateways similar enough to suggest some single blueprint (I Kings 9:15). At Megiddo two substantial buildings have been attributed to Solomon's architects; both have survived only at foundation level. One, set within its own enclosure wall, may be identified as a palace, built to a Syrian model with columned entrance portico, in finely dressed stone. A rectangular building just to the west, outside the enclosure, seems to be an administrative complex.

Of Solomon's palace, in a court adjacent to the Temple at Jerusalem, the author of Kings says relatively little and that is not entirely clear. One building, the "House of the Forest of Lebanon," was detached from the main complex. It was a rectangle of about 150 by 75 feet divided into aisles by three or four rows of Lebanese cedarwood columns, 15 to a row. Windows and doors were symmetrically

Restoration of fortified gate at Megiddo, first built by Solomon. The salient and recess city wall dates from later.

arranged. Golden vessels and shields were used and stored here, but for what purpose remains obscure. The description of the palace is best understood by analogy with the earlier palaces of Alalakh and Ugarit in Syria, and near contemporary ones excavated in Syria. The visitor passed through a pillared entrance hall or portico into the great rectangular "Hall of Judgment," probably through a door in its long side. This was the main ceremonial chamber, with the King's throne set against one of the short walls, probably to the left. The throne was a magnificent object of ivory overlaid with gold. Six steps approached the throne, each flanked by lions similarly made, while the throne seat was also flanked by them. Less elevated thrones shown on the carved ivories from Megiddo and on Ahiram's sarcophagus from Byblos are similarly decorated. Beyond this hall, through a door in the other long wall, the visitor passed into an interior courtyard around which were grouped the private apartments of the king, his queen and harem.

Though not a stone of Solomon's Temple has been excavated, it is possible, as with the palace, to offer a hypothetical reconstruction of it by supplementing the detailed, if not always explicit description in the Bible (I Kings 6) with a diverse range of archaeological evidence. Work began on the building in Solomon's fourth regnal year and was completed in his eleventh. Its exact location is uncertain, though most probably the foundations of the "Holy of Holies" were set on the rocky protuberance now covered by the Dome of the Rock, with the Temple entrance to the east. Timber came from the Lebanon; stone was quarried locally. Israelites were conscripted as laborers, Phoenicians hired as skilled craftsmen. Thus it is assumed that in style the building was predominantly Phoenician.

The most distinctive feature of the planning, found in Canaanite temples at Alalakh and Hazor, and in a 9th-century temple at Tainat in Syria, was the setting of the rooms one behind the other in a straight line, the building retaining the same width for its entire length. Internally it was divided into three chambers, each one leading into the next: a vestibule or porch, a room for worship, and finally a "Holy of Holies" for the Ark. Around three sides were a series of galleries and side rooms arranged in three stories, each a cubit wider than the lower one, in a manner not easy to reconstruct from the Old Testament narrative. The only parallel so far for this building in Palestine is a temple, first built in the 10th century BC, at Arad. Here there was a courtyard with an "altar of burnt offering," built of earth and undressed stones in accord with ritual requirement; a porch with two columns and low masonry "benches"; a "Holy of Holies," where two incense altars probably flanked the entrance, with a stone stela further in bearing traces of red paint; and an area paved with stone.

Small terracotta models of shrines from Cyprus suggest that the pillars of Yakin and Boaz were freestanding like the traditional *massebot*. These names have yet to be certainly explained, but are either dynastic names or phrases invoking strength in the name of Yahweh. The main room of the Temple had large outer doors and a set of double wooden doors before the "Holy of Holies," richly decorated with carvings overlaid with sheet gold. Its walls, as also those of the "Holy of Holies" beyond, were lined with cedarwood, again elaborately carved with patterns of gourds, palm trees and flowers, and various mythological creatures. Some idea of these designs, in miniature, may be gleaned from numerous fragments of carved ivory, inlays for wooden furniture, made also by Phoenician craftsmen, that have been recovered in quantity from Assyrian royal palaces in Iraq.

In the "Holy of Holies" stood the Ark of the Covenant.

Above it were two great wooden figures of cherubim, plated with gold, which stretched right across the width of the room and reached halfway to the ceiling. Elsewhere the name cherubim denotes a creature who advised the gods and was an advocate for the faithful. The best surviving clue to their appearance, again among the carved Nimrud ivories, suggests a winged creature with a leonine body and a human head. The cherubim and the Ark were seen as the throne and footstool of Yahweh who, according to the tenets of Israelite religion, might not be represented by a graven image. Neither this arrangement nor the idea is without parallel. In Canaanite iconography cherubs flank the thrones of gods and kings. In other Near Eastern countries empty thrones were on occasion to be found among temple furnishings. The Ten Commandments, official instrument of the pact between Yahweh and his people, were put into the Ark, as it were at Yahweh's feet. This again followed established tradition. Ramesses II, speaking of his treaty with the Hittite King, remarks:

"The writing of the oath [pact] which I have made for the Great King, the King of Hattu, lies beneath the features of the god Teshup [a Hittite deity]: the great gods are witnesses to it." The other Temple furnishings described in the Bible, though they have no exact contemporary parallels, may be visualized with the help of less impressive temple furnishings from sites in Palestine and Cyprus.

The sharpest commentary on the nature of Solomon's kingship was the precipitate division of the monarchy at his death. Outstanding as were David's achievements as soldier and planner and Solomon's as builder, administrator and merchant prince, neither had resolved the fundamental conflict between the old tribal traditions and the new institution of dynastic kingship. In the north particularly the dynastic claims of the House of David were deeply resented and Solomon's government regarded as tyrannical. Already before the end of Solomon's reign Jeroboam, northern overseer of works, had been forced to flee to Egypt as a refugee when northern opinion viewed him as a possible future king of Israel.

The Kingdoms divide. Had it not been for the intransigence of Rehoboam, Solomon's son, it is possible that the realm's unity might have survived a little longer. As it was, Rehoboam (c. 922 to 915 BC) succeeded to the throne of Judah at Jerusalem; but when he proceeded to Shechem for acclamation there by representatives of the northern tribes of Israel he alienated them at once by totally refusing to lessen the burdens levied by his father. He was forced to retreat southwards, and Jeroboam, who had returned from Egypt, was elected to the northern throne as King of Israel (c. 922 to 901 BC). Virtually at a stroke the broad realm of David and Solomon was gone, leaving Israel and Judah as minor powers surrounded by hostile rivals, their economy severely weakened by the loss of tribute and monopoly control of overland trade routes, and by internecine strife. If Rehoboam had ever intended to recover the northern

Left: lower story of a store-house in the 9th-century city of Hazor in northern Israel.

Above: a "Proto-Aeolic" stone capital from Iron Age Hazor, one of the few decorated elements in early Israelite architecture.

kingdom, such aspirations were shattered in the fifth year of his reign by the invasion of Sheshonq, pharaoh of Egypt.

Despite a great topographical list of cities visited by the pharaoh, inscribed at Karnak, the detailed course of his campaign is still debated. Rehoboam rapidly submitted, paid heavy tribute and saw Sheshonq's army move northwards, leaving Jerusalem untouched. Elsewhere there was much devastation; destruction levels recognized in excavations at places such as Tell Beit Mirsim, Beth-Shemesh, Tell Jemmeh, Tell Abu Hawam, Shechem and Megiddo have been associated with this invasion. Sheshonq installed himself in Megiddo, where only a fragment survives of the massive victory stela he set up. Jeroboam, traitor to his earlier Egyptian friends, had fled across the Jordan. Far to the south Egyptian forces were sent into the Negev and Arabah to destroy the network of Solomonic forts and trading stations, including sites like Arad and Ezion-geber. But for Egypt it was all rather a flash-in-the-pan. Sheshonq eventually withdrew, laden with booty (perhaps his only purpose), and it was long before Egypt again sent armies into Palestine.

As their subsequent history was plainly to reveal, Israel and Judah were in crucial respects fundamentally different. Judah had a relatively stable dynastic tradition; not so Israel which was to prove chronically unstable. Judah, though smaller and geographically less favored, was better insulated from foreign threats and internally more homogeneous. Israel had borders in the north and east exposed to powerful, predatory neighbors and contained within it a large Canaanite population. In the mid-8th century Israel was the first to feel those forces that were to overtake both kingdoms. Israel's history is the more confused; indeed its complexities sometimes baffle the historian.

Jeroboam had both to create the organs of a state and to establish an official religious cult. The capital was first at Shechem and then at Tirzah (modern Tell el Far'ah (North)), both originally non-Israelite towns without strong tribal affiliations. Although he was equally astute in selecting two ancient cult centers at opposite ends of his kingdom, Bethel and Dan, for the official shrines, Jeroboam's religious policies were less sure. The golden bulls he set up, as pedestals for the invisible deity (Yahweh), were too easily identified with the fertility cults of Canaan and neighboring states for the king to escape charges of heresy and idolatry.

But, able as Jeroboam was, he could not alone create a stable order of succession. In the following quarter of a century (c. 900 to 875 BC) army officers regularly and successfully challenged the succession of the previous king's son, accompanying their triumphs with systematic butchery of the superseded faction. This self-destructive trend was reversed for a period by Omri (c. 876 to 869 BC), whose rule at a vital moment gave much needed stability. To the north the Aramaean kingdom of Damascus under Ben-Hadad I was slowly encroaching on Israel's northern border, while away to the east in Assyria a potentially far more formidable foe was entering upon one of the dynamic and expansive periods in her history under Assurnasir-pal II. Omri shrewdly realized that such external threats required strong diplomatic ties with immediate neighbors like Judah and Phoenicia (both sealed by royal marriages) and control of kingdoms such as Edom and Moab.

Omri's reign was brief, but his son Ahab (c. 869 to 850 BC), married through his father's diplomacy to the Phoenician princess Jezebel, reaped the benefits of parental statesmanship. Momentarily united in the face of a common foe, the local kingdoms of Syria, with 2,000 chariots and 10,000 infantry provided by Ahab, checked the advance of Shalmaneser III of Assyria, about 853 BC, in a battle at Qarqar on the river Orontes.

The archaeological record of this period in Palestine is richer than for the earlier phase of the Iron Age. Excavated levels in the 10th-century town of Tell El Far'ah (North), ancient Tirzah, have revealed a violent destruction, with simple private houses replaced by the foundations of a large-scale building, with massive walls, that remained unfinished. This looks like Omri's destruction of the city held by Zimri in about 876 BC, and his proposed reconstruction, abandoned when superseded by plans for a new capital on a fresh site at Samaria.

The new capital, better placed geographically for communications with Phoenicia and Judah, was ideal for fortification and unencumbered by earlier structures. A small natural plateau was surrounded with a defensive casement wall within which was set the royal palace and ancillary buildings. The earliest pottery is immediately subsequent in type to the latest from Tirzah, which seems

Above: a Phoenician ivory plaque with Egyptian designs and cavities for multicolored inlays of glass or frit. It was found at Samaria and may date to the reign of Ahab, though excavated from a much later destruction level.

Left: 9th century BC stela from Moab with an inscription of its king Mesha, recording wars with Israel.

Right: general view of the hill of Samaria to which Omri transferred the capital of Israel from Tirzah. It lay in an ideal strategic position for the new capital.

for a time to have been depopulated by the move to Samaria. Initial building extended well into Ahab's reign and, though little but foundations and a few scattered proto-Ionic capitals for pilasters have survived, they indicate work of the highest quality, perhaps by Phoenician masons. Remains of a large alabaster vase with the cartouches of Pharaoh Osorkon II (c. 874 to 850 BC) may indicate diplomatic rather than just commercial links.

From the debris left by the later Assyrian sack of about 721 BC the excavators retrieved fragments of ivory furniture inlays, enriched with gold leaf and colored inlays, that have been associated with the Biblical description of Ahab's "house of ivory," though these pieces may not be so early. As Phoenicia, home of his queen, was renowned for its skill in this craft, such furniture and also possibly decorated wall plaques might well have been provided to suit Jezebel's taste. To Ahab, or his successor's reign, belongs a radical reconstruction of the palatial area at Megiddo to create an enclosed quarter as at Samaria. Storehouses (formerly known as "Solomon's stables") and a great water-shaft with approach tunnel suggest that the importance of this site as a strategic garrison town was the chief consideration in these changes. At Hazor also the city was strengthened to meet Aramaean threats, and a massive water-system with elaborate shaft and tunnel access was created to provide water in time of siege.

Prophets and pagans. Yet now internal tensions, as is clear from the Biblical account, were the most serious

threat to Israel's integrity. Jezebel had brought with her worship of such Phoenician deities as Baal, Melkart and Asherah, establishing priests and shrines for them wherever the court was established. Her fervent missionary zeal for these pagan gods and the strong surviving undercurrent in Israel of Canaanite tradition, of which they were a part, threatened for the first time to overwhelm official Yahwism. Throughout the country open-air shrines and altars were established, sacred trees planted for the fertility goddess, incense burners set up and mass-produced baked-clay figurines of women, nude and draped, were made in the old Canaanite manner. In this emergency the prophets of Yahweh divided. The compliant, nominally at least, accepted the new order; the intransigent, led by Elijah, formed a powerful, if at first isolated, opposition.

From its inception sometime in the period of the Judges the prophetic movement had been almost as much concerned with moral and political reform as with religious revival. Its members were men who believed themselves called by God to a special purpose communicated directly to them by divine inspiration. Their lives were transformed; their mission compulsive. At first in the 9th century, like Elijah and Elisha, they were men of ecstatic faith moved to deeds, as the Biblical account of their careers so vividly reveals. In the 8th century, though heirs to this tradition, they were more men of words, oracular prophets of doom. There was the poor peasant Amos, with an overpowering sense of social injustice and economic exploitation, seeking a revival of traditional religion and social morality; Hosea, himself sorely tried by an unhappy marriage, conceiving Israel as an adulterous wife who rejects her solemn covenant with the beneficent Yahweh, and urging a return to pure, primitive Yahwism; above all there was Isaiah, the noble statesman, caught up in the very events which presaged the onset of Divine judgment, with his powerful visions of an awesome Yahweh and a strong sense of impending disaster.

When Ahab died in battle against the Aramaeans, first his son Ahaziah, and then on his premature death, another son, Jehoram, succeeded to the throne. Abroad Jehoram was threatened by Moab as well as by the Aramaeans. In 1868 a stela was found by chance on the southeast corner of the tell at Dhiban, ancient Dibon, upon which the Moabite king, Mesha, had related his victories over Israel and the (re)building of "Qarhoh" – possibly Dibon or part of it.

Within Israel the prophet Elisha now led mounting opposition to the pagan court religion sponsored by the Queen Mother, Jezebel. Increasing tension finally exploded in an army *coup d'état* led by Jehu in about 842 BC. Jehu had been anointed king by Elisha, uniting against the House of Omri all the conservative elements in the court and country. When the kings of Israel, and of Judah as well, came to make terms with Jehu both were assassinated. This was a sign for a bloody purge, with few parallels in the country's history, of Ahab's family and court (including Jezebel), and of the priesthood and adherents of Baal.

Judah, though never reaching such extremes, did not escape comparable religious disputes. Under Rehoboam

A detail of the "Black Obelisk" found by Layard at Nineveh in Iraq, now in the British Museum. It shows Jehu, King of Israel, prostrate before the Assyrian King Shalmaneser III.

9th century BC ivory plaque from Arslan Tash in Syria, possibly showing Hazael, the King of Damascus, who fought Shalmaneser III of Assyria.

the king's mother, an Ammonite, and his favorite wife Maacah, of Aramaean descent, practiced and disseminated their native pagan cults. Under Maacah's sons Abijah (c. 915 to 913 BC) and Asa (c. 913 to 873 BC) her party held sway until Asa, on attaining his majority, officially purged the pagan cults. Strife with neighboring Israel had now ceased and under Jehoshaphat (c. 873 to 849 BC) Judah again enjoyed peace and prosperity. The judicial and fiscal systems were reformed, bringing closer government supervision and thus helping in some measure to avoid the social and economic grievances which had grown up in Israel against the Omrides. The alliance with Israel secured by the marriage of another Jehoram, of Judah (c. 849 to 842 BC) to Athaliah, a member of the House of Omri, now brought the cult of Baal to Judah. Ahaziah, her son, had barely ruled a year before his murder during Jehu's revolt in Israel, as already mentioned. The forceful Queen Mother seized the vacant throne, purged the opposition and extended the influence of Baal's priesthood. Within five years an infant son was enthroned – Joash, brought up by his aunt, wife of Jehoiada the chief priest, in alliance with the royal guard. Queen Athaliah was executed, and the shrines of Baal destroyed.

The reign of Joash (c. 837 to 800 BC) is little documented. Gradual weakening of royal support for Yahwism and military failure seem to have stimulated opposition which led eventually to his assassination and the succession of his son Amaziah (c. 800 to 783 BC). Amaziah, following his reconquest of Edom, became involved in a war with Israel over his treatment of Israelite mercenaries. Jehoash of Israel, though victorious, was satisfied with Amaziah's humiliation and did not seek to overrun Judah.

In the meanwhile, Assyria had made her growing authority felt in the north. In about 841 BC Shalmaneser III had campaigned in Syria, probably destroying Hazor, before reaching Mount Carmel and turning north into Phoenicia. Jehu paid him tribute, an event recorded and portrayed on the famous Assyrian "Black Obelisk," now in the British Museum. In the inscription on the obelisk Israel is known to the Assyrians as "Land of the House of Omri," and Jehu the usurper as "son of Omri" – an ironical twist of the true position. After Assyria withdrew Israel was dominated from Damascus under its vigorous ruler, Hazael, who also overran Transjordan and took tribute from Judah. But after the invasion of Syria and the imposition of tribute on Israel by the Assyrian king Adadnirari III in the later 9th century, the power of Damascus waned. With Assyria internally weak and preoccupied with its great rival, Urartu, in eastern Turkey, Israel and Judah enjoyed a tranquil period under relatively able kings.

With the two countries at peace, Jeroboam II of Israel (c. 786 to 746 BC) and Uzziah of Judah (c. 783 to 742 BC) restored the area of their combined authority to something like its extent under Solomon. Internal and foreign trade flourished. The port at Ezion-geber was refurbished, and

Iron Age shrine for an unorthodox cult near the Virgin's Spring on mount Ophel, Jerusalem.

fortresses, as at Kadesh-Barnea and Horvat Uzza near Arad, were erected to protect caravan routes through the desert. Settlement now flourished in much of the Negev. To the reign of Jeroboam II probably belong the records of oil and wine consignments written in ink on potsherds found during excavations at Samaria. These receipts for taxes in kind include almost as many personal names compounded with Baal as with Yahweh, a small, if telling, clue to those trends in contemporary society that the classical prophets, who emerge for the first time in the middle of the 8th century, were increasingly to condemn.

Archaeology has yet to reveal any very clear evidence for the shrines and rituals of the unorthodox cults which figure so prominently in the Biblical history of this period. One possible center of such worship has been revealed low on the eastern slopes of Ophel at Jerusalem, just outside the city wall, near the Virgin's Spring. Here a series of natural caves was found filled with pottery and baked clay statuettes of women and animals, but there were no bones to suggest funerary deposits. Adjacent to at least one of the caves was a stone-built shrine set against the rock, with two pillars, perhaps *massebot*, in one of its small rooms, and an altar on a rocky ledge above. The pottery would seem to have been thrown into the caves so as not to be profaned by secular uses after playing a part in religious rites. The extra-mural position of these shrines, and the human statuettes, reminiscent of Canaanite fertility figurines, almost certainly indicate pagan cults. Most of the related pottery may be dated about 700 BC.

The Assyrian menace. Until the middle of the 8th century BC Assyrian raids to the west had been only for the acquisition of plunder and tribute, through regular, devastating campaigns. With the accession of Tiglath-Pileser III (c. 745 to 727 BC) a policy of territorial acquisition and population transfer, increasingly exploited by his successors, was applied against all signs of resistance to Assyria's emergence as the military and economic overlord

of Syria and Palestine. Now, increasingly, Assyrian royal inscriptions, and later the Babylonian Chronicle, supplement historical information recorded in the Old Testament.

At Jeroboam's death the inherent tendency to anarchy in Israel reemerged. Five kings in 10 years schemed and murdered their way to the throne. Law and order collapsed; paganism was rife. In 743 BC, at Arpad in Syria, Tiglath-Pileser III had received the formal submission of Menahem, King of Israel (c. 745 to 738 BC), but not, however, of Uzziah of Judah, listed among the rebels. Before such a predator as Assyria even a strong ruler might have cowered; only a foolish one would have initiated an open conflict. But Pekah of Israel (c. 737 to 732 BC), in order to buttress his plans for resistance to Assyria, resorted to arms to coerce Judah into positive resistance to the foreign threat. Edom in the east, Philistia in the west, were also drawn in against Judah. Thus pressed, Ahaz of Judah (c. 735 to 715 BC), ignoring Isaiah's cautious and, as it proved, farsighted plea against such a course, invoked the aid of Tiglath-Pileser III against his enemies, bribing him with a splendid gift. The Assyrian ruler's reaction was swift and terribly effective. Israel, overrun, was reduced to a small area around Samaria, with Assyrian governors ruling the provinces of Dor, Megiddo and Gilead. Hazor, the vital bulwark in the north, was destroyed.

A pro-Assyrian revolt in Samaria led to Pekah's murder and the accession of Hoshea (c. 732 to 724 BC) who, for the moment, capitulated and paid tribute to Assyria. But when Tiglath-Pileser died after successfully defeating a Babylonian rebellion, Hoshea revolted against the new Assyrian king, seeking the ineffectual aid of an Egyptian pharaoh, probably Osorkon IV. Shalmaneser V, though he died in the hour of his triumph, moved west, took Shechem, captured and deported Hoshea, and then took Samaria in 722 to 721 BC. His successor, Sargon II, crushed further signs of rebellion and brought what remained of Israel into the Assyrian provincial system. Many inhabitants were deported to east and west of the Euphrates in Syria; in subsequent years they were replaced by peoples from southern Iraq who mingled with the natives to become ancestral to the later Samaritans – thereafter despised by Judah as a mixed race. For the prophets the fall of Samaria – only exceeded in their view by the later Babylonian captivity – confirmed their interpretation of Israel's history; the destruction signifying divine judgment on Israel's violation of the covenant with Yahweh.

Ahaz had bought his revenge on Israel at the price of liberty. Crippling tribute demands fell all the heavier on a country that had now lost Edom and its port on the Red Sea. Subservience to Assyria meant subservience to the gods of Assyria as well, who were brought into the Temple at Jerusalem. Now astral cults, the dedication of horses and chariots for the sun-god, and other Assyro-Babylonian rites were introduced. Nor was this all, for Ahaz generally favored the foreign cults, even on one occasion offering his son as sacrifice in fulfillment of a vow. Fresh political pressures on Judah came with the establishment of the 25th Dynasty in Egypt, whose pharaohs were eager to interfere in Palestine against Assyria. When Ashdod and other cities in Philistia revolted in 714 to 712 BC, with promises of Egyptian aid, Judah held aloof. Ashdod, where fragments of an Assyrian stela have been found in excavations, was captured and the region reorganized as an Assyrian province. The rebel leader, who had fled to Egypt, was handed over to Assyria. At Nineveh Layard found a sealing of the contemporary Pharaoh Shabako, showing the Egyptian ruler triumphant, with his titles inscribed above.

At Megiddo archaeology has vividly revealed the more general effects of Assyrian influence. On the debris of the royal and administrative buildings of stratum IV was built a town of small private houses laid out in approximately rectangular plots, clearly a conscious piece of town planning of a kind not previously seen in Palestine. Not only private houses but also some public buildings were now built to plans that have an Assyrian source. A governor's palace at Tell Jemmeh had brick vaults which may also have been designed by Assyrian builders. The presence of very high ranking Assyrian officials is marked in some cities by the presence of a finely-made pottery, so-called "palace ware," closely matched in the palaces at Nimrud in Assyria, destroyed about 614 BC, and contrasting markedly with the normal tradition of Palestinian potting at this time. A small town of the later 8th century, perhaps destroyed by Sennacherib's army, is now being revealed at Beersheba. The plan is dominated by a street running the entire circuit of the town just inside its walls. Houses were set between the casemate defensive wall and the road; houses on the

road's other side are generally four-roomed, with one broad and three long rooms divided by a row of pillars. Storehouses for grain, wine and oil are situated near the city gate, which was also equipped with a small shrine. The main public buildings stood in the center of the city on slightly raised ground.

Hezekiah, reformer in religion, anti-Assyrian in politics, succeeded his father Ahaz on the throne of Judah about 715 BC and ruled until 687 to 686 BC. Pagan cult practices and images were purged from Jerusalem and an unsuccessful attempt was made to close local shrines where the unorthodox cults had so long flourished. Of contemporary social and economic reforms very little is known. Archaeological evidence of administrative innovation at this time may be provided by the much-discussed storage-jar handles stamped with the four-winged royal scarab symbol,

the word *lmlk* "royal" and a place-name, either Hebron, Ziph, Socoh or the enigmatic *mmšt*. Other measures were more clearly designed to promote Hezekiah's anti-Assyrian policies. Jerusalem's fortifications were strengthened and water brought from the Virgin's Spring (Gihon) into the walled city of Ophel through a rock-cut tunnel that reached to the Pool of Siloam. In the tunnel was carved a famous inscription, now in Istanbul, at the point where teams tunneling in from opposite directions finally met. Albright translates part of it:

"[A]nd while there were still three cubits to be cut through, (there was heard) the voice of a man calling to his fellow. . . . And when the tunnel was driven through, the quarrymen hewed (the rock), each man toward his fellow, axe against axe." The central cities of Judah were provisioned, borders extended at the expense of Gaza and

Left: detail from an Assyrian relief showing the siege of Lachish by Sennacherib's army.

Above: Israelite prisoners taken by King Sennacherib's army at Lachish, on the reliefs in his palace at Nineveh in Iraq.

Remains of a small stone 5th century BC palace for a Persian governor on top of the mound at Lachish (Tell ed-Duweir).

The Inner gate of the city of Tell ed-Duweir (ancient Lachish) as revealed by British excavators in the 1930s.

Edom, and letters sent in an unsuccessful bid to secure the support of Israelite populations in Megiddo and Samaria.

When Sennacherib succeeded Sargon in 704 BC Hezekiah, involved in a network of plots from Egypt to Babylonia to unseat the new king, formally refused tribute. Sennacherib's campaign – if indeed there was only one and not two as some scholars believe – is known reasonably well, both from the Assyrian and the Biblical record. In 701 the Assyrians advanced down the coast, forced Ashkelon and Ekron to surrender, and then turned towards Judah to lay siege to Lachish. This event is vividly portrayed on a series of carved stone reliefs from Sennacherib's palace at Nineveh, now in the British Museum. Numerous cities in Judah were taken and from Jerusalem Hezekiah sent heavy tribute. Sennacherib, investing Jerusalem, demanded surrender. Then suddenly the Assyrians withdrew, either crippled by an epidemic or troubled by events at home. Within a few years Hezekiah was dead and his young son Manasseh (c. 687 to 642 BC) succeeded, with a policy of loyalty to Assyria throughout, even when Sennacherib was assassinated.

The middle years of Manasseh's reign were marked externally by a more or less continuous decade of Assyrian campaigns against Egypt under Esarhaddon and Ashurbanipal (c. 673 to 663 BC). Assyrian records mention Manasseh as a vassal contributing material for his royal master's building projects at home and the wars in Egypt abroad. Such conventional aspects of vassalage were matched by a return of the Assyrian gods to Judah. Indeed Manasseh completely repudiated his father's religious reforms. Everywhere pagan cults flourished again: the age-old fertility rites and ritual of sacred prostitution, the arts of divination and the practices of magic. Not without reason was Manasseh, in the eyes of the rigorously ortho-

dox authors of Kings, considered the worst monarch the country had ever known. By the time of his death, however, the Assyrian Empire had begun to disintegrate. Amon, Manasseh's son, was murdered after a brief two-year reign and was replaced by Josiah, a mere child of eight. Josiah's advisers began to shake off allegiance to Assyria, at first cautiously and then, as the great power became more obviously preoccupied elsewhere, more decisively. The provinces of Samaria, Megiddo and Gilead were preempted and the king's authority was extended to the sea coast.

Striking evidence of Josiah's control of the coastal region was provided by excavations in an L-shaped fortress at Mesad Hashavyahu, which yielded both Hebrew documents and an abundance of East Greek pottery, dating its occupation to the last third of the 7th century BC. Whether the Greeks settled here were a merchant community or, as seems more likely, mercenaries from Ionia and Caria in western Asia Minor like those known to have been employed by the Pharaoh Psamtik I, is arguable. The longest of the inscriptions is a letter, found in the debris of the guardroom, addressed to the local governor by a poor reaper seeking the return of a garment seized by an overseer. Greek mercenaries (kittim) are again referred to in an inscription from Tell Arad of about 600 BC. Ostraka of this date from Arad are primarily concerned with requesting supplies of wine, oil or grain from a man named Eliashib in charge of military supplies for the area. They also contain what seems to be a direct reference to the Temple in Jerusalem – "the House of Yahweh."

Josiah's orthodoxy secured for him a very favorable place in tradition. He set in train the most thorough religious reform yet attempted. The Temple at Jerusalem was purged and restored; out went the Assyrian deities, solar and astral cults, divination and magical rites, native pagan rituals, and with them their priests, eunuchs and prostitutes. At last, high places and shrines outside Jerusalem, among them the small temple excavated at Arad, were closed and their clergy absorbed into centralized worship at Jerusalem. The policy was pursued with equal zeal throughout the newly-added northern provinces deep into Galilee.

Babylonian overlords: exile and return. By the time the full impact of these changes had become apparent, Judah was once more threatened by an aggressor from Mesopotamia. In 612 to 610 BC an alliance of Babylonians and Medes had first overrun Assyria, storming Nineveh, and then, by taking Harran, eradicated the final traces of Assyrian government. However, an Egyptian army under Necho II marched in support of Assyria through the coastal plain of Palestine to Megiddo where, for reasons unknown, Josiah tried to stop it. He was killed in battle and for a few years Egypt exercised authority over Israel and Judah through a vassal king, Jehoiakim, who was forced to raise heavy tribute for his overlord. Under such pressures the religious reform movement petered out and its opponents were free to revert to their earlier practices. Despite the economic pressures on him Jehoiakim, with forced labor, built himself a new palace which can probably be equated with a building of this period excavated at Ramat Rahel, south of Jerusalem.

Meanwhile Nebuchadnezzar II of Babylon, defeating the Egyptians, had marched through Syria into Philistia, destroying Ashkelon and deporting its inhabitants. About 603 BC Jehoiakim transferred his allegiance to the new invader and Judah went unscathed. But Jehoiakim was clearly in two minds. When Nebuchadnezzar returned home to Babylon after a Pyrrhic victory over Egypt, Jehoiakim revolted, but then died. His young son Jehoiachin surrendered Jerusalem in 597 BC and was taken to Babylon with most of his court and vast quantities of booty, including the Temple treasury. Clay tablets found by German excavators at Babylon, dating from the 10th to the 35th regnal years of Nebuchadnezzar II, list oil issues for prisoners of war and dependents of the royal household, among them Jehoiachin, his sons and other Judaeans. In Judah the king's uncle Zedekiah was enthroned in his place.

Zedekiah's position was uneasy, for many still regarded Jehoiachin as the legitimate ruler of Judah and there was a strong undercurrent of anti-Babylonian feeling which, within five years, had precipitated Judah into its final, disastrous revolt. Early in 588 BC the Babylonian army was again in Judah and was gradually advancing on Jerusalem. Archaeological research at various sites in its path has provided evidence of the devastation then wrought. Many towns were destroyed, never to be rebuilt, and their population deported. At Lachish (Tell ed-Duweir), for instance, excavation has uncovered a substantial town

Above: a potsherd from Lachish bearing a message reflecting tension at the impending Babylonian attack.

Below: ruined Ophel terraces after Nebuchadnezzar's attack.

German excavations at Babylon in the early part of this century revealed these cellars of mudbrick thought to have supported great terraces on which were planted the legendary "hanging gardens."

devastated by assault and fire in 596 BC, then its rebuilt walls and reconstructed houses again destroyed less than a decade later. In one of the gate towers of this final city were found some letters between officers and the commandant written in ink on potsherds, vividly evoking the imminent disaster: "And let (my lord) know that we are watching for the signals of Lachish, according to all the indications which my lord hath given, for we cannot see Azekah."

After its capture in the summer of 587 BC Jerusalem was sacked and its walls leveled. Excavation on the eastern slopes of Ophel has revealed something of this destruction, when houses along the narrow summit of the ridge, and the great stone terraces supporting them, were tumbled down the slope. The administrators, if not summarily executed, were deported with much of the population to Babylonia. A brief attempt to incorporate Judah as a province in the Babylonian Empire under a local governor proved abortive, and after further deportations in 582 BC Judah was absorbed into the neighboring province of Samaria. Some Jews found their way to Egypt at this time, most notably those who were formed into a military colony at Elephantine at the first cataract on the Nile, probably by the Pharaoh Apries.

In Babylonia the exiles, perhaps in all about 15,000 to 20,000 people, were settled in villages of their own, free to earn a living as best they might, to pursue some form of communal life and to maintain their traditions. Although the prophets Ezekiel and Jeremiah urged resignation, political aspirations endured, focusing, after Jehoiachin's death, on his grandson Zerubbabel. It could hardly be otherwise among communities which included the leading figures of Judaean civil and religious life. In Palestine itself archaeology has shown the poverty of settlement and material culture at this time.

Within the first year of his triumph over Babylon in 538 BC the Persian king Cyrus restored the Jewish community and cult to Palestine. Ezra 6:3–5 preserves the original Aramaic memorandum of the king's oral decision on the matter, while Ezra 1:2–4 gives in Hebrew the royal proclamation of the decision as it would have been conveyed by heralds to those it most closely concerned. The Temple was to be rebuilt, to certain specifications, with funds from the royal treasury, and the Temple vessels taken by Nebuchadnezzar were to be restored to it. The first party to return, under Shesh-bazzar, son of Jehoiachin – as governor, not king – may be assumed in the absence of any records to have laid the foundations for effecting the Persian king's decisions in circumstances that cannot have been easy. Many Jews, however, were to remain voluntarily in their new Babylonian home.

Shesh-bazzar died, to be replaced by his nephew Zerubbabel. After years of slow progress and uncertainty, Darius eventually confirmed the original decree of Cyrus, which was found in the royal archives at Ecbatana in Iran, and instructed the local Persian governor to facilitate the construction of the Temple in every way. The new building was consecrated about 515 BC. Visitors to Jerusalem may today see, about 30 yards to the north of the present southeast corner of Herod's Temple platform, a straight joint in the masonry – Herodian to the south of it, but to the north markedly different. This stonework is so like masonry of the Persian period at Sidon and Byblos as to suggest the work of Zerubbabel's masons. Though the Temple rose again the Judaean monarchy did not, and Zerubbabel's eventual fate is not known. Palestine was now part of the vast Persian Empire.

Persepolis: The palace of the Great King

When Alexander the Great set fire to Persepolis in 330 BC, whether at the whim of a courtesan during a feast or in revenge for the Persian sack of Athens in 480 BC, he destroyed the supreme symbol of the last and greatest of the ancient Near Eastern Empires. Yet Persepolis remains something of a puzzle. It was never the administrative capital of the Persian Empire, nor even a favored summer residence, and Greek authors hardly mention it. Created by Darius I, it became the place where the Achaemenid kings came at regular intervals to celebrate the achievements of their royal ancestors in religious ceremonies and diplomatic receptions, and where they were buried. Most of Persepolis had been built by the time of Artaxerxes I and relatively little further work was carried out until approaching the end of the Persian Empire.

Below: head of a young Persian prince, made of Egyptian blue frit, wearing a crown battlemented like a wall. The eyes were originally inlaid. It was found at Persepolis and dates to the 5th or 4th centuries BC.

Right: despite intensive excavation and study the exact function of each building on the Persepolis Terrace remains debatable. It is not even known whether the palaces were residential or reserved for ceremonial occasions, the King and court living meanwhile in palaces and tented encampments on the plain below. It seems likely that all major processions took place on the plain.

Left: aerial view taken in the 1930s of the great terrace at Persepolis, showing the rocky headland at the foot of mountains that formed the heart of the city. It was once surrounded by massive mudbrick walls. Within, set side by side at random, were palaces, assembly halls, storerooms, administrative buildings and barracks.

Right: work in progress in front of the restored Harem building during the American excavations at Persepolis under Dr Erich Schmidt during the 1930s. The restored building acts as museum, storeroom and workshop. Although the task of excavation and restoration still continues, Schmidt's monumental publication of his work, in three volumes, remains one of the great masterpieces of Near Eastern archaeology.

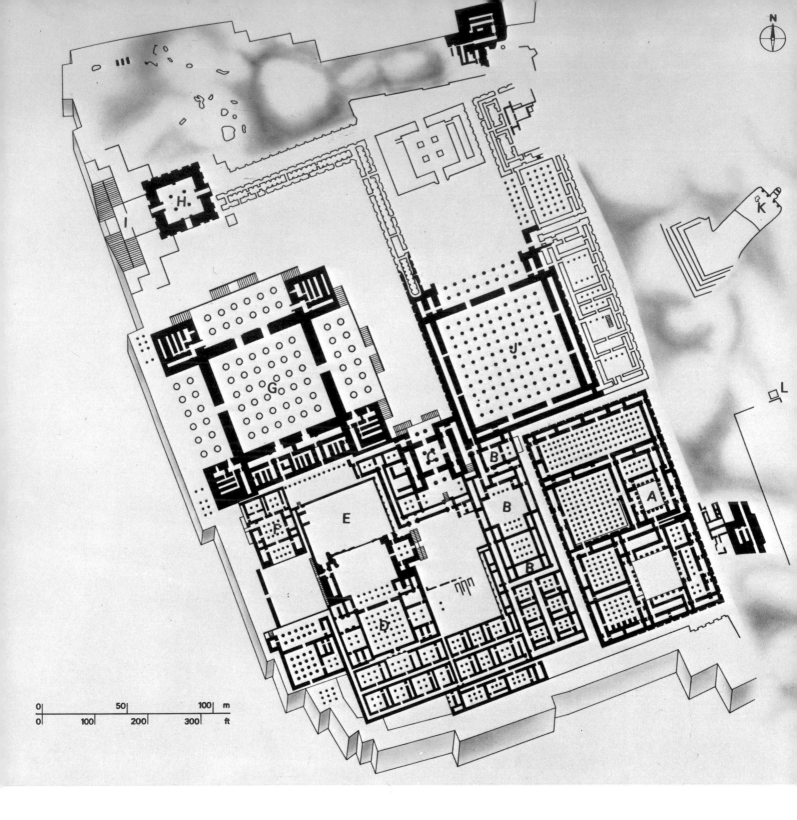

When looking at a plan of Persepolis it is not easy to detect the clear overall scheme of architectural development initiated by Darius I and virtually completed by his two immediate successors. Indeed some building was left unfinished and much seems somewhat haphazard. The great entrance gateway with its winged bull guardians was built by Xerxes. On the western side of the Terrace is the reception hall or Apadana with an adjoining series of private palaces and their ancillary buildings. To the east is the many-columned Throne Hall with adjacent storerooms, offices and barracks.

A Treasury
B Harem
C Tripylon (Triple Gateway)
D Palace of Xerxes
E Ruined building
F Palace of Darius I
G Audience Hall of Darius I (Apadana)
H Gate-house of Xerxes
I Stairway to Terrace
J Throne Hall of Xerxes
K Royal Tomb
L Cistern

Below: this is another view of the 1930s excavations at Persepolis, this time in the porch of the Throne Hall, the construction of which was begun by Xerxes and finished by Artaxerxes I.

Above: the Tripylon lies at the southeast corner of the Apadana. The walls of its smaller staircase are carved with servants, the larger with Median and Persian nobles and soldiers.

Right: a magnificent capital from one of the many columns which made the Apadana one of the most impressive buildings in the ancient world. Work here began under Darius and went on under Xerxes and Artaxerxes I. Today its high painted mudbrick walls have vanished, leaving only battered vestiges of its massive stone columns and doorways.

Far right: the Apadana reliefs show delegations from many parts of the Persian Empire. Here the Syrians (no. 6) pass through mustered files of Median and Persian guards. Each delegation is distinguished by dress and, to a lesser extent, by the gifts it brings, usually gold plate or jewelry, or rich textiles and animals.

Below: the main panel of the sculptures on the Apadana stairs originally showed the Persian king enthroned, his crown prince standing behind, with attendants, as if receiving the delegations sculpted elsewhere on the stairs. This was moved to the Treasury and these relief panels substituted, perhaps by Artaxerxes I.

Left: file of servants carrying dishes and young animals, perhaps sacrifices rather than food, carved on the southern stairs of the Palace of Darius.

Right: the Persian King and two servants carved on the jamb of the southern door of the main hall in the Palace of Darius. A beardless attendant with cosmetic bottle and towel carved on the jamb of the west door of room 12 in the Palace of Darius.

Above: delegation no. 15, the Bactrians, led by a Median usher, is seen here in distinctive local costume bringing gold plate and the camel so characteristic of their homeland to the east of Iran.

Below: delegation no. 3, the Armenians, led by a Persian usher. They are shown bringing textiles, gold plate, and one of the short sturdy horses for which their region was renowned.

Left: any kind of floral decoration on the reliefs is relatively rare, and where it does appear highly stylized and purely ornamental.

Above: the King's horses (followed off this picture by his chariots) moving in procession with Median and Persian noblemen, from the great stairway of the Apadana.

Right: an inscription of Artaxerxes III (359–338 BC) in Old Persian on the western stairway of the Palace of Darius. It records his titles, ancestry and the fact that he built the stairway.

Top: this reasonably accurate restoration of the Harem corrects the strange impression created today by the complete destruction of all original mudbrick walls at Persepolis.

Above: this view of the unrestored Harem illustrates exactly how stone was used only for door and window frames, stone bases and capitals.

Right: a detail of the finely decorated sword-scabbard worn by the King's arms bearer from the relief, found in the Treasury, which originally formed the centerpiece of the sculptural scheme on the Apadana stairway.

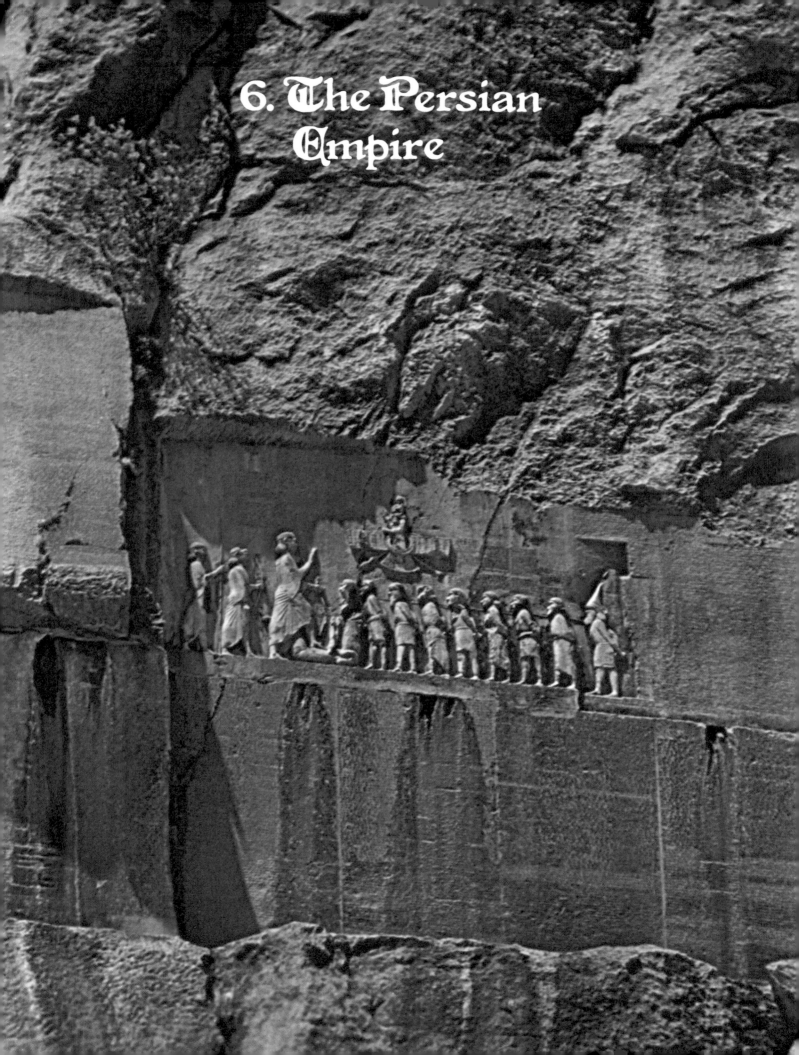

6. The Persian Empire

Origins of the empire. It was only when they came into conflict with the Assyrians in the Zagros mountain valleys of western Iran that the Iranian-speaking peoples entered the pages of history – the Persians in 844 BC, the Medes in 836 BC, in the reign of Shalmaneser III. At this time the home of the Persians lay somewhere in Kurdistan, extending down to the Great Khorasan Road running through the Zagros mountains from Iraq to the Iranian plateau. By the 7th century they were settled further to the southeast in the modern province of Fars. Media was located around a capital at Ecbatana, modern Hamadan, at the eastern end of the Great Khorasan Road as it passed through the Zagros mountains on to the plateau.

By the 7th century a Median confederation, in some way allied with the Scythians and Cimmerians, had become so dominant in the region that when Assyria crushed Elam, in modern Khuzistan, and was then herself destroyed, Media rapidly extended its authority over all southwest Iran. Under an able and ambitious ruler, Cyaxares II, the army was reorganized, the Persians subordinated, and diplomatic ties established with the Babylonians as they sought to overthrow the declining Assyrian monarchy. Once this was achieved, by the Medio-Babylonian alliance in 614 to 610 BC, Cyaxares marched into eastern Turkey to overthrow the kingdom of Urartu (Ararat) and attack Lydia. Babylonia, disturbed by Media's mushrooming ambitions, arranged by treaty for the frontier between Lydia and Media to be set at the Halys River. Among the battles between the Medes and Lydians was one which provides a very rare fixed point in the history of this period. Herodotus tells us that:

"Among their other battles there was one night engagement. As, however, the balance had not turned in favor of either nation, another combat took place in the sixth year [of the war], in the course of which, just as the battle was warming up, day was suddenly turned into night." The eclipse referred to is dated by astronomers to 28 May 585 BC.

For the space of half a century, from about 600 to 550 BC virtually nothing is known of Median history. Her culture is almost equally obscure, though it certainly played a considerable part in the later Persian Empire. The ancient Greek geographer Strabo explicitly states that Persian royal usage was derived from the Medes; for instance the word for governor – satrap in its Greek form – comes from the Median term *khshathrapan-. The many-columned halls of Persepolis and Pasargadae have precursors in Media at sites like Godin Tepe and Tepe Nush-i Jan, where there is also an 8th to 7th-century fire-temple, a type common in later Persia. Its fire was quenched and the building, perhaps on the death of a king, systematically packed with rubble and abandoned.

The same deficiency of information would apply to the Persians were it not for the accounts of their history and customs left by ancient Greek authors, and scattered references in the Old Testament. Inscriptions of the Achaemenid royal house, save for the great rock relief at Behistun, are neither very numerous nor very informative. It is consequently very difficult to write of the last and greatest of the ancient Near Eastern empires without imperceptibly assuming Greek eyes and Greek prejudices. Herodotus has provided us with an account of Persia and Persian history, until about 480 BC, of unparalleled excellence and fascination. Thucydides has chronicled Persian involvement in the Second Peloponnesian War (431 to 404 BC) between Athens and Sparta. Xenophon, an Athenian in the service of Cyrus the Younger, has left a superb account (known as the *Anabasis*) of the retreat of the ten thousand Greek mercenaries from Mesopotamia to Trapezus on the Black Sea after the defeat and death of Cyrus at Cunaxa in 401 BC. Xenophon also wrote an historical "novel," the *Cyropaedia*, with Cyrus the Great as its hero, in the guise of a model ruler. Ctesias, the Greek doctor of Artaxerxes II, on the opposite side to Xenophon at Cunaxa, wrote a not entirely trustworthy history of Persia that has only survived in bits. Valuable supplementary evidence may be gleaned from such later works as Arrian's *History of Alexander*, Strabo's *Geography*, Plutarch's *Lives* and the *World History* of Diodorus Siculus. Much is thus known of events in the west of the empire, notably in Turkey, Cyprus and the Levant, but the east is rarely clearly documented, not least the endless and complicated court intrigues that did so much to weaken the Achaemenid Persian monarchy.

In its beginning, as throughout its history, the Persian Empire ultimately depended on the vigor and intelligent direction of its ruler, the Great King. For more than 200

p.117: the rock relief at Behistun on the road into Iran from Iraq, showing King Darius I triumphant over rebels, c. 520 BC.

Left: gold model of an Achaemenid chariot from the "Oxus Treasure" found on the banks of the river Oxus in 1877; perhaps originally a temple treasure.

years (c. 550 to 330 BC) members of a single noble Persian family, founded by one Achaemenes, ruled the largest Empire until then created, stretching from Greece to India, from Egypt into the Caucasus at its widest extent. Its creator was Cyrus. Writing of Alexander, Arrian noted "but no one else ever invaded India, not even Cyrus, son of Cambyses, though he made an expedition against the Scythians and in all other ways was the most energetic of the kings of Asia" – high praise indeed from so great an admirer of Alexander.

The family of Cyrus had ruled the Persians for generations. He bore the title "King of Anshan" – a part of Fars only recently identified for certain – when he succeeded in about 558 BC, at the age of 40 or so. Within ten years he had overthrown his grandfather, the Median King Astyages, and occupied the Median capital at Ecbatana. Lydia, taking advantage of the Median defeat, moved eastwards across the Halys river. Cyrus, now firmly established at home, marched into Turkey and about 545 BC captured the capital of Lydia, at Sardis, and its famous ruler Croesus, whose life was almost certainly spared, despite graphic Greek accounts of his suicide on a funeral pyre. Persian power was now brought into direct contact with the Ionian Greek city states of western Turkey which were to play so crucial a role in the empire's later history.

Cyrus now turned his attention to Babylon. He did not move directly against King Nabonidus, who had supported Croesus, but waited cannily for his growing unpopularity with his own subjects over religious affairs to undermine his position. Babylon's Elamite subjects (living in southwest Iran) first went over to Cyrus, and then in 539 BC he peaceably occupied Babylon. The Babylonian Chronicle records:

"[T]he shield-bearers of Gutium guarded the gates of Esagila [the great temple of Marduk]; not one spear was brought near to Esagila, nor entered its sanctuary; not one ceremony was disturbed."

It was here particularly that Cyrus established his enduring reputation for tolerance and clemency by honoring the god Marduk of Babylon, demoted by Nabonidus in favor of the god Sin, as recounted on the famous "Cyrus Cylinder," now in the British Museum. Even better known is his decision at that time to free the Jews from their Babylonian captivity. Former subjects of the Babylonian king in Syria and Palestine submitted to the new overlord who, as the Book of Ezra clearly shows, astutely sought and gained their enduring support. From his capital at Ecbatana Cyrus laid the foundations for the administration of his realm with a skill that sustained it for so long, despite the varying quality of its rulers. The eastern frontier was not so easily stabilized as the western and Cyrus died fighting the Massagetae in northern Iran in 530 BC. He was buried in the city he had founded at Pasargadae.

Greeks and Persians. His son and successor Cambyses (c. 530 to 522 BC) had already been enthroned as titular king of Babylon for about 10 years and was no longer a young man. His brief reign was largely occupied with preparing and achieving the conquest of Egypt planned by his father. In the campaign of 525 to 522 BC the ancient Egyptian capitals of Memphis and Thebes were taken, but planned expeditions against Carthage, Ethiopia and the Siwa Oasis proved either, in turn, impractical, a partial failure or a total disaster. An extremely hostile account of Cambyses is given by Herodotus, probably explained by the nationalism of Egypt's priests, who were his main informants, and by his own anti-Persian bias. Cambyses was accused of

Below: baked clay cylinder recording the surrender of Babylon to Cyrus the Great in 539 BC.

slaying the sacred Apis bull, a supreme act of sacrilege in Egyptian eyes. In fact, in true pharaonic tradition, he provided a magnificent sarcophagus for the bull that had died naturally in the sixth year of his reign. Though temple revenues and buildings suffered in the war, Cambyses seems generally to have followed his father's tolerant and statesmanlike policies. He died in Syria, after a riding accident, as he returned to suppress a revolt that had broken out in Iran. His successor, Darius, had accompanied him to Egypt as his spear-bearer, but seems to have been back in Iran when Cambyses met his death.

The circumstances surrounding the accession of Darius are shrouded in mystery. The primary historical source is his own account, inscribed in 520 to 518 BC high on the rock of Behistun on the Great Khorasan Road through the Zagros mountains. Here, in carved relief much in the Assyrian manner, Darius is shown standing, his spear and bow-bearers behind him, with his left foot on the body of the usurper Gaumata. The King's right hand is raised to the god Ahura-Mazda hovering in a disk above. Before Darius, arms bound behind their backs, yoked together at the neck, stands a file of nine rebel leaders. The accompanying inscription is given in three languages, Old Persian, Elamite and Akkadian, all in the cuneiform script. So important did Darius regard this inscription that copies were despatched throughout the Empire, an example in Aramaic written on papyrus is known from Egypt, in Akkadian on a baked clay tablet from Iraq. Many scholars have consequently regarded it as propaganda, a clever attempt to conceal his own dubious right to the throne.

Cambyses' long absence in Egypt had clearly provoked a revolt at home. The Magian Gaumata had seized the eastern Empire, claiming to be Bardiya, a younger brother of Cambyses, though Darius claims that this man had already been slain by Cambyses. If Darius is to be doubted, the rebel may indeed have been the true Bardiya (Greek Smerdis) rebelling with the aid of some Magi (a priestly caste) against his absent brother. Whatever the exact truth, Darius overthrew Gaumata, who was assassinated in 522 BC. According to Greek sources Darius later married both Atossa, sister of Cambyses and wife of Gaumata, as well as Parmys, daughter of the true Bardiya. Then in a remarkable series of lightning campaigns, from 522 to 518 BC, Darius crushed one rebellion after another, notably in Elam, Babylonia and Egypt, and thus reunited the Empire. From his earliest years as king, Darius (a "shopkeeper" Herodotus called him) organized and taxed the Empire systematically, always keenly aware of the financial assets of each newly-conquered province.

On his Egyptian campaign in 519 to 518 BC Darius restored temples and fostered local religion, codified the law and recut a canal at Suez that facilitated sea links with Iran for tribute ships. The Greek, Skylax of Caryanda, was commissioned to explore the sea route to India prior to the great campaign there of 514 BC, which made Darius ruler of the Punjab. This became the most heavily taxed of the provinces. Only an excursion in quest of gold into European Scythia beyond the Bosporus, perhaps in 519 BC rather than after the Indian offensive, brought military stalemate. The nomadic Scythians led him ever onwards, scorching the land as they retreated. Darius was more successful later against Scythians on his eastern frontier.

It was in starting hostilities with European Greece that Darius was to sow the seeds of fatal discord on his western frontier. Since the triumphs of Cyrus in Turkey, the Greek

A Persian palace guard, shown carrying his bow and quiver on his back, portrayed on a multicolored glazed-brick frieze at Susa in Iran. This 5th century relief gives us a good idea of the appearance of the Persian warrior.

city states of Ionia had been under Persian tutelage. In about 500 to 494 BC they revolted to regain their political independence and earlier commercial prosperity in the Aegean. Sardis was sacked and Cyprus joined the revolt. The Persians combined the operations of their army and fleet, the latter largely derived from the Phoenician cities, and recaptured Cyprus, defeated the Ionians and their allies at sea and stormed the center of opposition at Miletus. Satrapal authority over Ionia was restored and a major campaign launched to punish mainland Greece for assisting Ionia. This culminated in the Persian defeat at the battle of Marathon in 490 BC, which steeled Greek resolve and convinced Darius that he could only succeed in conquering Greece with a massive and carefully prepared operation by land and sea. In the midst of such preparations he died, in 486 BC.

It fell to his less able son Xerxes (c. 486 to 465 BC) to pursue the war with Greece; but first he had to contend with opposition from more traditional sources. Already under Darius Egypt, always restless when subordinated to foreign rule, had taken the opportunity of his involvement in Greece to rebel. In his second regnal year Xerxes had harshly crushed the uprising and set his brother Achaemenes over the country. When in 484 to 482 Babylon followed suit Xerxes reacted even more strongly. Babylon was pillaged by his army, its walls dismantled, its major shrines wrecked. The golden statue of the god Marduk was removed, crippling the cult that had so long encouraged regular attempts to revive an independent Babylonian kingdom under a native king.

In 481 BC Xerxes took up residence at Sardis to prepare for the invasion of Greece. He assembled the vast army memorably described by Herodotus, and a fleet with the Phoenician navy at the heart of it. The Hellespont was bridged with boats and a canal dug through the Athos peninsula. The campaign began auspiciously for Xerxes. His fleet was victorious at Artemisium. Despite the heroic defence of the pass at Thermopylae in 480 BC by Leonidas, king of Sparta, the Persian army forced its way through into Attica, which was devastated, took Athens and sacked the Acropolis. The Greeks were driven back on their final line of defence at the Isthmus of Corinth. But at a stroke the naval victory of Themistocles at Salamis turned the tide. With his supply lines perilously threatened Xerxes was forced to retreat back into Turkey. First the remaining Persian army under Mardonius was routed at Plataea and the general killed, then Greeks landed north of Miletus in Turkey and defeated another Persian army under Tigranes. The Ionians went over to the side of the mainland Greeks and the Persian defeat was complete. After 479 BC when Herodotus is no longer available as a source, the career of Xerxes is obscure. He seems to have been content with building projects in Iran at Persepolis and the affairs of his harem that slowly, and fatally, came to dominate the Dynasty. In 465 BC he was assassinated.

Through court intrigues Artaxerxes I emerged as king, much under the disruptive influence of the Queen Mother, Amestris. What was soon to become a familiar pattern of events followed. In the east he had to overcome disaffection at court and in Bactria. In the west Egypt revolted in 460 BC with Greek support. In 449 BC, after intermittent conflict, a delegation under Callias, an able Athenian diplomat, went to Susa to sue for peace terms. By defining their areas of influence the Greeks and Persians sought to establish a provisional *modus vivendi*. Persia agreed not to send a fleet west of the Bosporus or of Phaselis in southern Turkey, nor an army within three days' march of the coast, while Athens left all east of that line, including Egypt and Cyprus, to the Persians.

In reality it was little more than a ceasefire. Friction between the Ionian city states and the Persian satrap at Sardis was endemic and a fresh conflagration was only averted by Greek preoccupation after 431 BC with the Second Peloponnesian War between Athens and Sparta. At first Persia remained a spectator. In 424 BC both Artaxerxes and his queen died. His policies, as seen in his

A Greek relief dating from the 6th century BC showing Greek warriors in combat.

The tomb of Cyrus the Great (died 529 BC) at Pasargadae in Iran. It was probably designed and built by stonemasons from western Turkey. Alexander the Great visited it and ordered its restoration. Even in its present desolate state it has great dignity.

honorable treatment of the exiled Athenian leader Themistocles and various racial minorities, were more akin to the firm magnanimity of a Darius than the petulant fury of a Xerxes; but his reign marks a turning point in the history of the Persian Empire. The signs of eventual disintegration now began to appear.

Decline of the empire. On the death of Artaxerxes one of the bloodiest of Achaemenid court struggles for the succession broke out. Xerxes II, son of Artaxerxes and his queen, survived only 40 days before being murdered by a half-brother, Secydianus, son of a Babylonian concubine, who then aspired to the throne. From Babylon another half-brother, Ochus, supported by the satraps of Hyrcania and Egypt, proved more powerful. Declared King of Babylon as Darius II in 423 BC, he took supreme power and purged Secydianus and his faction. But the empire was now dangerously unstable. Satraps revolted and warred with one another; in Egypt a war of independence was at last successfully waged and one of the richest provinces lost. At court Queen Parysatis schemed for the succession of her favorite son, Cyrus the Younger, against the eldest, and declared heir, Arsaces. In 408 BC Cyrus, a mere youth of 16, superseded the able and influential satrap Tissaphernes as supreme commander in Turkey and intervened decisively in the Peloponnesian War on Sparta's side.

Matters were brought to a head when Media revolted and Darius II, falling ill on campaign, returned to Babylon to die there in 404 BC. Arsaces, taking the throne as Artaxerxes II, was soon seen to be much under the influence of his wife, Queen Stateira. Cyrus, who had been called east to participate in the Median campaign, was allowed to return to Sardis. There, on the pretence of

gathering forces for an expedition against Pisidia, he enlisted the support of local satraps and assembled a mercenary army, including the Greek Xenophon, to make an attempt on his brother's throne. Marching east and then southwards down the Euphrates, he was defeated and killed by the armies of Artaxerxes and Abrocomas, satrap of Syria, at Cunaxa, 60 miles north of Babylon, in 401 BC. This is the campaign, and its aftermath for the 10,000 retreating Greek mercenaries, so well described in Xenophon's *Anabasis*. Cyrus emerges from the Greek accounts as a most able and charming man, who might well have proved a better ruler than his brother.

Cunaxa well illustrates the growing threat to the ruling dynasty posed by the great strength and incipient independence of the satraps of Turkey. Their skill in exploiting Greek rivalries on their western frontiers, both with arms and money, might all too easily be turned eastwards against the Great King himself, or more insidiously against one another. Long heirs to the independent traditions of local kingdoms like Lydia, Lycia and Phrygia, the satraps were increasingly Hellenized in dress, manners and culture. The whole administration was gradually moving away from its eastern roots. At the same time Greek influence was once more stimulating the separatist aspirations of Egypt, Phoenicia and Cyprus.

Although in the earlier part of his reign Artaxerxes II succeeded in imposing peace terms on mainland Greece (in 387 BC), effects were transient. Xenophon records:

"King Artaxerxes thinks it just that the cities in Asia should belong to him, as well as Clazomenae and Cyprus among the islands, and that the other Greek cities, both small and great, should be left independent, except Lemnos, Imbros and Scyros; and these should belong, as of old, to the Athenians. But whichever of the two parties does not accept this peace, upon them will I make war, in company with those who desire this arrangement, both by land and sea, with ships and with money.''

The machinations of the Greek states, the intrigues and rivalries of the satraps, the restlessness of conquered peoples in Judah and in northern Iran caused endless strife and friction, crippled all attempts to recover Egypt and threatened the western Empire with collapse. When a revolt of the king's sons, led by Darius the heir, was forestalled and its leader executed, Ochus, a younger son, succeeded in setting his rivals at odds with the king and one another, so that on Artaxerxes' death in 359 BC he was able to seize the crown as Artaxerxes III.

The full extent of the Empire's devolution was now to be revealed, not through a weak king but through a strong one's failure to restore any real semblance of enduring stability. In a reign of 20 years the dynamic and resourceful Artaxerxes III (359 to 338 BC) vigorously reasserted central control over his dangerously fractured dominions. When an attempt to recover Egypt failed, Cyprus, Phoenicia and Cilicia rebelled. In 345 Artaxerxes assembled a huge army at Babylon and marched triumphantly against Phoenicia, then Egypt; Cyprus capitulated. But the eunuch Bagoas poisoned the king before Persia could become deeply involved in the struggle between the Greek city states and Philip of Macedon, father of Alexander the Great. Artaxerxes III had failed to destroy his dynasty's two most enduring enemies, the Greeks abroad, and at home the intrigues of court and harem.

The train of events took an increasingly melodramatic turn. Bagoas, who could not take the throne himself, placed on it Arses, son of Artaxerxes; but he survived barely two years, falling victim himself to poison intended for the all-powerful eunuch. With the main royal line now exterminated, Bagoas perforce turned to a collateral branch and placed Darius III, grandnephew of Artaxerxes II, on the throne. He clearly misjudged his man, for Darius was not only energetic, but as ruthless as the eunuch king-maker himself, who at last fell victim to one of his own poisoned draughts. In an interval provided by Macedon's preoccupation with its own security after the murder of Philip in 336 BC and the accession of the young Alexander, Darius was able to reconquer Egypt, which had reacted rapidly to the murder of Artaxerxes III by once more declaring its independence.

By then Alexander of Macedon, launched at last on his great Asiatic campaign, had shattered Persian authority in Turkey. In 333 BC he defeated the Persians at the Battle of Issus, close to the sea north of modern Iskenderum in

Cyrus, of the Achaemenid family, brought into being the vast Persian (Achaemenian) Empire, which extended all the way from Sogdiana in the northeast to the Aegean Sea in the west.

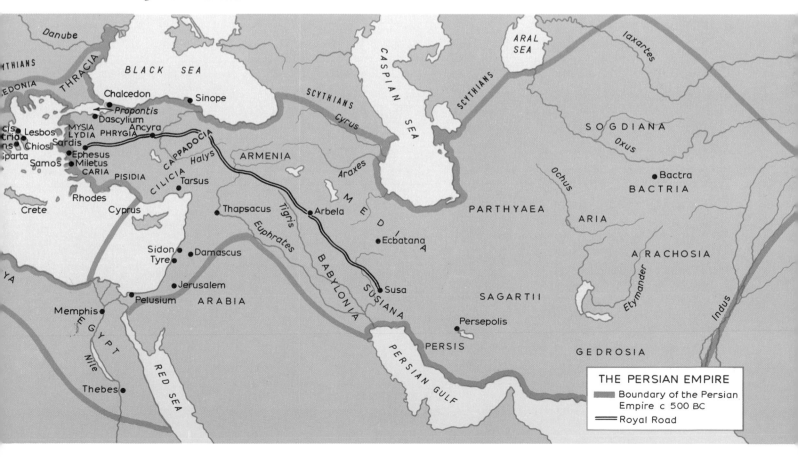

Turkey. In 333 BC he defeated the Persians at the Battle of Alexander. Alexander moved triumphantly through the Levant and conquered Egypt. Then, returning north and turning east into Mesopotamia in 331 BC, he fought a final great battle with Darius at Gaugamela, just to the east of Nineveh and Nimrud, the ruined cities of the Assyrian Empire destroyed three centuries earlier by the Medes. Again a fugitive, Darius fled eastwards across northern Iran, only to be murdered by his own, now desperate, court. The satrap Bessos succeeded as Artaxerxes IV. In turn hunted down and executed by Alexander, his death brought an end to the native Persian dynasty. Fire, on Alexander's orders, had already devastated the great dynastic center at Persepolis. Ironically, it is Greek and Roman interest in Alexander and his eastern campaigns that has preserved for us so much information on the later Achaemenid dynasty.

The Great King and his court. To a Persian it was unimaginable that society should operate without a king to ensure the proper order of things. He alone could provide victory in war, the rule of law, productivity in agriculture and husbandry, and protection from supernatural powers through his special relationship with the supreme god, Ahura-Mazda. So far as it is possible to judge, the Persian king had to be born of Achaemenians on both sides of the family, or at least of a mother belonging to one of the seven most noble families. As the later history of the dynasty has shown, the Queen Mother exercised great

authority. On accession the king assumed a throne name, generally one of three: Darius ("Holding firm the good"), Xerxes ("hero among rulers") or Artaxerxes ("having just rule"). Not worshiped as a god in his lifetime, the king was nevertheless set apart by his supposed direct access to the deity and entitled to full obeisance from his court. His person was also regarded as sacred. Divine instructions were believed to reach him in dreams; thus it was said Xerxes received instructions to begin the invasion of Greece. In any major rite the king was the leading participant. Xerxes, before crossing to Europe, conducted a ceremony of propitiation. As the sun's disk rose over the horizon at dawn he poured a libation from a golden goblet, which he then threw into the sea with another golden vessel and a Persian sword, to consecrate his army to the service of Ahura-Mazda.

Court protocol endorsed this supernatural status. On carved reliefs the king is shown larger than any other human being, his crown and that of the crown prince is distinctive, similar to that of Ahura-Mazda, and his square-cut beard is matched only by that of the crown prince and of supernatural beings. Ritual required, if circumstances did not always allow, that a king's feet should never touch the ground outside his palace; within it he walked on special carpets forbidden to others. To sit on the king's throne was a capital offence. The royal robe, with which he was endowed at his coronation, was both unique and talismanic. Generally of purple and white, it was worn over a tunic embroidered with the winged symbols of

Winged monster on a multicolored glazed-brick frieze from a royal palace at Susa.

Ahura-Mazda. According to Xenophon, eager though Cyrus the Younger was to usurp the throne, he refused to allow Artaxerxes to be assassinated when wearing the coronation robe. The king's daily life was governed by a whole series of taboos; he lived apart, eating special food off special dishes. Both the Old Testament and Greek authors agree on this. The *Book of Esther*, for example, recounts that:

"All the king's servants and the people of his provinces know that for a man or woman who approaches the king in the inner court without being summoned there is one penalty; death, unless, by pointing his golden scepter toward him, the king grants him his life."

Even more illuminating are various passages in *The Wisemen at Dinner (Deipnosophistai)*, a book completed about 200 AD by Athenaeus of Naucratis in Egypt. It assembles accounts of convivial occasions culled from numerous ancient sources of varying reliability. Many of its references are exaggerated, particularly to the opulence and indulgence of the Persians, but some of it is basically accurate and vivid:

"All who attend upon Persian kings when they dine first bathe themselves and then dress in white clothes, and spend nearly half the day on preparations for the dinner. Of those who are invited to eat with the king, some dine out of doors, in full sight of anyone who wishes to look on; others dine indoors in the king's company. Yet even these do not eat in his presence, for there are two rooms opposite each other, in one of which the king has his meal, in the other the invited guests. The king can see them through the curtains at the door, but they cannot see him. Sometimes, however, on the occasion of a public holiday, all dine, in a single room with the king, in a great hall. . . . In most cases the king breakfasts and dines alone, but sometimes his wife and some of his sons dine with him. And throughout the dinner his concubines sing and play the lyre."

The royal court had no fixed abode. The king had palaces and estates throughout the empire, as did his family. The primary administrative centers were at Babylon and Susa, though Ecbatana held a special position as the former Median capital and a favored summer resort. From early in the dynasty a key position at court was held by the commander of the king's bodyguard, dominating an enormous hierarchy of officials and domestic functionaries. Apart from them were the members of the royal family and their households, the king's harem and its staff, and at the capitals the whole personnel of government and administration at all levels. Such varied courtiers as Babylonian astronomers and "wisemen," Phoenician admirals and explorers, Greek doctors, scientists and philosophers gave it a cosmopolitan character. They were all, as a rich legacy of tales makes clear, splendidly housed, lavishly entertained and in a perpetual ferment of intrigue and gossip.

Army and administration. Throughout the empire Persian authority, and the power of individual kings and

A Greek view, painted on a vase in southern Italy, of King Darius enthroned among his courtiers; Greek gods above.

satraps as well, rested ultimately on the army. In the early empire its allegiance to the central administration, in the person of the ruler, was generally reliable; but as the satraps grew more independent and the Achaemenian family more factious, the loyalties of local military forces became divided and unpredictable, while later on mercenaries, primarily Greek, provided wealthy rebels with their own forces. In peacetime there was a standing army, made up largely of Medes and Persians, with a royal guard of cavalry and the famous "Immortals," foot soldiers always held to the number of 10,000, who provided the supreme royal guard, the final bastion of the monarch's authority. For war the army became a mosaic of contingents as ethnically varied as the empire itself, though foreigners rarely rose very high in rank. Most officers were Iranians or Babylonians. Divided into lancers, archers and cavalry by nationality, the army depended generally on superior manpower rather than subtle tactics. Garrisons, again multinational, were divided like the army into standards, each bearing its commander's name, and these in turn were divided into centuries. Owing to an accident of survival one of the most obscure and distant of these garrisons is now the best known. At Elephantine in southern Egypt papyrus documents have survived belonging to an Aramaic-speaking Jewish colony engaged there in military service.

For administrative purposes the empire was divided into provinces, known to the Persians as "lands," and to us, after the Greek, as satrapies; some at least dated from the time of Cyrus. Darius increased their number by subdivision and conquest, giving the ancient kingdoms of Babylonia and Egypt special positions which were taken away by Xerxes. The Persians, as the empire's masters, always enjoyed a privileged role. Herodotus lists 20 satrapies. (Surviving Persian lists, often inappropriately compared with his, are of peoples and have no specific reference to the system of administration). Each province was ruled by a satrap, always a member of the royal family or of the highest nobility, who was responsible above all for security and tax collection. Insofar as local conditions allowed, the satrapal courts and administrations mirrored those of the Great King. Some idea of a satrap's life and duties are revealed in a series of letters, written in Aramaic on leather, surviving from the archives of Arsames, satrap of Egypt under Artaxerxes I and Darius II. They concern one of his estates in Egypt, though the use of leather rather than papyrus suggests they were written in Iraq or Iran where Arsames, leaving his Egyptian business to deputies and agents, was often to be found with the royal court. As a member of the royal family his authority may well have extended beyond his particular satrapy.

Throughout the empire the king's writ concerned itself with things great and small to a degree that is often surprising. The weakness of the later kings of the dynasty arose in part from their inability to maintain the level of scrutiny established by Darius. A few examples will

The "Alexander Mosaic" from Pompeii copying a fine 4th century BC Greek painting of the Battle of Issus, 333 BC; the moment when the tide of victory turns in Alexander's favor.

illustrate its extent. When Oroites, satrap of Lydia, proved recalcitrant, Bagaios, a Persian official, was selected for the task of bringing him to heel, not through force of arms but through exercise of royal authority alone. Arriving before the satrap in his palace at Sardis, Bagaios delivered one by one to his secretary, who then read them aloud, the sealed royal despatches. He started with routine matters of little moment. Then, Herodotus goes on:

"His object was to test the loyalty of Oroites's bodyguard to see if they might be willing to act against their master. When, therefore, he noticed that they regarded the documents with respect – and, still more, the words they heard read from them – he passed one to the secretary which contained an order purporting to come from Darius, to the effect that the guards were to refuse service to Oroites. The order was read out and the guards promptly laid their spears at Bagaios's feet. Then Bagaios, seeing the written order obeyed, ventured to hand to the secretary the paper he had reserved to the last. This contained the words: 'King Darius commands the Persians in Sardis to kill Oroites.' The guards immediately drew their swords and killed him."

No less decisive was the King's action in a much more minor matter called to his attention by the injured party. His letter was later inscribed in stone and set up by the priests of the sanctuary of Apollo in Magnesia in western Turkey, whose plea over the head of the local satrap, Gadatas of Ionia, had been favorably answered. It shows Darius' concern both for religious observance and for the cultivation of trees and crops – a vital royal responsibility for Persian kings, noted by other Greek sources:

"King of Kings, Darius, son of Hystaspes, to his 'slave' Gadatas says: I hear that you are not obeying my orders in all things; I commend your policy in cultivating my land and in introducing food-crops from beyond the Euphrates into Lower Asia, and for this great credit will be given you in the house of the King. But as you are causing my intention on behalf of the gods to be forgotten, I shall give you, if you do not change your course, cause to know that I am angered; for you have demanded tribute from the sacred gardeners of Apollo, and ordered them to dig profane ground, not knowing my feelings towards the god, who spoke truth to the Persians."

The Jews rebuilding the Temple in Jerusalem also successfully appealed to Darius over the local satrap's head. The King's hand is to be detected even in the affairs of the Jewish colony at Elephantine; and the administrative tablets from Persepolis reveal his close interest in payments large and small.

An efficient postal service using mounted couriers along patrolled roads secured excellent communications, giving royal directives the necessary immediacy. Aramaic served as the international language in which royal edicts went forth throughout the empire to be translated as required into the local tongue for administrative purposes.

"Then on the thirteenth day of the first month the royal scribes were summoned, and copies were made of the orders addressed by Haman to the king's satraps, to the governors ruling each province and to the principal officials of each people, to each province in its own script and to each people in its own language. The edict was signed in the name of King Ahasuerus [Xerxes] and sealed with his ring, and letters were sent by runners to every province of the realm." (Esther 3:12–13.)

The Old Testament has made the "law of the Medes and Persians which changeth not" proverbial. The Achaemenid kings were not so much great lawgivers and innovators as codifiers, particularly Darius. With the empire newly created it was essential that in each satrapy local laws should be systematically recorded so that the new administration of Persians could effectively operate them. Here again great wisdom was shown in not imposing foreign law and customs, but in treating the subject peoples according to their own traditions. The Achaemenid rulers comment in many of their inscriptions on their concern for law and its proper execution. The king was the chief judge of crimes against the state, but generally justice lay in the hands of local courts, where it was rigidly and efficiently practiced. As was common at the time, punishments were very severe.

Religion. Neither inside Iran nor out was there a single religion in Achaemenid times. In the diverse provinces of the empire old forms of worship were honored and openly tolerated by the Persian rulers. Vigorous controversy has for long prevented any clear understanding of the religion of the king and his court. The sources to which all scholars must perforce appeal are not yet sufficient to allow for agreement even on the most basic issues. In a famous, but sadly concise passage on Persian religion, Herodotus describes, from a Greek standpoint, the external characteristics of a religion that in essentials is that of the *Avesta* (Law), the corpus of Old Persian religious texts still preserved by the Parsees of India.

"The erection of statues, temples, and altars is not accepted practice amongst them. . . . Zeus in their system, is the whole circle of the heavens, and they sacrifice to him from the tops of mountains. They also worship the sun, moon and earth, fire, water and winds, which are their only deities: it was later that they learnt from the Assyrians and Arabians the cult of Uranian Aphrodite. . . . As for ceremonial, when they offer sacrifice to the deities I mentioned, they erect no altar and kindle no fire; the libation, the flute-music, the garlands, the sprinkled meal – all these things, familiar to us, they have no use for; but before a ceremony a man sticks a spray of leaves, usually myrtle leaves, into his headdress, takes his victim to some open place and invokes the deity to whom he wishes to sacrifice. The actual worshipper is not permitted to pray for any personal or private blessing, but only for the king and for the general good of the community, of which he himself is part. When he has cut up the animal and cooked it, he

Gold daric coin of Darius showing the king, or the royal "genius," with bow and a spear with a golden pomegranate on its base.

makes a little heap of the softest green-stuff he can find, preferably clover, and lays all the meat upon it. This done, a Magus (a member of this caste is always present at sacrifice) utters an incantation over it in a form of words which is supposed to recount the birth of the gods. Then after a short interval the worshipper removes the flesh and does what he pleases with it . . . a male Persian is never buried until the body has been torn by a bird or dog . . . the Persians in general, however, cover a body with wax and bury it . . . the Magi not only kill anything, except dogs and men, with their own hands but make a special point of doing so; ants, snakes, animals and birds – no matter what, they kill them indiscriminately. Well, it is an ancient custom, so let them keep it.''

Unlike the Old Testament, the *Avesta* literary tradition contains no historical information, only ritual instructions and hymns including a wealth of mythological detail. It is moreover (in this respect like the Old Testament) a compendium of texts composed at various times and assembled in its present form long after the Achaemenid period. The Persians of the *Avesta* believed themselves to be obeying the commands of God as revealed to their prophet Zoroaster, whose hymns or songs, the *Gathas*, in a language more primitive than the rest, form the foundation of the *Avesta* tradition. Some scholars believe that Zoroaster was born in the later 7th century BC and practiced his ministry, possibly as an exile from Media, in eastern Iran and beyond. His conversion, in about 588 BC, of the local king Vishtaspa to the religion of the *Gathas*, marked the real start of his prophetic career. The *Gathas* proclaim a single, supreme God, creator of all things material and spiritual, who is beyond the reach of evil forces. The world is divided between two opposite poles, offered as free choices to men, Truth and Lie, Good and Evil. Eternal rewards are promised to those who choose the way of good deeds, eternal torment to evil-doers. Since the supreme symbol of Truth is fire, fire altars became the major cult symbol of Zoroastrianism.

The acceptance of Zoroastrianism in western Iran in the 6th century may have been the work of the Magi, a priestly tribe or caste among the Medes who were considered indispensable to the performance of any religious ceremony. Their inscriptions suggest that both Darius and Xerxes formally accepted the principal doctrines of Zoroaster; but it was not until the reign of Artaxerxes I, when the civil calendar was reformed about 441 BC with months named after the leading deities of the cult, that Zoroastrianism may clearly be seen as the official religion of the ruling dynasty. Older cults certainly survived and were in time greatly to modify the prophet's teachings. In worship carried out at the royal and satrapal courts the cults of the ancient Iranian religion continued, not seriously modified by orthodox Zoroastrianism.

The most famous rite in Indo-Iranian religion, the use of an intoxicating drink called *haoma* (*soma* in India), prepared by pounding in a mortar a plant of unknown identity, possibly wild rhubarb, goes unmentioned in Herodotus. This was an oversight. A seal design found at Persepolis on several clay tablets, dated to the reign of Xerxes, has been convincingly identified as the haoma

Post-Achaemenid fire-altars at Naqsh-i Rustam, near Persepolis, burial place of the Achaemenid kings from Darius I.

Looking down into part of the Median fire-temple at Tepe Nush-i Jan in Iran, packed with shale when abandoned.

ceremony. Indeed the ancient historian Douris may have been referring to it when he wrote, "at the festival of Mithra alone, of all the festivals celebrated by the Persians, the king gets drunk and dances the (Persian) dance." On the relevant Persepolis sealings, below the winged disk of Ahura-Mazda two people flank a fire altar and a stand bearing a mortar and pestle, identical in form with a whole series of green stone vessels, inscribed with brief phrases in Aramaic, also found at Persepolis. The inscriptions suggest that the *haoma* ceremony was largely a celebration in honor of the god Mithras, held particularly by, and for, the army.

Trade and economics. The Persians always accepted that the vast complex of their empire embraced an enormous variety of social and economic conditions, ranging from the long-established and highly sophisticated urban societies of Babylonia, Turkey and Egypt to the predominantly agricultural and nomadic communities of the Iranian homeland. No attempt was made to centralize or unify the methods and structure of economic and commercial life so long as taxation was efficiently and regularly collected. With good security and excellent overland communications trade flourished. Prosperous Phoenician cities minted their own silver coinage in the 4th century. Luxury goods in precious metals, glass and fine pottery were exported from specialist centers of manufacture throughout the empire and deep into what is now Russia. Large quantities of Greek, primarily Athenian, coins of the 5th and 4th centuries are found all over the empire down into Arabia. Fine Greek pottery followed a similar pattern of distribution. From various centers in the western empire merchant communities, again mainly Greek, traded western luxuries for oriental ones brought west by the

Below: surviving buildings at Pasargadae: palaces (B & C), gateway (A), together with a watercourse (D) and canal (E).

Above: Pasargadae with the ruin of the Zendan-i-Suleiman in the foreground. It may have been a temple or a treasury.

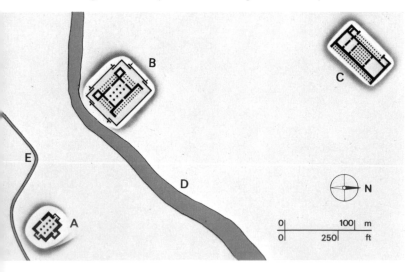

caravan trade. Basic commodities like grain, in which Babylonia, Syria and Egypt were so rich, were exchanged for Greek wine and olive oil.

In theory all land belonged to the king. The private royal domain, including hunting parks, was extensive. Estates were granted to members of the royal family, to satraps and to high officials on various terms, as also to lesser officials and army officers – commonly in return for services to the crown and a portion of each harvest. This system was akin to the feudalism of medieval Europe. But already by the earlier 5th century increased rents were demanded more often than military service. Progressively, banking houses took over management of estates, paying the landlords' rent and rendering dues to the crown as required. This change was eased by moves towards a monetary economy, especially in western provinces where contacts with Greece were closest. Most of the empire used miscellaneous bullion, passing by weight, for its transactions and only in Turkey did both the crown, and more rarely the satraps, conform to local practice and mint

coins. After about 517 BC the Persian treasury issued the famous gold "darics" that were the only substantial gold coinage minted before that of Philip II of Macedon. The lesser silver sigloi and shekels bore a distinctively Persian figure, a king or royal hero variously armed. Satraps, especially in time of war in the later empire, occasionally had coins minted with their own portraits. In the 4th century various cities in Cilicia, notably Tarsus, had coins inscribed with the satrap's name in Greek or Aramaic.

A unique series of documents for studying banking practices and economic pressures in this period has survived from Nippur in southern Iraq, where excavations revealed the archives, inscribed on clay tablets, of the banking house of Murashu, active about 455 to 403 BC. Indeed there are many such documents from Iraq, not so readily studied as the Murashu group but clearly showing the country's highly developed economic administration. They indicate, among other things, how disastrous Achaemenid monetary policy was. Heavy taxation in cash and kind caused a shortage of goods and precious metals that

stimulated continuing inflation throughout the period. If the royal treasury had reissued in coinage the taxes it gathered, a fully-fledged monetary economy might have emerged far faster than it did, and reduced this trend. But the Persian monarch followed the instincts of his kind and the traditions of his age by hoarding it all in great treasuries at Babylon, Susa and Ecbatana, both in bullion and plate. It was these treasure-houses which so amazed the Greeks when they fell to the armies of Alexander.

Cities and palaces. Archaeological investigation of Achaemenid culture has concentrated so far on the achievements of the royal court and its satellites. Palaces of kings and governors have been explored, but virtually nothing else. Even they vary, so that no coherent picture has yet emerged. At Babylon, where some idea of a great administrative city might have been hoped for, the German excavators found few buildings which could confidently be attributed to the Persian period. Later building in the Seleucid period had obliterated what Xerxes' army had not destroyed in 482 BC. Then again at Susa, the other administrative capital, only palaces have so far been excavated. There on the Apadana mound, a vast artificial platform over the earlier Elamite city, Darius and Artaxerxes II created monumental palaces, largely of mudbrick decorated with polychrome glazed bricks including friezes of animals, real and imaginary. Only columns, their capitals and bases, and a restricted range of sculpture are of stone. The city itself was walled and possibly surrounded by a moat linked to the local river. Across the river in its own parkland was another palace, built later by Artaxerxes II or III, with large many-columned halls, its walls and columns decorated with painted plaster.

Susa has yielded, in various editions, a trilingual building inscription in Old Persian, Elamite and Akkadian, carved on foundation tablets of baked clay and stone, that described the construction of palaces there by Darius. The particular interest of this text lies in its account of the foreign materials and craftsmen employed by the king. Cedarwood came from the Lebanon, brought to Babylon by Syrians and then from Babylon to Susa by East Greeks (Carians and Ionians); *yaka* wood came from Ghandara and Carmania (southern Iran). Gold from Sardis in Lydia and Bactria, lapis lazuli from Sogdiana, turquoise from Chorasmia, ivory from Ethiopia, Sind and Arachosia, were all worked on the spot. Unspecified decorative elements for the terraces came from Ionia; stone columns, worked at Susa, from a village in Elam. Ionians and Sardians worked the stone, Medes and Egyptians the gold, Sardians and Egyptians the wood. Babylonians baked bricks and Medes and Egyptians adorned the terraces.

This exploitation of foreign resources and specialist craftsmen followed established Near Eastern imperial traditions. But, so far as it is possible to judge from the meager surviving remains of all this splendor, cosmopolitan craftsmen worked under such close local supervision that once on the spot their individual styles were rarely to be detected save in details of workmanship and technique.

A headless statue of Darius recently discovered at Susa, with triligual cuneiform and Egyptian hieroglyphic inscriptions, well illustrates this. Though it has some of the traditional features of Egyptian statuary, notably the back pillar against which the King's standing body is set, and was indeed made in Egypt according to the inscription, the style of the monarch's costume is Persian both in fashion and execution. Such also was the pattern over the mountains in Fars, where at Persepolis Darius was initiating the most ambitious of all Achaemenid architectural and sculptural programs.

The famous Median capital of Hagmatana – The Place of Assembly – and favored Achaemenid summer residence, known to the Greeks as Ecbatana, lies under the modern city of Hamadan and has yet to be excavated. Spectacular finds of Achaemenid plate and jewelry have been reported from illicit digging there. Outstanding among them are two inscribed foundation tablets, one of gold, one of silver, two lion-headed drinking vessels of gold and various bowls and dishes. The most famous surviving monument is a very battered stone lion, most probably carved at the orders of Alexander to commemorate his favorite, Hephaestion, who died at Hamadan, much to the King's great distress.

Of all surviving cities of this period in Iran, that at Dahan-i-Ghulaman (Gateway of Slaves) far away in eastern Iran – possibly Zarin the capital of ancient Drangiana – is the most obviously spectacular. It seems only to have been occupied for a relatively short period of time. Excavations have revealed, on a terrace 4 to 5 meters above the surrounding land, private houses with four oblong and four corner rooms set round a central hall or court, public buildings with porticoed courtyards and a unique religious building. This is of mudbrick with a single entrance to the south, away from the fierce prevailing winds. A central courtyard is flanked by four porticoes, each with a double row of square column bases and subsidiary altars and offering tables; staircases are set in square rooms at each corner. In the center of the court is a row of three rectangular altars, hollow inside and set on low pedestals approached by steps. Burnt animal bones may be the remnants of sacrifices conducted here.

It is, however, the sites of Pasargadae and Persepolis in the Persian homeland, the modern province of Fars, that epitomize for posterity the particular character and achievements of the Achaemenid monarchy. But even they are far from fully understood. Pasargadae, high on the Murgab plain, very cold in winter and often scorching in summer, was the capital established by Cyrus, the coronation city of the dynasty. If there were buildings at Pasargadae before about 550 BC they remain to be discovered. The existing remains are of a city largely constructed between about 546 and 530 BC, with parts left unfinished

Persepolis, where Darius moved the home of the Achaemenid dynasty. He and his successors were buried at or near this terrace.

when Cyrus suddenly died. Although Cyrus imported craftsmen from recently-conquered Ionia and Lydia in western Turkey to assist with the stone working, the overall character of the site, its design, layout and function, were part of a local Iranian tradition.

Despite a number of excavations the overall plan is still elusive. Dominating the site is a huge, unfinished stone platform of well-wrought ashlar masonry, intended no doubt to bear a royal palace but altered to take a less substantial building of mud-brick when Darius started his ambitious building program at Persepolis. Below this terrace, in an apparently random setting on the plain within a large walled area, may now be seen a very ruined tower, the enigmatic Zendan-i-Sulaiman, and three buildings set in carefully designed and watered gardens. One, a monumental gateway flanked by protective bull colossi in the Assyrian manner, contains the famous relief of a winged genius in a long robe wearing an elaborate Egyptian royal crown, once thought to represent Cyrus himself. Two palatial buildings with long porticoes have the character of pavilions, designed for leisurely strolling or sitting, overlooking gardens and pools that anticipate one of Persia's greatest legacies to civilization. Slightly detached, and standing in its own enclosure, is the rectangular stone tomb of Cyrus set up on a six-stepped plinth, a rosette carved high above the door at the gable peak. As with all the Achaemenid royal tombs, nothing of the burial has survived.

Persepolis. Cyrus or Cambyses may have built palaces in the plain at Persepolis, but it was Darius who began the more extensive development of the huge site. Although so often only remembered for the great terrace with its ceremonial buildings, Persepolis embraces a very much wider area still largely unexplored by excavation, in which the buildings on the terrace, known in antiquity as a "fortress," are but the best preserved. From the reign of Darius the Achaemenid kings were buried first in rock-cut tombs at Naqsh-i-Rustam, four miles northwest of the Persepolis terrace, then later in similar tombs cut in the rocky cliff behind the terrace. Facing the tombs at Naqsh-i-Rustam is a freestanding tower, the Ka'bah, exactly like the Zendan-i-Sulaiman at Pasargadae but better preserved. The function of these towers is debated, though a later, Sasanian inscription on the Ka'bah calls it a storehouse. They may then have been some kind of dynastic treasury, perhaps incorporating a shrine in memory of deceased members of the royal house.

Persepolis is only obliquely mentioned by Greek authors before the time of Alexander and played no obvious part in the politics or administration of the empire. It was never apparently a regular residence of the court for any length of time. Indeed after the first half of the 5th century BC when most of the buildings on the terrace were built, the Achaemenid kings added little to them. The city seems to have been reserved for annual festivities, rites and banquets

Baked clay head of a man wearing a fur-trimmed hat from excavations at Persepolis; possibly a Persian.

in honor of the royal house and its achievements, and for the royal burial ceremonies. Ingenious attempts to reconstruct these activities from the disposition of the terrace buildings and their sculptured reliefs are confounded by the sheer variety of explanations advanced. The rather cryptic contemporary building inscriptions offer no guide; even the names of the buildings and their functions are largely a matter of modern inference.

The heart of Persepolis is a rocky headland projecting into the plain from a range of low mountains. Darius encased this natural platform in a massive wall of well-wrought blocks, with a monumental approach by double flights of stairs on the western side looking out over the plain. Of the great mud-brick defensive wall that once ringed the terrace and ran up the mountain behind, and the similarly constructed walls of the buildings on the terrace, nothing now survives. What remains is a battered skeleton of stone columns, column bases and capitals, doorways and staircases with sculptured friezes. It requires a great exercise of the imagination to envisage the magnificent

134 | *The Persian Empire*

assembly of buildings, so opulently furnished, to which Alexander put a torch in 330 BC.

The nature of the site is best grasped by a rapid glance at its ground plan, always remembering that what is now revealed by excavation grew slowly over a number of years and probably does not represent the original design drafted by Darius and his architect. The buildings on the terrace, south of the great entrance portal, fall into two main groups, an eastern and a western one. The main gateway, with its monumental winged bull-guardians, bears an inscription of Xerxes: "By favor of Ahura-Mazda, this colonnade of All Lands I built. Much other good (construction) was built within Persepolis, which I built and which my father built." On the western side of the platform stands the great royal audience hall, the Apadana, with a series of private palaces and ancillary buildings, including the harem, behind it. Public access, always very restricted, was through a large triple gateway on the southeast of this group of buildings. On the eastern side, approached through an unfinished gateway and across a large courtyard, is the multi-columned "Throne Hall" with adjacent storerooms. In the southeast corner is a large, self-contained rectangular building, developed in stages, that accommodated the treasury, royal storehouses and armory in columned halls, rooms and porticoed courtyards. In the architectural details, Ionian Greek or Egyptian traits may be detected, but the predominance of columned rooms and multi-columned halls is derived from a Median architectural tradition.

The Apadana is a multi-columned building about 167 feet square. It has doorways in each wall, massive corner towers, porticoes on three sides, chambers on the fourth. Stairways lined with sculptured reliefs lead up to the porticoes on the north and east sides. Foundation boxes in the northeast and southeast corners of the hall each contained a thick sheet of gold and another of silver with trilingual inscriptions of Darius, in the cuneiform script, recording the extent of his realm. Work here was completed by Xerxes and Artaxerxes I. Existing remains give little idea of the original forest of columns, each 65 feet high, with their double bull-headed capitals, surrounded by massive mud-brick walls some 17 feet thick, plastered and painted. The timber roof beams inside would have been painted and the walls either draped with richly embroidered tapestries or painted. Here, as throughout Persepolis, the spectator today easily forgets that the rather dull gray of the stone (when it had not been polished), and the buff of the baked brick were once a riot of rich color. The great double-leaf wooden doors of the Apadana were lined with reliefs in gold and bronze.

The stairway reliefs of the Apadana, the most famous range of Achaemenid sculpture, depict representatives of 23 peoples of the Persian Empire bringing tribute to Darius, who was originally shown enthroned in the central panel with the crown prince Xerxes standing behind him. These panels were subsequently removed, for reasons unknown, perhaps under Artaxerxes I, to the "Treasury," where excavators found them. The present central panels on the Apadana stairways show confronted Median and Persian guards standing below the winged disk of Ahura-Mazda. In the original design the enthroned king and his heir were flanked by panels showing a lion attacking a bull, a very ancient motif long associated with monarchy. Its exact magical significance has been much debated; some give it an elaborate astronomical explanation, some see it as a warning that beyond this point only the privileged might go into the Great King's presence. Nor is it certain whether these reliefs show the order of events on a particular annual festival, perhaps at the New Year, or whether, following an age-old Near Eastern tradition, they were intended as a perpetual panorama of the empire – the Great King forever receiving homage and tribute. In the reliefs, which are more varied than a superficial glance at selected sections might suggest, appear the mustered files of Median and Persian guards through which the tribute bearers of many regions, from Arabia to Armenia, from the Danube to the Oxus, move in succession, headed by a Median delegation. Each delegation is distinguished by costume and to a lesser extent by the gifts it brings.

South of the Apadana is the Tachara, a small private palace of Darius, set on the highest part of the platform facing south. Along its lower southern facade and access stairs the lion and bull in conflict flank a procession of confronted guards. Up the side walls of the stairs carved servants take food into the palace. At the top, an entrance portico with two rows of four columns has guards carved on the door jambs leading to adjacent rooms. The jambs of the central door leading into the small central columned hall, with its highly polished masonry, are carved with standing figures of the king beneath a sunshade held by an attendant. One was labeled Darius in the garment folds, to the other the name of Xerxes, who completed the work here, was added. The royal hero killing a beast is carved on some inside door jambs – an apotropaic motif (for averting evil). On the door jambs of two private rooms on the northern side are shown in one case an attendant with unguent jar and towel, in the other an attendant with brazier and vessel. Elsewhere the king appears holding a scepter and flower-shaped pomander, followed by an attendant with a fly-whisk. Artaxerxes III added a staircase on the west side of this palace.

On the same level across at the southeast corner of the Apadana is the "Triple Portal." The walls of its smaller staircase are decorated with reliefs of servants carrying food and drink, just possibly for sacrifices, the larger with Median and Persian nobles and soldiers in processional friezes. Southwards are the remains of various palatial buildings, conspicuous among them the Palace of Xerxes. It is a larger version of the Tachara, decorated on door and window jambs with servants bearing food and equipment. This whole area is enclosed on the south and east by rows of identical storerooms.

Part of a 5th century BC silver drinking set which consists of bowl, ladle and juglet and is executed in the Greco-Persian style favored in the workshops of western Turkey.

Beyond a wall directly to the east of the Apadana lies the other large building on the terrace, the "Throne Hall" – perhaps better described as the "Hall of One Hundred Columns," as it is difficult to see how, through the numerous closely-set columns, a throne placed inside would be conspicuous to any but a small group of people. A foundation inscription records that it was begun by Xerxes and completed by Artaxerxes I. A long portico with a double row of columns, flanked by end walls with colossal bull statues, fronted the courtyard. The door jambs on the north and south sides show the king enthroned beneath a canopy and the winged disk of Ahura-Mazda. On the north doors five tiers of guards are shown, while on the south the ruler's throne is supported by representatives of the subject peoples, as on the royal tomb facades. On the eastern and western door jambs the royal hero drives his sword into the chests of various rampant beasts, real and imaginary. In the northeast corner of the terrace, in rooms in the fortification wall, was found a batch of clay tablets written in Elamite dealing with administrative transfers of food commodities in the years 509 to 494 BC. They apply to a large region extending to the south and well into Elam, though not normally including Susa. They treat equally the Elamite gods Humban and Shimut, the Persian Ahura-Mazda and Mithra, and the Semitic Adad.

In the southeast corner lies the "Treasury," with the reliefs moved from the Apadana. It was hereabouts that the excavators found in the debris left by Alexander's sack of 330 BC all that had survived of the Achaemenid kings' legendary hoards. Of precious metals there was virtually nothing; stone vases bearing the names of Egyptian pharaohs of an earlier age, of a Hittite king and of Ashurbanipal of Assyria may well have been looted long before Darius from the palaces of Assyrian kings in northern Iraq. Only a marble torso of a seated female figure was left as a reminder of loot from Greece. Stone dishes from the table services of Xerxes and various other pieces of equipment hardly match the splendor that astonished the Greeks. Here also was another group of tablets, this time dated between 492 and 458 BC, again in Elamite, recording issues of silver from the Persepolis treasury, chiefly in place of rations in kind, to various places in Persia. They show clearly the problems faced by an administration coping with a change from payments in goods to payments in cash.

Minor arts and crafts. As in the arts of government, in religion and the economy, in commerce and society, much craftsmanship in the provinces of the Achaemenid Empire went on as of old. Only slowly did fashions set by the opulent equipment of the Great King and his court begin to inspire local craftsmen working in such materials as base metal and pottery, instead of the original precious metals, glass and semi-precious stones so plentifully available to court artisans. Most of the surviving objects commonly called "Achaemenid" are in the international style developed under court patronage.

Men and women throughout the empire wore a rich variety of personal ornaments. The Persian troops, according to Herodotus, "glittered all over with gold, vast quantities of which they wore about their persons." Earrings, bracelets, anklets and neck-rings were distinguished by animal motifs, the terminals often cast as animal heads or bodies. Some were richly inlaid with colored stones or pastes. Achaemenid gold and silver plate was of legendary variety and splendor. Herodotus noted that after the Persian army's defeat at Plataea the camp contained "many gold bowls, goblets and other drinking vessels. On the carriages were bags containing gold and silver spouted vessels." Precious metals were given as tribute to the king, who also dispensed them to his aristocracy, to foreign guests and to ambassadors; in this, weight mattered as much as fine craftsmanship. Here again there was a marked taste for elaborate animal-shaped handles and spouts, for bowls and dishes with decoration inspired by the lotus flower or radiating rosettes. The distribution of such vessels is illustrated by identical silver bowls from Rhodes off the southern coast of Turkey and Kazbek in the Caucasus, decorated with S-spirals, each terminating in a bird's head. They may well have been produced in workshops in western Asia Minor, perhaps in Lydia, which was also making superb amphoras with animal handles like the one found in Bulgaria at Duvanli.

A whole range of metal shapes was also closely imitated in cut glass produced for a luxury market in satrapal courts across the empire, from Cyrenaica to Iran. Metal forms again influenced stone vessels, and pottery of great fineness was produced for rich customers. Distinctive Achaemenian "court style" designs may also be recognized on seals, both those shaped as cylinders for rolling an impression in the old Mesopotamian tradition, and those made to stamp an impression. Some of the silver tableware and stamp seals associated with satrapal courts in western Turkey show how profound an influence Greek styles exercised on workshops in that part of the Empire.

Conclusion. The collapse of the Persian Empire before Alexander's army marked the end of the traditional political and cultural boundaries in the Near East. Alexander's generals, though they divided up his vast domain, retained his ideal of fusing ancient eastern traditions with those of Greece. Absorption of Greek culture and Greek ways of thinking accompanied an influx of Greek traders and scholars, soldiers and adventurers, particularly in the Levant. In the "Biblical Lands" fresh seeds of political and religious conflict were sown – between the Jews and their Hellenized rulers; and in religion between those Jews who accepted the new world without compromising their old faith and those who were so seduced by its ways as to find their traditions an embarrassment. When the political and religious struggles were over, the religion known today as Judaism emerged, forged from the faith and historical experience this book has briefly surveyed.

Further Reading

CHAPTERS 1 AND 2

Aharoni, Y., *The Land of the Bible* (London, 1967).

Aharoni, Y. and **Avi-Yonah, M.,** *The Macmillan Bible Atlas* (London, 1968).

Glueck, N., *Rivers in the Desert* (London, 1959); *The River Jordan* (New York, 1968); *The Other Side of the Jordan* (Cambridge, Mass., 1970).

Kenyon, K. M., *Digging Up Jericho* (London, 1965).

May, H. G. (Ed.), *Oxford Bible Atlas* (Oxford, 1974).

Prescott, H. F. M., *Jerusalem Journey* (London, 1954); *Once to Sinai* (London, 1957).

Wheeler, M., *Walls of Jericho* (London, 1956).

Wheeler, R. E. M., *Archaeology from the Earth* (London, 1954).

Wilkinson, J., *Egeria's Travels* (London, 1971).

CHAPTERS 3 AND 5

Albright, W. F., *The Archaeology of Palestine* (3rd Edn, London, 1963).

Archaeological Institute of America (sponsors), *Archaeological Discoveries in the Holy Land* (New York, 1967).

Avi-Yonah, M., *The Holy Land* (London, 1972).

Bright, J., *A History of Israel* (2nd Edn, London, 1972).

Edwards, I. E. S. and others, *The Revised Cambridge Ancient History*, Vols I and II (1970–3).

Gray, J., *The Canaanites* (London, 1964).

Kenyon, K. M., *Archaeology in the Holy Land* (3rd Edn, London, 1970); *Jerusalem, excavating 3000 years of history* (London, 1967); *Royal Cities of the Old Testament* (London, 1971); *Digging Up Jerusalem* (London, 1974).

Lapp, P., *Biblical Archaeology and History* (Cleveland, Ohio, 1969).

Negev, A. (Ed.), *Archaeological Encyclopedia of the Holy Land* (London, 1972).

Pritchard, J. B., *Gibeon, where the sun stood still* (Princeton University Press, 1962); *The Ancient Near East in Pictures relating to the Old Testament* (with supplement; Princeton University Press, 1969); *Ancient Near Eastern Texts relating to the Old Testament* (3rd Edn with supplement, Princeton University Press, 1969).

de Vaux, R., *Ancient Israel: its Life and Institutions* (2nd Edn, London, 1965).

Winton Thomas, D. (Ed.), *Documents from Old Testament Times* (Oxford, 1958); *Archaeology and Old Testament Study* (Oxford, 1967).

Wiseman, D. J. (Ed.), *Peoples of Old Testament Times* (Oxford, 1973).

Wright, G. E., *Biblical Archaeology* (London, 1957); *Shechem: the Biography of a Biblical City* (London, 1965); (with **Fuller, R.**), *The Book of the Acts of God* (Penguin Books, 1965).

CHAPTER 4

Harden, D. B., *The Phoenicians* (London, 1962; revised Edn in Penguin Books).

Moscati, S., *The World of the Phoenicians* (London, 1968).

CHAPTER 6

Collins, R., *The Medes and Persians* (London, 1974).

Culican, W., *The Medes and Persians* (London, 1963).

Frye, R. N., *The Heritage of Persia* (London, 1963).

Ghirshman, R., *Persia from the Origins to Alexander the Great* (London, 1964).

Porada, E., *Ancient Iran* (London, 1965).

Wilber, D. N., *Persepolis* (London, 1969).

Acknowledgments

Unless otherwise stated all the illustrations on a given page are credited to the same source.

Ad Windig, Amsterdam 13, 16, 20, 31, 33, 38–39 (center), 45 (left), 56, 88 (top)

Professor Y. Aharoni, Institute of Archaeology, Tel Aviv University 86 (bottom)

American Numismatic Society, New York 129 (top)

Ashmolean Museum Oxford 22, 23 (bottom), 26 (top), 43 (left), 49, 59, 60, 61, 62, 63, 64, 71, 73, 74, 77 (top), 78, 81 (top), 84 (bottom), 85, 88 (bottom), 90 (bottom), 92, 101, 105 (bottom), 107, 117, 135

E. Böhm, Mainz 81 (bottom), 106, 108 (top), 108–9 (top), 111 (top), 112 (top), 122, 129 (bottom left), 130–131

Trustees of the British Museum, London 46 (right), 50 (top), 51 (right), 68, 69, 79 (bottom), 80, 89 (bottom left), 100 (top), 118, 119

Cleveland Museum of Art, Purchase, J. H. Wade Fund 75 (right)

Elsevier archives 2, 17 (top), 27, 47 (bottom), 51 (left), 70, 84 (top), 89 (bottom right), 95, 96, 98 (right), 102, 103, 105 (top), 114 (bottom), 124, 132

French Archaeological Institute, Beirut 67

Hatay Museum 44

A. A. M. van der Heyden, Amsterdam 9, 10, 11, 12 (top), 14 (bottom), 15, 17 (bottom), 19, 21, 24, 25, 30, 41, 46 (left), 47 (top), 83, 90 (top), 91, 93, 99, 121

Photo Hillel Burger, Jerusalem 39 (bottom)

Holle Bildarchiv, Baden-Baden 45 (right), 54, 55, 100 (bottom)

From the collections of the Israel Department of Antiquities and Museums, Jerusalem 65

Dr. V. Karageorghis, Director, Department of Antiquities, Nicosia, Cyprus 76

J. Koch, Lucerne 48

Mansell Collection 126–7

Musée du Louvre, cliché des Musées Nationaux 42, 72 (bottom), 98 (left), 120

Museo Nazionale, Naples 125

National Museum, Copenhagen 79 (top)

Negenman, Nijmegen, 16

Ny Carlsberg Glyptotek, Copenhagen 72 (top)

Oriental Institute, University of Chicago 108 (bottom), 109 (bottom), 111 (bottom), 112 (center and bottom), 113, 114 (top), 115, 116, 133

Palestine Exploration Fund, London 14 (top), 26 (bottom)

Paters Montfortanen, H. Landstichting, Nijmegen 57, 104

Radio Times Hulton Picture Library 23 (top)

Service de Documentation Photographique des Musées Nationaux, Versailles 53

D. Stronach, British Institute of Persian Studies, Teheran 129 (bottom right)

Walters Art Gallery, Baltimore 75 (left)

Prof. Y. Yadin 34, 37, 38 (top & bottom), 39 (top), 40, 97

Drawings on pages 35, 36, 52, 86, 87 and 89 are by John Hofer; those on pages 29, 50, 110 and 130 are by Oxford Illustrators.

The Publishers have attempted to observe the legal requirements with respect to the rights of the suppliers of photographic material. Nevertheless, persons who have claims to present are invited to apply to the Publishers.

The Publishers are grateful to the following for permission to quote copyright material: Dame Kathleen Kenyon, for a passage from her article in the "Palestine Exploration Quarterly" of 1939 (Ch. 2); The Loeb Classical Library (Harvard University Press: William Heinemann) for a passage from *Pliny's Natural History*, trans. H. Rackham, W. H. S. Jones & D. E. Eichholz (Ch. 4); Penguin Books Ltd for passages from Herodotus' *The Histories*, trans. Aubrey de Sélincourt (Ch. 4 & 6); passages from James B. Pritchard (ed.) *Ancient Near Eastern Texts Relating to the Old Testament*, 3rd rev. edn. with supplement, copyright © 1969, reprinted by permission of Princeton University Press (Ch. 1, 4 & 5).

Glossary

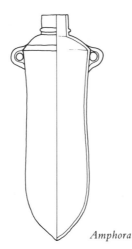

Amphora

Note: asterisks indicate separate entries on words thus marked

Adonis The Phoenician god of vegetation, his name was derived from the word for "lord." His life was symbolic of the natural life of vegetation – withering and dying in the heat of high summer and reviving in the spring. His death and survival were widely celebrated in the Lebanon, particularly by the River Adonis (modern Nahr Ibrahim), near Beirut. In Greek mythology both Aphrodite, goddess of Love, and Persephone, Queen of the Underworld, claimed him when he was killed boar-hunting. Zeus⋆ decreed that he should spend half the year with each – part on earth and part in the underworld.

Ahura-Mazda The name means "wise lord" in the Old Persian language. In the inscriptions of the Achaemenian Persian kings he is the supreme god – creator of the world, of men and of their peaceful prosperity. He is shown on sculptured reliefs in human form rising from a winged disk. He was the chief divinity in Zarathustra's teachings and his name is rendered in Persian as Ormuzd or Ormazd (*see* **Zoroastrianism**).

Albright, W. F. (1891–1971) The leading American Biblical scholar of his time. He was outstandingly versatile. As a distinguished linguist he made contributions to the study of ancient Egyptian, Akkadian, Ugaritic and other Semitic languages. His deep interest in the religion of Canaan and Israel was equally productive. In excavations at Tell Beit Mirsim between 1926 and 1932 he combined careful observation of succeeding occupation levels with a thorough study of the pottery each contained. The published results rapidly become a basic working tool for all Palestinian archaeologists.

Amphora A large baked-clay jar, usually tall and slender, with two shoulder handles, a tall narrow neck and a base tapering to a point. Designed for easy transport and storage both by land and sea, they normally carried liquids. Though more usually used to describe such jars in Graeco-Roman archaeology, the term is sometimes applied to similar vessels of earlier date. For administrative reasons an amphora could have inscriptions stamped on the handle denoting either the nature of the contents (as with a modern vintage mark on a wine bottle) or its destination.

Amulet A tiny object designed to give protection or to ward off evil. They were usually pierced to enable them to be suspended from a bracelet or necklace. Though not explicitly mentioned in the Old Testament, save perhaps at Isaiah 3:20, they are found everywhere in excavations. Variously made of stone, baked clay, metal, faience⋆, glass, bone and ivory, those found in Palestine and Syria are commonly Egyptian in style and inspiration. They mainly represent gods, animals, fruits, flowers and parts of the human body.

Antediluvian The term refers to the legendary time before the Flood recounted in Genesis and the literary tradition of the Sumerians in southern Iraq. The first fragment of the Babylonian flood legend was recognized inscribed on a clay tablet in the British Museum in 1872 by George Smith, who established its place in the great national Epic of Gilgamesh. In excavations at Nineveh he later found more pieces. He died prematurely at Aleppo in 1876 on his third expedition to the east.

Apis bull Worshiped at Memphis in Egypt from earliest times as the god of fertility. A representative bull was chosen by the priests of the cult, and for its lifetime received all the honors due to such a god. When this bull died it was mummified and buried with due ceremony, the date being carefully recorded.

Apotropaic motif Any picture or symbol believed by the person who drew or carved it to avert evil. The term apotropaic derives from a Greek verb meaning "to turn away." Modern "hippies" have adopted the ancient Egyptian "ankh" (life) sign for exactly these reasons (*see also* **amulet**).

Ark of the Covenant The wooden chest containing the stone tablets upon which were inscribed the Ten Commandments. They were given by Yahweh in Sinai to Moses with instructions for making the Ark in which they were to rest (Exodus 25:10ff). It was the most sacred religious object in Israel, eventually housed in the "Holy of Holies" of Solomon's Temple in Jerusalem. It disappeared forever in 586 BC, when the Babylonians sacked Jerusalem. It was regarded as a portable throne for the invisible presence of Yahweh.

Arrian: *History of Alexander* The most important source for the career of Alexander the Great, as earlier works are only known at second or third hand. Arrian (c. 95–175 AD) was a Greek and wrote in later middle age (c. 150 AD). He had read widely, including the books by Ptolemy (Alexander's friend from boyhood and after his death ruler of Egypt), Nearchus (a Cretan who had also known Alexander from boyhood and became his admiral), and Aristobulus (possibly an architect, who on Alexander's orders had repaired the tomb of Cyrus at Pasargadae). (Translation in Penguin Classics.)

Artifact Any object made by man for his own use.

Asherah The name both of a Canaanite (and Phoenician) goddess and of the cult⋆ object by which she was represented in shrines. Asherah, a mother-goddess, was worshiped under similar names in many parts of the Near East, but is best known from the Ras Shamra texts. In this city she was wife of the supreme god El⋆ and mother and counsellor of the other gods. She also had some special connection with the sea. The Old Testament does not always clearly distinguish between the goddess and her image. The latter was made of wood, but is nowhere described and has yet to be certainly identified in an excavation as wood usually decays completely. It was a man-made object (not a growing tree), stood vertically, and may have carried some features of the goddess. It stood near an altar.

Ashlar masonry This consists of square cut stones laid regularly either as a wall in itself or as the facing for a rubble or brick-built wall.

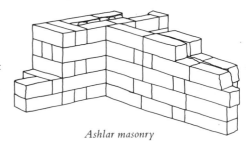

Ashlar masonry

Astarte The Greek name for the Canaanite (and Phoenician) fertility goddess rendered Ashtoreth in Hebrew. Like her Babylonian counterpart Ishtar she had some connection with the stars. In the Ras Shamra texts she is regularly associated with Baal★. In art she was commonly shown nude, sometimes with a lion's head or standing on a lion, and flanked by flowers or snakes. Numerous baked clay statuettes and relief plaques from excavations in Palestine and Syria showing such figures are believed to portray her (Astarte plaques). They are found in both houses and temples and were meant to invoke the help and protection of the most popular of goddesses. There are more precious representations in molded glass, silver and gold.

Baal The name means "master." He was the chief fertility god of Canaan and Phoenicia, associated particularly with winter rain and storm. The Ras Shamra texts include many nature myths involving him. His cult animal was the bull, whose horns adorned his helmet. He was called "he who mounts the clouds," strongly reminiscent of the description of Yahweh in Deuteronomy "riding the clouds in his glory" (33:26). He is commonly thought to be represented on a stela★ from Ras Shamra showing a helmeted warrior in a kilt, striding forward with a thunderbolt as a spear and carrying a mace. Many uninscribed copper and bronze statuettes of warrior gods from excavations in Palestine and Syria probably represent him.

Babel, Tower of The great ziggurat★ of the temple of the god Marduk★ in Babylon (Babel) in Iraq. It is described by the Greek historian Herodotus★ as having six stages of decreasing size set one on top of the other, crowned by a small temple approached by a spiral staircase. The ground plan was recovered by the German excavators of Babylon, but its exact form is still doubtful. Genesis 11:1–9, with the story of God's confusion of languages, involves a wordplay on the place-name "Babel" and the Hebrew word "*bālāl*" (to mix).

Bamah A Hebrew word used for places of worship on natural hills, or for the variously sized mounds of stones built in temples, as at Megiddo, to simulate them (*see also* **High place**).

Bedouin The desert-dwelling nomads of the Near East, who now account for about a tenth of the area's population, though under ever increased pressure to settle permanently. Their chief means of livelihood depends on herding sheep and goats assisted by asses, horses or, in modern times, camels. They live in tents and have a regular pattern of movement in autumn, winter and spring, camping more permanently in summer where water is available. They are grouped in tribes under autocratic sheikhs. Much has been learned of the way of life of such people

in antiquity, long before their almost universal adoption of the Moslem religion, from the baked clay tablets found in a palace of the 18th century BC at Mari in Syria (*see also* **Parrot**).

Bes Represented as a bandy-legged dwarf with broad face, protruding tongue, a beard like a lion's mane and animal ears and tail, he was the primary domestic god of ancient Egypt. He was supposed to contribute to the happiness and well-being of the household, dancing to amuse the gods. The figure of Bes or his grotesque, smiling face regularly decorated furniture, cosmetic equipment and jewelry. He was widely adopted in the Near East outside Egypt, but is often represented in fresh ways which suggest that his character may have been modified as he traveled outside the immediate sphere of Egyptian religion.

Betyl The word comes from the Greek *baitylos*, and means specifically a meteoric stone, held to be sacred because it fell from heaven. The term is used loosely by archaeologists to describe conical stones set on altars shown in ancient pictures of Phoenician temples. Actual surviving examples have yet to be confidently identified.

Bliss, F. J. The eldest son of Daniel Bliss, founder in 1866 of the Syrian Protestant College, now the American University of Beirut. He suffered from lifelong ill health and never engaged in a regular profession. He excavated at Tell el-Hesi, first with Petrie★ and then alone (1891–2), at Jerusalem with A. C. Dickie (1894–7), and on a number of tells★ in the Shephelah with Macalister★ as his assistant (1898–1900). He excavated to the best standards of his day and published promptly. His book *Development of Palestine Exploration* (London, 1906) remains the basic survey up to 1903, when the lectures on which it is based were given.

Breydenbach: *Peregrinationes* (Mainz, 1486) An early and finely printed illustrated book, with colored woodcuts representing various places on the way to the Holy Land, and some of the peoples to be found there. The text was largely written by a certain Friar Martin Roth, who had not made the journey, and illustrated by Erhard Reuwich, an artist who had accompanied the nominal author on his pilgrimage in 1483. It is typical of the many standard pilgrim accounts, though it devotes an exceptional amount of space to challenging the beliefs of Moslems, Jews and Christian heretics. (No modern edition.)

Burdett Coutts, Angela, Baroness (1814–1906) In 1837 she inherited the main share in the great London Bank of Coutts from her

step-grandmother, to become "the richest heiress in all England." She refused all offers of marriage until 1881, including one, it is said, from the aged Duke of Wellington, and then happily married a much younger American. Throughout her life she entertained numerous friends in all ranks of society and devoted her vast fortune, which she managed personally, to charitable causes all over the world. She was particularly devoted to the Church of England and its international interests, but was not doctrinaire, and her concern for Jerusalem sprang directly from this.

Capital The upper part of a column or pillar used to support the superstructure of buildings. They were often highly decorated, as in the three "orders" of classical architecture: Doric, Ionic and Corinthian. In the ancient Near East, with such rare exceptions as the great double-bull capitals of Persepolis, they were not so elaborate. In Iron Age Palestine they had simple volute decoration based on a palm-tree motif earlier used in Canaanite art.

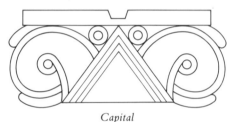

Capital

Cartouche An oval-shaped bracket with a bar across one end used to enclose, and thus emphasize, the hieroglyphs which rendered the main elements in the names of ancient Egyptian kings. In its earliest and most pictorial form it shows a double thickness of rope with knotted ends. It symbolized royal power over all "which is encircled by the sun." Phoenician craftsmen borrowed it as a decorative motif, often putting meaningless but picturesque Egyptian hieroglyphs inside it.

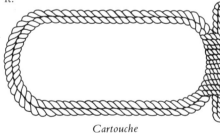

Cartouche

Casemate wall A wall consisting of two parallel outer faces, divided up inside by cross walls to form chambers within the thickness of the wall. A feature of Iron Age fortifications in Palestine.

Casemate Wall

Chateaubriand, F-R (1768-1848) The great French writer, who himself divided his life into three parts: Traveler and Soldier, Man of Letters and Man of Action. He lived through, and participated in, the most vital period of modern French history as ambassador and political publicist. The journey which produced his *Itinéraire de Paris à Jérusalem*, written between 1809 and 1811, was hurried, and the book not one of his best, but it is very typical of the attitudes of his time. His masterpiece is the autobiographical *Mémoires d'Outre-Tombe*, in which by skilful selection he created the work of art he had vainly striven to make out of real life.

Clermont-Ganneau, Charles (1846-1923) One of the greatest French scholars of his day. Palestine (for long his home) was his main interest, but he traveled widely, studying the antiquities of Phoenicia (1881), the Red Sea area (1886), Cyrenaica and Crete (1895) and Egypt (1906-7, 1907-8). He recovered the stela★ of Mesha, King of Moab for the Louvre in Paris, as well as numerous other antiquities. He was a pupil of Renan★ and in time as influential a teacher as his master. His publications were numerous and wide-ranging, marked by great insight and originality, whether in the treatment of the archaeology, history, art or languages of the ancient Levant.

Constantinople: Imperial Ottoman Museum (*See* **Istanbul: Archaeological Museum.**)

Corbeled vault A method of roofing in stone or mudbrick, whereby the courses laid on each side of a room or passageway are set so that each one extends beyond the one beneath it. Thus they gradually form a bridge across the void that can easily be closed at the top by a single, relatively small slab. It was commonly used before the discovery of the true vault.

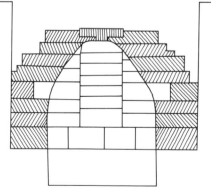

Corbeled vault

Crimean War (1853-6) Waged by Britain, France, Turkey, and later Sardinia on one side, against Russia, who was hoping to expand through the Dardanelles to ports on the Mediterranean at the expense of the weak Turkish Empire. She also claimed to be protecting Christianity in the Turkish Empire, including the Holy Places of Palestine then controlled by Turkey. After much confused and inept fighting in the Crimea, peace was made in 1856, confining Russia to the Black Sea. The War aroused great public interest in England and directed attention to the decayed state of the Holy Places.

Ctesias A Greek doctor from western Turkey who, in the early part of the 4th century BC, lived at the court of the Persian King Artaxerxes II. He wrote a history of Persia (*Persica*) in 23 sections, of which only a small part has survived in extracts made by later authors. Ctesias has been accounted unreliable, but this may be largely due to the butchered way in which his work has come down to us. (No modern edition in English.)

Cubit A unit of measurement, of about 48 centimeters (18 inches) or slightly more, based on the distance from the elbow to the tip of the middle finger.

Cult Any system of religious worship. When used as an adjective by archaeologists it refers to any object used in religious ceremonies.

Cuneiform script

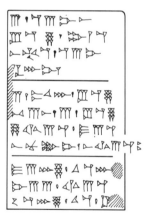

Cuneiform script The wedge-shaped writing system originally developed (from c. 3000 BC) by the Sumerians of southern Iraq to write on clay tablets. It was later adapted for writing a number of languages, notably Akkadian, spoken by the earliest Semitic inhabitants of Iraq, and then used as the international diplomatic language of the Near East until superseded by Aramaic under the Persian Empire. At Ras Shamra the script was specially modified to write the Ugaritic alphabet, and in Persia to write Old Persian and Elamite.

Curzon: *Visits to Monasteries in the Levant* (1849) An account of travels in Egypt, Palestine and Greece between 1833 and 1838. Save for his journeys as a young man, the Hon. Robert Curzon (1810-70), lived the retired life of a Victorian country gentleman. He was a great collector of books and visited the monasteries of the Near East to obtain the rare manuscripts their libraries still contained. His superb collection was bequeathed to the British Museum in 1921. His book is one of the most spirited and witty accounts of Near Eastern travel ever written, greatly enriched by a variety of highly entertaining stories and anecdotes. Curzon had a sharp eye and keen ear, conveying with simple directness in an easy literary style the character of Oriental life as he saw it. (Reprinted by Arthur Barker Ltd, London 1955.)

Cyclopean masonry Huge, often untrimmed stones, set one on top of the other, and not usually bound together by any form of cement.

Cyrus Cylinder A solid, barrel-shaped object of baked clay about 23 centimeters long from Babylon in Iraq, now in the British Museum. It is inscribed in cuneiform script with a text of Cyrus the Great, King of Persia (c. 550-529 BC). It originally formed part of a foundation deposit in a major building. It describes how the god Marduk★ rejected Nabonidus, King of Babylon, for impious behavior and appointed Cyrus to replace him in 539 BC, when Babylon surrendered peacefully to the Persian invaders. The inscription goes on to describe the new policy of religious tolerance introduced by Cyrus.

Dagon A god especially associated with the Philistines. The "Ark of the Covenant"★ was deposited in his temple at Ashdod when captured by the Philistines. Much earlier he was well known among the Amorites of Mesopotamia, and had a temple at Ras Shamra matching in size that of Baal, with whose cult he was closely associated. His role as a vegetation god is marked by the probable derivation of his name from the Semitic common noun for "corn."

Daric A Persian gold coin commonly said to take its name from the Persian King Darius I (c. 522-485 BC). In the Bible it is not only the first coin mentioned, but also a general term for a gold coin, both under Cyrus and even under King David, long before the introduction of coinage. This may support the view that the name in fact derives from the Akkadian words (*darag mana*) for one sixtieth of a mina, a standard unit of weight in Iraq.

Darwin, Charles: *On The Origin of Species* (1859) A landmark in the history of biology and one of the most controversial books of the 19th century in Christian eyes. In a detailed and carefully mustered argument,

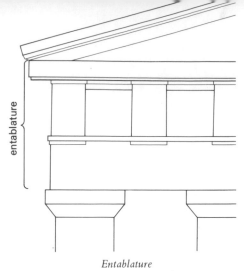

Entablature

supported by a mass of evidence, Darwin demonstrated and explained the theory of evolution in nature through "the survival of the fittest" (in T. H. Huxley's famous phrase). The whole Darwinian theory denied any sudden creation of man and therefore any literal interpretation of the fall of man, with momentous consequences for theologians. As a reaction increased interest was shown in Palestinian archaeology by Christians seeking to undermine Darwin's theory. (Available in the Everyman Library and many other editions.)

Diodorus Siculus: *World History* This work covered the history of the world from mythical times to Caesar's conquest of Gaul. The author was a contemporary of Julius Caesar in the first century BC. Only 15 of the 40 books comprising the *History*, written in Greek, have survived. They cover the crucial period c. 480 to 323 BC, during the Persian supremacy. Diodorus abbreviated original histories in a haphazard fashion and selected events more for their moral lessons than for their historical significance. (Translation available in the Loeb Classical Library.)

Egeria A female pilgrim who visited the Holy Land between about 381 and 384 AD, and wrote an account of her journey which only survives in part. Nothing is known of her save the facts that emerge in her writing. She was an enthusiastic Christian tourist, little concerned with anything that did not increase her understanding of the gospel. She wrote a rather conversational Latin. (*Egeria's Travels* translated by J. Wilkinson, London, 1971.)

El The primary Semitic word for "god," describing the divine power that inspires men with awe and dread as in the Old Testament story of Jacob's dream (Genesis 28:17). In the Ras Shamra texts El appears as the supreme god, father of all the gods, lord of heaven and storm. He is called "the Father of Men," or "the Bull," signifying both his creative and his majestic roles. His authority also had moral force, for he was "the Kindly, the Merciful."

Entablature A term used primarily in descriptions of Greek and Roman architecture to denote the horizontal elements in a building which rest on the columns and support the actual roof.

Eshmun The god of the city of Sidon in Phoenicia. In origin a fertility god, he also presided over health and healing like the Greek god Asklepios with whom he was subsequently identified. He was also much revered at Carthage, where the last defenders of the city against the final Roman attack of 146 BC are said to have burned themselves alive in his temple rather than surrender.

Eusebius: *Onomasticon* A geographical dictionary of Biblical place-names consisting of short articles mentioning the historical events for which the place was famed and in certain cases proposing identifications with actual sites. It was compiled by Eusebius, Bishop of Caesarea, who lived about 260 to 340 AD and is known as "the Father of Christian History." It was later translated from Greek into Latin, and amplified, by St Jerome (c. 342 to 420 AD), who is better known for his translation of the Old Testament from Hebrew into Latin. Despite its errors the *Onomasticon* has been fundamental to all modern study of the historical geography of Palestine. (No modern edition.)

Faience An artificial material consisting basically of powdered quartz covered by a vitreous, alkaline glaze varying in color. It was widely used for the manufacture of beads, amulets and small vases, particularly in Egypt.

Fellahin The country people of Egypt – "the agriculturalists." When the Turks ruled Egypt the name was used as an abusive term to describe Egyptians in general.

Fisher, C. S. (1876-1941) He graduated from the University of Philadelphia (his birthplace) as an architect, but became interested in archaeology and spent most of his life in active fieldwork in Iraq, Egypt, Palestine and Jordan. In Palestine he worked at Samaria, Beth-Shan, Megiddo and Beth-Shemesh. His fine draughtsmanship and mastery of informal teaching, supported by increasingly varied experience, contributed a great deal to the development of American excavations in the Near East.

Flaubert: *Salammbo* (1862) A conscious attempt by one of the greatest of French novelists to evoke the atmosphere of life in ancient Carthage, and its life-and-death struggle with Rome. In 1849 Flaubert visited Egypt and Syria, and in 1858 he went to Carthage. He then made an extensive study of archaeological and historical sources. In the

novel, as in the best richly colored film epics, he recreated vividly, credibly and sympathetically, with a masterly handling of crowd and battle scenes, the city and its struggle for survival. (Translation in Everyman Library.)

Foundation trench A trench cut into the subsoil by the builders of a wall, and into which its foundations are set. It is important for an archaeologist to recognize such a trench and to isolate the sherds of pottery or small finds from it, for they are vital to dating the construction of the wall and building of which it formed a crucial part.

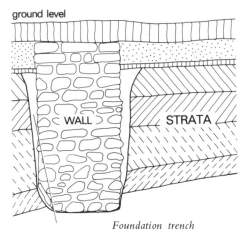

Foundation trench

Frit An artificial compound made by heating together silica, a copper compound (generally malachite) as colorant, calcium carbonate and natron (salt). It was widely used in the Near East as a pigment, most commonly blue.

Gardiner, Sir Alan (1879-1963) The leading British Egyptologist of his day. He had sufficient private means to enable him to devote his life entirely to the study of the ancient Egyptian language. In a long life of thorough and systematic work he published many basic texts, as well as a monumental *Egyptian Grammar*. His most significant discovery was the recognition of a link between the Egyptian hieroglyphic script and the Semitic alphabets through the inscriptions incised on rocks in Sinai by Semitic labourers employed there by the Egyptians as miners.

Garstang, John (1876-1956) Most widely known for his excavations at Jericho between 1930 and 1936. In 1920 he became Director of the British School of Archaeology in Jerusalem and first Director of Antiquities, creating the Department of Antiquities for the British Mandate government. After World War II he became the first Director of the British Institute of Archaeology at Ankara in Turkey – a country with which he had long been associated. His books *The Land of the Hittites* (1910) and *The Hittite Empire* (1929) were pioneering works of enduring value.

Glueck, Nelson (1900–71) An outstanding teacher, administrator and archaeologist, he was a pupil of Albright★ and for many years the most active exponent of his teacher's discoveries in the chronology of Palestinian pottery. He conducted extensive surveys in Transjordan and the Negev, using the pottery he found on the surface to date the main periods of settlement in these regions. At Tell el-Kheleifeh, thought by some to be Solomon's port of Ezion-geber, he found an Iron Age fortress in excavations. His excavations at Khirbet et-Tannur in Jordan revealed a wealth of information about the Nabataeans – a people who, with their capital at Petra, controlled the rich caravan trade from Arabia in the time of Christ.

Granulated decoration A jeweler's technique. Minute grains of gold or silver are soldered in patterns onto strips of sheet metal. A similar technique using wire instead of granules is known as *filigree*.

Hadad The Amorite god of winter rain and storms, later referred to as Baal★.

Herodotus: *Histories* Written, according to the author, "that the great deeds of men may not be forgotten . . . and especially the causes of war between them." It has earned him the posthumous title "Father of History." He was born between 490 and 480 BC in Halicarnassus in southwestern Turkey, and died in Italy in 425 BC. As a young man he traveled widely in Egypt and the Near East, and his comments on countries in the Persian Empire and their history are of outstanding importance to modern scholars. (Translation in Penguin Classics.)

High place The general rendering of the Hebrew *bamah*★.

Holy of Holies The name originally referred specifically to the innermost room of the tented tabernacle in which the Ark of the Covenant★ was kept during travels in the wilderness. Later it described the innermost room (*debir*) of Solomon's Temple in Jerusalem, serving the same purpose. It was a cube about 20 cubits★ each way. Apart from the Ark, it contained two olive wood cherubims whose wings reached from wall to wall.

Homer: see *Iliad* and *Odyssey*.

Iliad An epic poem by the ancient Greek poet Homer, whose identity and career are still much debated. He probably lived in one of the Greek cities of western Turkey about 700 BC. The poem's title is derived from Ilion, the city of Troy in northwest Turkey. It recounts the events of four crucial days in the tenth and final year of the siege of Troy by the Greeks under their leader Agamemnon about 1200 BC. But its themes are far more universal, and its details a rich (if at times disputed) source of valuable information for archaeologists. (Translation in Penguin Classics.)

Istanbul, Archaeological Museum Until World War I much of the Near East formed part of the Turkish Empire ruled by the sultan from Istanbul. Official excavations were carried out with his permission, and finds went to the major museum of the Empire in Istanbul, where they remain.

Kenyon, Dame K. M. Renowned for her excavations at Jericho (1952–8) and Jerusalem (1961–7), she was formerly lecturer in Palestinian Archaeology in London University (1948–62) and Principal of St Hugh's College, Oxford (1962–73). In 1931–4, as a member of the British expedition to Samaria, she helped to introduce the careful methods of digging and recording perfected with Mortimer Wheeler★, with whom she was then also cooperating in excavations at St Albans (Verulamium) in England. Later, by cutting massive trenches deep into the mound at Jericho and into the precipitous slopes of Ophel at Jerusalem, she was able to correct previous errors of interpretation and add enormously to knowledge of both cities. In a number of books (see Further Reading here) she has made her findings widely available to the general reader.

Kinglake: *Eothen* (1844) The account of a journey made in 1834–5 through the Turkish Empire by A. W. Kinglake (1809–91), a lawyer and member of Parliament, who was later to write the standard history of the Crimean War★. *Eothen* is no ordinary travel book filled with facts and information. The title is a Greek word meaning "from the early dawn" (ie from the East). The book was designed as a pattern of impressions and anecdotes which would evoke in a reader's mind the special character of the Near East and its people as Kinglake saw them. The great Arabian traveler (Sir) Richard Burton called it "that book of books," and it remains to this day the finest introduction to the Near East in English. (Various editions: Dent, London, 1954; edited R. Fedden, Methuen, London 1948.)

Kronos The youngest son of Heaven and Earth in Greek mythology and leader of his brothers the Titans. He married his sister and proceeded to swallow all their offspring save Zeus, who escaped by a trick. He was later forced to disgorge the rest and was overcome by them in a great struggle. His rather grim and, some scholars argue, untypically Greek character has led him to be attributed to the older mythology of Turkey. He was identified with particularly formidable gods encountered by the Greeks in other religions of the Levant.

Lapis lazuli A semi-precious stone of bright, deep blue color, often flecked with gold, much prized in antiquity for decorative purposes. Chemically it is a complex silicate containing sulphur. It is a relatively rare stone, and its primary source in the ancient Near East and Egypt lay in the area of Badakhshan, deep in the mountains of modern Afghanistan. It had consequently to be transported over great distances and was a highly valued commodity, which the Egyptians became very skilful at imitating in faience and glass.

Lapis specularis Specular stone – a type of mica or talc. It is transparent or semi-transparent and was used as glass or for ornamental purposes.

Layard, Austen Henry (1817–94) One of the most brilliant and controversial figures of Victorian England – pioneer archaeologist, member of Parliament and government minister, diplomat and ambassador, art-historian and author. In two enduringly readable books, *Nineveh and its Remains* (1849) (referring in fact to ancient Nimrud) and *Nineveh and Babylon* (1853), he recounted the pioneer excavations he conducted in Iraq between 1845 and 1852 that made him world famous. At Nimrud and Nineveh he explored the palaces of the great Assyrian kings (about 880 to 650 BC) with their monumental sculptured reliefs, their carved ivory furniture inlays and their richly varied metalwork. There and in southern Iraq he recovered many inscribed tablets giving valuable impetus to the currently developing science of Assyriology. Nothing in his ensuing stormy political and diplomatic career was ever to match this achievement, which revealed his great energy, enterprise and sense of adventure as well as an unusual talent for writing about his work.

Lear, Edward (1812–88) Renowned throughout the English-speaking world as a writer of nonsense verse and limericks. It is sometimes forgotten that this strange, melancholy man was an inveterate traveler, and produced some memorable watercolors (and subsequently oil paintings) of the landscapes through which he passed. He went to Egypt a number of times, to Palestine and Syria in 1858 and again briefly in 1867. He regularly published illustrated journals of his travels in Greece and Italy, but his Near Eastern drawings were not reproduced in this way and are still not as well known as they deserve.

Macalister, R. A. S. (1870–1950) Director of excavations for the Palestine Exploration Fund in 1900–9 and 1923–4, working at Gezer (where his major contribution to Palestinian archaeology was made) and Jerusalem. He was best known in his time as an authority on Celtic languages and the Ogam script, serving from 1909 to 1943 as Professor of Celtic Archaeology in University College, Dublin, the city of his birth.

Marduk The name of the state god of Babylon, rendered in Hebrew as Merodach. He was the supreme creator god.

Massebah (plural *masseboth*) A Hebrew word adopted by archaeologists to describe vertical stones, usually monoliths, thought to have been set up as memorials or objects of worship.

Maundrell, H. *A Journey from Aleppo to Jerusalem . . .* This work recounts a journey made between February and March 1697 by Henry Maundrell (1665–1701), chaplain to the Levant Company at Aleppo in Syria, with fourteen male companions. Although originally written for private circulation, his account was published two years after his death and remained for 150 years the most popular guide to the more accessible parts of Syria and Palestine. It is one of the first careful accounts in English of the antiquities of the area. As Curzon★ aptly remarked in 1849, when it was being superseded by more popular literary works, "he tells us plainly and clearly what he saw . . . whilst other travellers . . . describe only what they think about it." (Reissued by Khayats of Beirut, 1963.)

Melkart The chief god of Tyre and, because of Tyre's predominance, chief god also of the Phoenicians. The name means "ruler of the city." In origin a sun god, he also acquired a close association with the sea and was particularly popular at Carthage and in the western colonies. The Greeks identified him with Heracles.

Molk (Moloch) A deity to whom human sacrifices were offered, particularly in the Valley of Hinnom, near Jerusalem (II Kings 23:10). In origin he was the national god of Ammon in Transjordan. It has also been argued that no specific god is referred to in the Bible and the relevant phrase should be translated "for an offering;" thus "so that no one might make his son or daughter pass through the fire *in honor of Moloch/* . . . pass through the fire *for an offering.*"

Morrison: *The Recovery of Jerusalem* (1871) The first major attempt to popularize the work of the Palestine Exploration Fund in Jerusalem, edited by Walter Morrison, member of Parliament, the Fund's Honorary Treasurer. It consists very largely of Warren's★ account of his work in the City. Though not as enthralling or well-written as Layard's★ accounts of his excavations in Iraq, Warren's "plain and unadorned" style exactly matches the rigors of his work, and his account is no less impressive as the record of pioneer excavations under the most trying and dangerous conditions.

Mummy From the Arabic, the word means an embalmed body, most commonly applied to those from ancient Egypt. This method was used for burying Joseph (Genesis 50:26). There is no ancient Egyptian account of the methods used in mummification, but many actual mummies have survived, and examination has shown that techniques, developed from period to period, varied with social class. They consisted essentially of removing the internal parts most likely to decompose and soaking the rest in natron (salt) before impregnating it with oils and resins.

Obelisk An architectural term applied to a tapering shaft of stone, often cut in one piece, of square or rectangular section with a pointed top in the form of a pyramid. They were most commonly used in ancient Egyptian temple architecture. The popularly named "Cleopatra's Needle" on the London Embankment is a typical example of an obelisk.

Obsidian A dark, vitreous stone, similar to bottle-glass, of volcanic origin. It was widely traded in the ancient Near East in prehistoric times from sources in eastern Turkey. It was worked like flint to form keen-edged tools, or else chipped and polished to serve as decorative inlays. Egypt had her own sources of supply.

Odyssey An epic poem by the ancient Greek poet Homer (*see* **Iliad**), recounting the return of Odysseus, son of the King of Ithaca in Greece, from Troy after the Trojan War, and the vengeance he took on the suitors of his wife Penelope. Like the *Iliad* it contains many details of interest to archaeologists. (Translation in Penguin Classics.)

Ossuary A receptacle for the bones of the dead. The term is usually applied by archaeologists to small, chest-like containers carved from such soft rocks as limestone. It may also be applied to a cave or charnel-house in which the bones of many skeletons have been deposited together.

Ostrakon The word means a potsherd in Greek, and is used by archaeologists to describe any fragment of pottery, bone or stone used for writing on. As papyrus was expensive, potsherds were commonly used both in Egypt and Palestine for everyday administrative purposes and for exercises by student scribes. They could only be used for the cursive forms of Egyptian hieroglyphic script and for the Canaanite and Hebrew alphabets, and not for cuneiform script.

Palestine Exploration Fund It was founded at a meeting in May 1865, with the purpose of "investigating the archaeology, geography, geology and natural history of Palestine." At a public meeting in June 1865, where the Fund was formally established, three basic principles were adopted:
1 whatever was undertaken should be carried out on scientific principles;
2 the Society should, as a body, abstain from controversy;
3 it should not be started, nor should it be conducted, as a religious society.
On these principles it continues, publishing the results of researches regularly in the "Palestine Exploration Quarterly."

Pantheon This means specifically a temple dedicated to all the gods, but has been more generally adopted by ancient historians to describe the whole range of gods among any particular people. The word is of Greek origin.

Parrot, André Honorary Director of the Louvre, he is renowned for his long series of excavations since 1933 at ancient Mari on the river Euphrates in Syria, and for a number of books on ancient Near Eastern art and archaeology. Although the architectural remains at Mari are varied and interesting, it is the numerous inscribed baked-clay tablets from an 18th century BC palace that have done so much to increase modern knowledge of the Western Semitic peoples at this time – the Patriarchal Age.

Pectoral An ornamental breastplate or broad necklace extending down onto the chest.

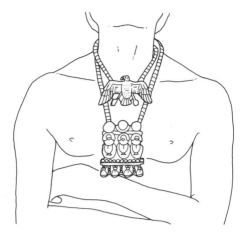

Pectoral

Petrie, Sir W. M. F. (1853–1942) He introduced scientific field archaeology to Egypt, and in numerous excavations and publications laid the foundations for all modern study of ancient Egyptian archaeology. Early in his career, at Tell el-Hesi (1890), and for a few years towards the end of it, at Tell Jemmeh (1926–7), Tell Farah (South) and Ajjul (1930–4), Petrie abandoned Egypt for Palestine. Although his work there was not as successful as his work in Egypt, the resultant publications have an honorable place in the study of Palestinian archaeology, and his collection of Palestinian antiquities, now in the Institute of Archaeology in London University, is invaluable for teaching and study.

Pictographic script This basically means any writing with pictures. Such drawings are designed to communicate a certain message in a way that will be immediately understood by the people for whom they are intended. Unlike other drawings they have no aesthetic purpose, and are distinguished by stereotyped execution and omission of details. In time they are formalized into linear symbols which bear only the most distant relation to their pictorial ancestors. The Egyptian hieroglyphic script is the best known example of a very sophisticated "pictographic" system of writing.

Plastered slope Also known as glacis fortification, this was a method of defending cities adopted in Palestine and Syria in the first half of the second millennium BC. It was a defence in depth consisting of an enormous rubble rampart with sloping face covered by a thick layer of plaster, on the summit of which the town wall was built. Such defences were probably designed as protection against battering rams.

Plutarch: *Lives* A description of twenty-three "pairs" of lives, and four single, written by the Greek philosopher Plutarch (c. 46–120 AD). The "Parallel Lives" set the life of an eminent Greek side by side with that of an eminent Roman, offering points of comparison between the two to bring out their moral character. It is valuable to modern scholars for the author's careful choice and honest use of his historical sources, many no longer extant. The famous English translation by Sir Thomas North (1579) was closely followed by Shakespeare in his three Roman plays.

Pococke: *A Description of the East* (1743–5) This work draws upon travels in Egypt, Palestine, Syria and Cyprus between 1737 and 1740. It has no literary pretensions, but is written by an industrious and well-informed young man with wide sympathies and a clear eye. He was primarily interested in archaeology and drew what he saw with unusual accuracy. (No modern edition.)

Postern gate A small or concealed entrance to a city or fortress.

Pritchard, J. B. Long associated with the University Museum at Philadelphia, he is best known for his excavations at el-Jib (Gibeon) and Tell es-Sa'idiyeh in Palestine, and at Sarafend (ancient Sarepta) in Phoenicia, south of Sidon. His popular book on Gibeon and his editing of major volumes of texts and pictures illustrating the contributions of Near Eastern archaeology to Biblical studies are among the best of their kind now available (*see* Further Reading).

Pylon An architectural term for a monumental gateway to an Egyptian temple, composed of two massive blocks of masonry

Pictographic script

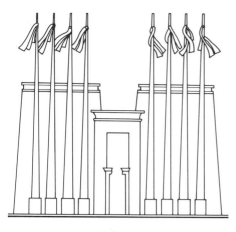

Pylon

with inclined walls joined by a doorway whose coping is at a level about half their height. They were usually decorated with tall, wooden poles from the top of which floated pennants and flags.

Quaresmio, Francesco: *Historia Theologica et Moralis* (1639) A massive compendium of information, with finely engraved pictures and plans, which may be judged the last major work on the Holy Land written in the medieval scholastic tradition. In eight detailed major sections it describes in turn the Holy Land, its sects and religious orders, the nature of pilgrimage and the various stages of the major routes of pilgrimage. The author made only restricted use of his own experience as a traveler. (No modern edition.)

Reisner, George (1867–1942) One of the outstanding American Egyptologists of his time. He dug briefly in Palestine from 1909–10 as Director of the Harvard Excavations at Samaria. His work was always meticulous and thorough, and his excavation reports, when completed, monumental. His most famous discovery was the tomb of Queen Hetep-Heres at Giza in Egypt (c. 2550 BC) in 1925, which aroused almost as much interest as that of Tutankhamun found less than three years earlier.

Reland, A.: *Palestine Illustrated by Ancient Monuments* (1714) Described by Robinson* as "next to the Bible the most important book for travelers in Palestine." It assembled for the first time, in Latin, as much relevant information as possible about ancient Palestine, assessing it critically. But naturally it only reached a very restricted public and, as the author had no personal experience to draw on, never had an impact on Biblical studies equal to Robinson's work just over a century later.

Renan, E. (1823–92) Professor of Hebrew at the Collège de France in Paris from 1861

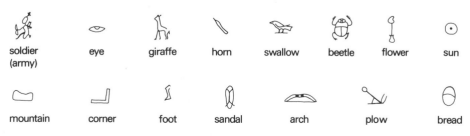

(with a brief break). He was one of the most distinguished, if the most controversial, scholars of Semitic studies in his generation. His rational, scientific approach in such finely written general works as his many-volumed *History of the Origins of Christianity*, which included his notorious *Life of Jesus* (1863), and his equally monumental *History of the People of Israel* (1888–94), marked a new era in Biblical Studies. But it is his report on his expedition to Phoenicia in 1860 that entitles him to be called "The Father of Palestinian Archaeology."

Repoussé decoration A metalworker's technique in which a design is hammered up from the back of a piece of sheet metal so that it appears in relief on the front. The work is normally carried out with a blunt tool against a yielding surface.

Revet (revetment) The process of providing a rampart with a retaining wall or face of masonry.

Rhyton A drinking vessel in the shape of a horn or an animal's head.

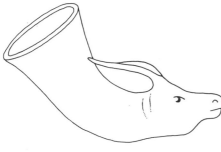

Rhyton

Robber trenches These are cut subsequent to the destruction of a building in order to extract the stone or brick of its walls for reuse. If the wall is removed completely to its very foundations, the earth-filled robber trenches will be vital for reconstructing the plan of a building, for they are the "ghosts" of its original layout.

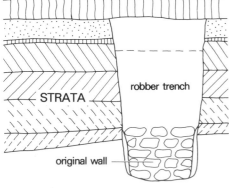

Robber trench

Roberts, David (1796–1864) A Scot who rose from humble origins as a scene-painter in the theater to become one of the most popular landscape painters of Victorian England. During his lifetime he found a good market for his pictures and for the lithographic reproductions of drawings made during his journeys abroad. Among the most successful of the latter was his publication "Sketches in the Holy Land and Syria" (1842).

Robinson, Edward (1794–1863) He came from an American family of farmers and preachers, and for some time combined both callings with the study first of Classical languages, then of Hebrew. Before assuming appointment as professor of Biblical Literature in the Union Theological Seminary, New York, he traveled in Palestine with Dr Eli Smith, long a missionary in Syria, from April to June 1838, and returned briefly in 1852. On the basis of five months' traveling he laid enduring foundations for the study of the "Physical and Historical Geography of the Holy Land" – the title his final comprehensive work would have received had he lived to complete it. His writings are not now easily accessible, as is the work of his most distinguished successor, George Adam Smith (see *Historical Geography of the Holy Land*, latest edition, Fontana, London 1973).

Rothenberg, Benno Born in Germany and educated at the Hebrew University in Jerusalem, he is now attached to Tel-Aviv University. He is best known for his work as Director of the Sinai Survey in 1956–7 and, since 1959, for survey and excavations in the Arabah and the Negev, with particular reference to the early history of mining and metallurgy.

Salient and recess fortifications These consist of a solid wall constructed with a

Salient and recess fortifications

succession of regularly set projections giving a pattern of "offsets and insets." They were commonly used in Palestine in the Iron Age (*see also* **Casemate walls**).

Sarcophagus A stone coffin, rectangular in shape. The outside was often decorated with reliefs and the inside cut so as to take the body and any funerary equipment.

Satrapy The term used in the Persian Empire to describe the major administrative provinces, each presided over by a satrap or governor. The word is of Median origin. The only certain list of satrapies is provided by

Herodotus for the reign of Darius, and lists twenty in all. The Persian kings have left us long, monumental inscriptions listing the peoples over whom they ruled, but these have no direct relation to the organization of satrapies.

Scarab/Scarab seal A scarab is an amulet* in the form of a beetle, associated in ancient Egypt with the sun-god Khepri, who is often depicted with a scarab as his head. The Egyptians believed that the sun-god was self-created like a beetle, which hatches from the ball of dung in which it lays its eggs. They saw in the beetle pushing its dung-ball along the ground an image of the sun's daily path across the sky. Most scarabs are relatively small, the underside bearing inscriptions or decorative motifs. Such seals were made of a wide variety of materials and used throughout the Levant.

Schaeffer, C. F. A. A leading French archaeologist who was for many years Director of the National Museum of Antiquities at St Germain-en-Laye near Paris. He is best known for his long series of excavations at Ras Shamra (Ugarit) in Syria and at Enkomi in Cyprus. In particular the tablets found at Ras Shamra opened a new era in Biblical studies.

Schliemann, Heinrich (1822–90) He pursued a career in commerce until he was 41, and then retired to devote himself to archaeology. In four campaigns of excavation between 1871 and 1890 at Troy in north-west Turkey he uncovered nine superimposed cities, and for the first time demonstrated the importance of stratigraphy* in understanding a Near Eastern *tell* (mound). His work aroused worldwide interest. He set high standards of recording, observation and rapid publication before which his errors of interpretation are rapidly forgotten.

Shekel Originally a weight, later a coin. In Israelite times it seems to have weighed about 0.403 ounces. The earlier Babylonian shekel had varied more in weight, ranging from about 0.3 to 0.62 ounces.

Sigloi (plural form) The Greek for the Hebrew shekel, meaning also a weight and a coin. Under the Persian Empire there were 20 silver sigloi to one gold daric*.

Silo A pit or airtight structure in which green crops are kept for fodder.

Slip A potter's term. It is a solution of clay mixed with water until it has the consistency of a thick soup, which is applied to the surface of a partly dried pot by pouring or dipping. It is generally of a different color from the body of the pot, and may be used to conceal the body color. When polished with a stone or bone it is said to be *burnished* – a technique common in Iron Age Palestine. Archaeologists sometimes use the word *wash* to describe a very thin slip.

Sphinx A winged monster with the body of a lion and a human head, usually female. The Biblical *cherubim* were probably such creatures.

Squeeze An impression taken from an inscription either by the use of damp paper or more commonly today with a rubber, or similar, solution.

Stanhope, Lady Hester (1776–1839) Niece of the Younger Pitt and, from 1803 to 1806, when he was prime minister, his hostess in London. "I let her do as she pleases; for if she were resolved to cheat the devil she could do it," he is said to have remarked, to which she added: "And so I could." Increasingly intolerant of social conventions, she left England for the Near East in 1810 with a party of friends and never returned. By 1814 she was established in the Lebanon. In time she adopted the pose and lifestyle of a benevolent, if autocratic, eastern princess, becoming a legend in her own lifetime thanks to many distinguished visitors and their accounts of her in books (see Kinglake's *Eothen*★) and European drawing rooms.

Stela An upright slab or pillar usually carved with inscriptions and reliefs. Stelae served a variety of purposes in the ancient world – as funerary monuments, as monuments commemorating royal victories, and as dedications to gods.

Strabo: *Geography* A description in Greek of the physical, geographical and historical development and more unusual customs of the main countries of the Roman world. Strabo (c. 64 BC to 19 AD) was a considerable traveler, but inevitably relied much on the work of earlier writers and the reports of his contemporaries. Though at times uncritical, his book is invaluable today for the range and variety of the information it has assembled and preserved. (Translation in Loeb Classical Library.)

Stratigraphy/Stratum Stratigraphy is one of the major interpretative principles of field archaeology, borrowed from geology. It depends on the fact that where one deposit of debris overlies another, the upper must have accumulated after the lower, since it could not have been inserted beneath it. In practice, however, there are numerous modifications to this general rule, for many acts of nature, from earthquakes to burrowing animals, will disturb any orderly sequence of deposit, as well as interference by man. It is the archaeologist's main purpose to distinguish one deposit from another by its texture, color or contents (which may of course be intruders from earlier or later levels), and to draw diagrams (sections) of his site's stratigraphy so that other scholars may check his interpretation. The various layers of debris recognized are conventionally called either *levels* or *strata*.

Survey of Western Palestine A map at 1″ to the mile drawn up under the auspices of the Palestine Exploration Fund and the Ordnance Survey between 1871 and 1877. Only four of these six years were spent in Palestine, as the surveying party was withdrawn for nearly two years after an attack by villagers in 1875. Twenty-six sheets were published in 1879, covering the area from the Mediterranean to the Jordan, from Beersheba to Tyre and Banias. They were printed with great detail in four colors, with relief in brown hachuring. The Survey was not superseded until 1936 when the first of a new 1/100,000 series was produced under the British Mandate Government. It remains one of the greatest achievements of the Palestine Exploration Fund.

Tanit This has long been confidently identified as the west Phoenician (Carthaginian) name for the Phoenician goddess Astarte★, but there is some information to show that she may also have existed independent of Astarte in Phoenicia itself. In Roman times in the western Mediterranean she was associated with Juno, who was primarily the goddess of women.

Tell The Arabic word used for artificial mounds which commonly represent the debris of ancient towns and villages in the Near East.

Topheth An area in the valley of Hinnom near Jerusalem. The name derives from the Aramaic word for a hearth or fireplace, for here children were sacrificed to the gods as burnt offerings. It has been adopted by archaeologists as a general description of such places in Carthaginian settlements. It is usually a burial ground with urns containing the bones of children and animals. Accompanying stelae★ are carved with crude designs and dedicated to the goddess Tanit★ or Baal★ (Hammon) (*see also* **Moloch**).

Trireme A warship driven by three banks of oars. Its Phoenician form is well illustrated by a baked clay model from Armant in Egypt.

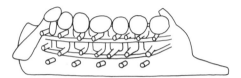

Trireme

Tumulus A burial mound of earth or stones, usually covering a stone-built chamber in which the body and its funerary equipment were placed.

Vergil Author of the great Latin epic poem the *Aeneid*. He wrote it in the last eleven years of his life, while living in seclusion in the Italian countryside, and left it unfinished at his death in 19 BC. It was composed to celebrate the origin and growth of the Roman Empire, using the legend of Aeneas as its theme. Aeneas was a member of the royal family of Troy, briefly mentioned in the *Iliad*,★ who escaped when the city fell to the Greeks and after long wanderings founded a Trojan settlement in Latium, the source of the Roman race. (Translation in Penguin Classics.)

Votive statue A statue offered or dedicated for a specifically religious purpose, perhaps in fulfillment of a vow to the gods or in order to win their favor.

Wadi The Arabic word for a rocky watercourse or valley, dry except in the rainy season.

Warburton: *The Crescent and the Cross* (1845). Though not a literary masterpiece like Kinglake's *Eothen*★, it still puts Warburton among the best writers in English on the Near East. His descriptions of landscape and atmosphere are much finer than his grasp of character – his Arabs do not spring live from the page as do Kinglake's. But if he did not have Kinglake's irony and dramatic sense, he was equally enthusiastic in his desire to portray the Near East for the reading public of High Victorian England. Nor has time rendered his book any less enjoyable. (No modern edition.)

Warren, Capt. (General Sir Charles), (1840-1927) He conducted the first excavations in Palestine sponsored by the Palestine Exploration Fund as a young man between 1867 and 1870. This work, which was carried out to the south and southeast of the Temple area in Jerusalem, was reported in *Recovery of Jerusalem*★ and *Underground*★ *Jerusalem*. Thereafter Warren had a distinguished career as a fighting soldier and administrator, much of the time in Africa.

(Wey, William): *Informatyon for Pylgrymes unto the Holy Land* (London, 1515) The book is exactly what its title implies, but appeared without any clear indication of authorship when printed in 1515. Closer examination shows it to be virtually identical to a much earlier manuscript entitled "The Itineraries of William Wey, fellow of Eton College, to Jerusalem AD 1458 and 1462 and to St James of Compostella (ie in Spain) in AD 1456." This is one of the earliest of guidebooks, full of plain, useful fact – rates of exchange, mileage between towns, lists of fees and tariffs to be paid in the Holy Land, and lists of useful words in the languages most likely to be encountered. It is more mercantile than religious in spirit, as shown in its thorough, businesslike listing of indulgences to be gained at the Holy Places.

Wheeler, Sir Mortimer His long and varied career has included spells as museum director in Cardiff and London, as archaeological administrator in London, India and Pakistan, as Professor in London University, as field arachaeologist in England and abroad, but above all he is known as a master of archaeological method and organization. By broadcasting, lecturing and writing he has contributed much to the present high status and popularity of the subject. His *Archaeology from the Earth* (Pelican) remains the most lively and instructive introduction to the subject.

Wilkie, Sir David (1785-1841) A Scot who, after a highly successful career as a painter of scenes of rural life, historical subjects and portraits, turned his attention to the Near East. He left England at the close of 1840 and, traveling through Constantinople (where he painted a portrait of the Sultan), reached Jerusalem late in February 1841. His letters home reveal the strong impact the countryside had on him as a fresh source of artistic inspiration. His avowed intent was to produce biblical pictures based on accurate observation of their true natural setting, but only a handful of sketches were ever made. He returned through Alexandria, Malta and Gibraltar, where he died and was buried at sea. His burial was portrayed in J. M. W. Turner's magnificent painting of the scene –

"Peace – burial at sea of Sir David Wilkie" (1842). (See A. Cunningham, *The Life of Sir David Wilkie*, London 1843, for his letters from the Holy Land.)

Woolley, Sir Leonard (1880-1960) The leading Near Eastern field archaeologist of his day, responsible for outstanding excavations at Carchemish (1912–14), at Ur (1922–34), where he found the famous Royal Cemetery, and at Tell Atshana and al Mina (1936–9, 1946–9). He combined the talents of a practical archaeologist and architect with those of a writer. His books, both academic and popular, described the results of his work clearly, accurately and vividly. His *Digging Up the Past* is an excellent brief introduction to Near Eastern archaeology. It has been published as a Pelican book in company with his *Ur of the Chaldees* and *A Forgotten Kingdom* (about Tell Atshana).

Wright, G. Ernest (1909-74) A leading American Biblical Scholar best known as an archaeologist for his work at Shechem (1956–74) and Gezer (1964–5) in Palestine, and at Idalion in Cyprus (1971–4). He was particularly concerned with the organization and direction of American archaeological research in the Near East, and with teaching a rising generation of field archaeologists. He also showed concern for the development of a wide and well-informed public interest in Biblical Studies and Palestinian archaeology, notably in his books *Biblical Archaeology, Shechem: Biography of a Biblical City* and (with R. Fuller) *The Book of the Acts of God* (Pelican).

Xenophon Born about 430 BC, he was a great admirer of the Greek philosopher and teacher Socrates. In 401 BC he joined the expedition of Cyrus "the Younger" in his abortive attempt to seize the Persian throne from his elder brother Artaxerxes. This memorable episode, and Xenophon's own heroic role in extricating the ten thousand Greek mercenaries from Iraq following the defeat and death of Cyrus at the battle of Cunaxa, is related in his *Anabasis* (translation in Penguin Classics). His *Cyropaedia* is an account of the career of Cyrus the Great, King of Persia (c. 550–529 BC), in which historical facts and personalities are modified to suit the purposes of a treatise on the ideal form of government and the perfect ruler. Cyrus is idealized, drawing much on Xenophon's acquaintance with Cyrus "the Younger," and Xenophon's own ideas are freely blended into his account of Persian government and administration. (Translation in Loeb Classical Library.)

Yadin, Yigael Professor of Archaeology in the Hebrew University of Jerusalem, he is renowned for his excavations at Masada and

Hazor as much as for his work on the study and publication of the Dead Sea Scrolls. A distinguished soldier and administrator, he is also master of the presentation of his work in written form and lectures for the general public. His excavations are marked by a spectacular deployment of manpower and resources, a keen appreciation of historical circumstances and great interpretative skill.

Zeus In Greek mythology he was the son of Kronos★, whom he overthrew and succeeded as supreme god. Primarily god of sky and weather, he was associated with most aspects of human life as supreme judge and legislator. He is normally shown as a mature man with benign, bearded face, carrying a thunderbolt and the *aegis* (often interpreted as a thundercloud) which, when shaken, brought terror to his enemies.

Ziggurats The staged temple-towers of ancient cities in Iraq. Although a number have been excavated, none is preserved in anything like its original form, and they are reconstructed from Herodotus'★ description of one at Babylon (*see under* **Babel**) and from representations on ancient Assyrian palace reliefs.

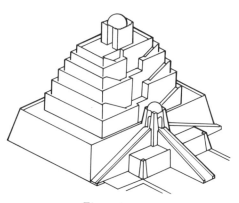

Ziggurat

Zoroastrianism Once the national faith of Iran and still practiced by small communities there and by the Parsees of India. Its great prophet Zarathustra (Greek: Zoroaster) is traditionally dated about 628–551 BC, but may have lived much earlier. He spent his life in eastern Iran, and his teachings have survived in some of his hymns (the *Gathas*). He proclaimed a single supreme god, creator of all things. The world he saw as divided between two opposite poles of Good and Evil, Truth and Lie, offered as free choices to all humanity. The supreme symbol of Truth is fire, and fire-altars are consequently the primary cult symbol of Zoroastrianism. The early history of this religion, particularly its role at the time of the Persian Empire, is still extremely uncertain and much disputed among scholars.

Index